OUTLINES

OF

LECTURES ON THE

HISTORY OF PHILOSOPHY

BY

JOHN J. ELMENDORF, S. T. D.,

UNIVERSITY PROF. OF PHILOSOPHY AND ENGLISH LITERATURE IN
RACINE COLLEGE.

NEW YORK:
G. P. PUTNAM'S SONS.
182 FIFTH AVENUE.
1876.

COL. COLL., NOV. EB.,

MAGISTRAE DILECTISS. ADOLESC. MEAE,

HAS PRIMITIAS AET. MATUR.

REVERENTER ATQ. OBSEQUENTER

DEDICO,

ALMAE MATRI

SALUT. ET FELICIT.

IMPRECANS.

PREFACE.

The object of this manual is sufficiently indicated by its title, "Outlines of lectures on the History of Philosophy." It aims at no more than to present, in condensed form, a syllabus of the course, for review and recitation. For *education*, the learning to philosophize, what can be a substitute for the living guide, elucidating the student's confused thought, and making him to grow in mind as he traces the development of human thought? It is surely enough to rest this on the pregnant words of the master; "nobler far is the serious pursuit of the dialectician who finds a congenial soul, and then with knowledge ingrafts and sows words which—are not unfruitful, but have in them seeds which may bear fruit in other natures, nurtured in other ways,—making the seed everlasting, and the possessors happy to the utmost extent of human happiness." (Phaedr., p. 276.)

Text-books, surely, will not do this. In the history of philosophy, the lecturer will have a principle, a clue by which to guide his scholar. It may be a different one from what the best text books supply. The most scientific of these, if brief, will be the driest and most divorce philosophy from that out of which it springs, and on which it most powerfully re-acts, the progress of civilization, literature, art, politics, religion. If, on the other hand, extensive enough to be both clear and attractive, such works are ill adapted to the brief period which an under-graduate course allows for this study, though the student must soon come face to face with those problems of the age whose answer must be based on some philosophy, true or false. Only the living teacher can direct every lecture towards those practical ends; books will not answer the purpose.

Also, there are some leading principles, some cardinal thoughts of the world's master-thinkers which the writer thinks that the student should have the opportunity of examining for himself, and his experience has shown him that, under favorable circumstances, a fair proportion of American youth will gladly avail themselves of the opportunity of doing so.

These outlines, then, are intended, first, to save the delay caused by much writing in the lecture-room, secondly, to aid a free use by lecturer and scholar of original sources; and, thirdly, to provide help in review and recitation; if *interleaved*, the manual may prove still more serviceable.

The extreme condensation sometimes needful may render the statement here given unsatisfactory, as indeed no two persons would find in an original thinker the same salient points; the lecturer will remedy that defect.

The writer is aware that he lays himself open to criticism in not infrequent changes of terms, and also in referring much of peripatetic principle to S. Thom. Aq. But practical considerations into which he will not enter, guided him in both respects.

It is perhaps due to himself that the writer should add that the completion of his work has been rendered far more difficult, and to himself less satisfactory than it otherwise might have been, through loss by fire of a not insufficient supply of materials, as well as through such hindrances as a thousand miles' distance from publishers must needs create.

Thanks and special acknowledgments are due to his friend, Mr. H. H. Martin, for valuable assistance in revisal.

Racine Coll., Sept., 1876.

CONTENTS.

Chapter 10.

DEVELOPMENT OF ENGLISH EMPIRICISM.

Chapter 11.

DEVELOPMENT OF RATIONALISM.

Chapter 12.

SKEPTICISM AND MYSTICISM IN THE SEVENTEENTH AND EIGHTEENTH CENTURIES.

Chapter 13.

FRENCH SENSUALISTIC SCHOOL OF THE EIGHTEENTH CENTURY.

Chapter 14.

SCOTCH PHILOSOPHY.

Chapter 15.

GERMAN CRITICAL AND IDEAL PHILOSOPHY.

Chapter 16.

ENGLISH AND FRENCH EMPIRICISM IN THE NINETEENTH CENTURY.

Chapter 17.

ENGLISH AND FRENCH PSYCHOLOGICAL AND SPIRITUALISTIC SCHOOL OF THE NINETEENTH CENTURY.

CHAPTER I.

INTRODUCTION.

1. TERMS AND DEFINITIONS.—2. SUBJECTS.—3. ORIGIN AND PROGRESS.—4. SYSTEMS.

[*References:*—Sir William Hamilton's Metaphysics, First Seven Lectures: Fleming's Vocab. of Phil., Ed. Krauth.]

1.—TERMS AND DEFINITIONS.

Philosophy, *i. e.*, Truth-seeking, a term said to have originated with Pythagoras. (?) Cic. Tusc. Quæst. v. 3. Plato's Phædrus, p. 278.

Its aim is the conditions, limits and ultimate principles of all knowledge concerning GOD, man, or the universe.

Distinguish (*a*) *empirical*, or historical, knowledge, *i. e.*, of facts or phenomena:

(*b*) *Scientific*, classifying these phenomena, and determining their relations, and laws or uniformities:

(*c*) *Philosophical*, *e. g.* of effects in their causes, back to a First Cause; of qualities as inherent in substance, etc.

(See further, § 4.)

The *possibility* of a solution of philosophical questions may be denied, yet the attempt is an historical fact of the utmost importance and widest influence, instructive even in its failure.

Relations of reason to faith, the one seeking truth by the aid of that "true Light which lighteth every man that cometh into the world;" the other finding it revealed, and "supernatural truth" grounded upon it.

(On the failures of Phil., see Cic. Tusc. Quæst. i. 11, etc.; De Nat. Deorum. iii. 39. S. Aug. Confess. iv. 4; vii. 9, 20, 21.)

2.—Subjects.

A. *Logic* is the theory of the laws of thought; of the instrumentality by which all knowledge is possessed, discovered or developed.

B. *Metaphysics,* "Philosophia prima," sometimes identified with philosophy, may be defined as the ultimate principles of necessary truth ("transcendental") common to all sciences, apart from all phenomena, or partial manifestations of them. (Ferrier's Institutes of Metaphysics; Introd.)

(1.) *Ontology, Aitiology:* the theory of true being, absolute existence.

(2.) *Epistemology:* the theory of knowing. and of its limits.

(3.) "*Agnaiology*" (Ferrier): the theory of ignorance.

C. *Theology.* "Theosophy," is the theory of God, the Infinite, the Absolute. the First Cause, the One, etc. (Arist. Met. x. 7); may be included in (B.).

Theodicea (Leibnitz): The relations of God to man.

D. *Anthropology* is the theory of man in every relation.

(1.) *Psychology*, (Goclenius), the science of the mind.

(*a*) Empirical.

(*b*) Rational; (may include Logic, Æsthetics, Ethics.)

(2.) *Ethics*, the theory of the good; (as such may be referred to (B.) or (C.); "Moral Philosophy," the obligations of man to GOD, his neighbor, and himself.

Politics and *Œconomics:* the science of man in society.

Sociology,

International Rights.

E. *Cosmology* is the theory of nature, of the Universe.

Æsthetics is the theory of the beautiful; (may be referred to (B.).

3.—ORIGIN AND PROGRESS.

A. Philosophy may be founded on sacred books, religious traditions, etc.; for these give the first answers to many of the questions raised.

B. But reason reflects, systematizes, eventually criticises; hence commentators, and *scientific theology.*

C. Reason finally emancipates itself, and attempts to arrive at independent conclusions, and may even be antagonistic, as—

(1.) Pyrrhonism.

(2.) Mysticism.

(Comte's three eras of progress.

(1.) Theological.

(2.) Metaphysical.

(3.) Positive, *i. e.*, reason confined to phenomena and their laws.

NOTE.—Does one of these exclude the others ?)

4.—PHILOSOPHICAL SYSTEMS.

I.

A. *Empiricism* bases all knowledge on experience, *i. e.*, remembrance of repeated phenomena,

(1.) Of external sensible objects,

(2.) Of internal operations of the mind.

It rejects *à priori* sources of knowledge. Hence:

(1.) *Sensualism*, deriving all knowledge from sensation. Truth is individual, relative. *Ideology* is the science of "ideas," *i. e.*, remembered and generalized sensations.

(2.) *Materialism*, the theory of one substance, which is matter.

Hylozoism.

(3.) Philosophical *Atheism;* no designing and directing mind can be known.

Teleology is impossible.

B. *Rationalism.* Some elements of knowledge, at least, are furnished by *pure* reason.—(Bacon's Apophthegms: 19.)

II.

A. *Dogmatism* asserts that knowledge is attainable by a right use of our faculties.

B. *Scepticism, Pyrrhonism,* asserts that knowledge is unattainable by reason; opinion is our only ground of assertion.

(NOTE.—Distinguish from religious skepticism.—Mansel.)

Probabilism. Hence:

(1.) *Nihilism*, the denial of all existence.

(2.) *Positivism*, knowledge limited to phenomena.

(3.) *Critical School* in which reason and understanding supply only the subjective forms of knowledge; *e. g.*, space and time. Phenomena are the only things objectively known. Pure metaphysics of GOD, the Soul, and the Universe, have no objective validity.

C. *Mysticism*, which makes truth attainable by immediate union with GOD.

(1.) Mysticism of *sentiment*, in which love is the only source of truth. Hence *Quietism*.

(2.) *Pure* mysticism, in which *ecstasy* is the union of the soul with GOD. Hence *Theurgy*. (Cousin: Hist. Gen. Phil., Sect. I. See also app. xi. to Henry's Cousin's Elem. Psychol.)

III.

A. *Realism* asserts intuitive cognition of the external object, or *non-ego*.

B. *Idealism* asserts that ideas are the only objects known.

(1.) *Subjective* Idealism; the *ego* and the *non-ego* are one thing. (Fichte.)

(2.) *Objective, Pantheistic* Idealism; the *ego* and the *non-ego* are manifestations of the Absolute. (Schelling.)

(3.) *Absolute* Idealism; relations are the only objects of knowledge. (Lewes' Hist. Phil. 10th Epoch, cc. i., ii., iii.

IV.

A. [Monism.] The theory that one principle is the ground of all being.

(1.) *Materialism.*

(a) *Evolution.*

(b) *Plurality of elements.*

(2.) *Idealism.*

(3.) *Pantheism ;* hence, *Emanation.*

B. *Dualism* asserts two principles : *e. g.*, mind and matter.

CHAPTER II.

INDIAN PHILOSOPHY.

1. General Characteristics.—2. Literary Sources.—3. Philosophical Schools.

[References: Sir Wm. Jones' Works, especially, Transl. Inst. of Menu; Transact. of the As. Soc., (Colebrooke, etc.,); F. Von Schlegel; H. H. Wilson's translations and prefaces; Müller's Chips, etc., vol. I; Cousin, Hist. Phil. Mod., 2d Ser., vol. 2, Sect. 6; Ritter II. 2; Contemp. Rev., June, 1872.]

1.—General Characteristics.

A. *Value,* for us, is found in the fact that, though independent of more familiar systems, *e. g.*, modern pantheism, Ind. Phil. is yet one with ours in methods and conclusions. Some tendencies of the present age very fully and philosophically developed.

B. *Underlying Unity.* (1.) In origin, from the theory of *Emanation,* which must not be confounded with (2.) *Pantheism;* in the latter, evil is non-existent, or is one of the qualities of the Divine Essence; in the former, evil is the result of decay, of degradation. Instit. Menu, i. 49-57; Schlegel, ii. 2; H. H. Wilson's trans. Vishnu—Purana, I. 19 et seq.

"All the kings who have been, and all who shall be, are but parts of the Universal Vishnu. The rulers of the gods . . .

and of the malignant spirits . . . the chief among beasts . . . men, etc., the best of trees, mountains, planets . . . are but portions of the Universal Vishnu."

The king's son at the end of his prayer says: "Glory to him whom I also am . . . I am all things; all things are in me. Brahma is my name," etc. "Thus meditating upon Vishnu as identical with his own spirit he became as one with him . . . he was freed from the consequences of moral merit and demerit, and obtained final exemption from existence."

(3.) In *means* to be employed.

(a) *Abstraction* from passions, cares, etc.

(b) *Science;* hence the need of philosophy.

2.—Literary Sources.

A. The *Vedas* (four). Each is of two parts;

(1) Mantras, or prayers.

(2.) Brahmanas, or precepts.

Especially noteworthy is the Rig-Veda; (circ. 1500, B. C. ?)

All systems profess submission to them, for they were revealed by Brahma, and preserved by tradition until arranged by Vyása (*i. e.*, compiler), (Colebrooke, in As. Trans., vol. 8.)

They are based on a pure monotheism; in them no idolatry, but a symbolic worship of the elements: *e. g.* Agni=fire, Indra=sky, Varuna=water, Soma=moon. (See Hymn to the Paramatma, Rig-V. vii. 10; see also the Gayatri, or, "holiest verse," which lifts man up to Brahma; Sir Wm. Jones. vol. xiii.)

B. The *Upanichads.* Theological Commentaries.

D. Brahmá-Soutras, and others of the *Uttara* (second) Mimánsá, or Vedánta, (vid. inf.)

E. *Institutes of Menu*, a son of Brahmá. They give a comprehensive system of Indian legislation, etc., based on the prevailing philosophy. They are of uncertain, probably, of various, dates. (Sir Wm. Jones, B. C. 800; cf. Ritter.)

F. *Bhagavat-Gita* is an episode of the great Indian epic, Mahábhárata. (Trans. 16 vols., 8vo., 1600 pp., by Fauche, 1860; B-G. trans. by Chas. Wilkins, 1785; Latin trans. by A. W. Schlegel. Vid. et. Cousin; Hist. Phil. Lect. 2, Ed. 1863.)

G. *Purándás* (eighteen) fully develop pantheism. (H. H. Wilson's Pref. to Vishnu-P.)

"Vishnu is the world;" "cause and effect"; "creator and the thing to be created," etc.

The chief P. is *Brahmá Purándá*. The universe is from the indiscrete cause, which is one with matter and spirit. From Pradhána, the chief principle, proceed,

(1.) *Mahat* =Intelligence; from M.,

(2.) *Ahankára* =Consciousness, or the *ego*, (cf. Hegel, and Cont. Rev. July, 1874); from A.,

(3.) The five elements; from these,

(4.) The divine egg, the abode of Brahmá, the Creator, who is also Vishnu the preserver, until the end of a kalpa, (Brahmá's day), when, in the form of Siva, he swallows up the universe, and reposes. After a season, awaking again, he renews the universe.

As the universe proceeds from *prakriti*, *i. e.* eternal nature, without sensible qualities, so at the end of the series of *kalpas, i. e.* Brahmá's life, all the gods and other forms of being will be annihilated, and the elements merged into primary being again.

3. Philosophical Schools.

A. *Vedánta, i. e.* end of the Védas, otherwise known as the *uttara* Mimánsá, has for its author, Vyasa.

(1.) *Its starting point* is orthodox interpretation of the Védas.

(2.) *Its method* is deduction from the Védas.

(3.) *Its principle* is emanation; Brahm is manifested as

(*a.*) Brahmá.

(*b.*) Vishnu.

(*c.*) Siva.

From (*a*) emanate gods, rishis, kings, etc. and the universe. He continually transforms and diversifies himself; "as the spider spins and gathers back again its web."

On this is based a system of *Idealism.*

(4) *Psychology;* individual souls are sparks from the one infinite light. Besides these there is the one supreme soul in all, which is not individual nor free. (As. Res. v. 8, p. 421, seq.)

"He who sees all things in the *Atman* (supreme soul) and the *Atman* in all beings, he will not despise anything." "They go on in thick darkness who adore *prakriti;* but they go on in thicker darkness, who delight in created and perishable nature." (Isa Oupan. 6–12).

Hence, *transmigration* of souls; and, for the wise at last, *Nirvána,* absorption in Brahm.

(5.) *Conclusion*, Mysticism. Transmigration is to be remedied by virtues, especially the ceremonial, and ascetic contemplation.

B. *Sánkhya*, (judgment, wisdom) of *Kapila*.

(1.) The *founder*, Kapila, is, perhaps, a mythologic personage. The best text is a treatise in verse called Káriká. (See trans. with comment by H. H. Wilson, and also As. Trans. vv. 1, 3.)

(2.) The *starting point* is not strictly orthodox, and called *nir-Isvara*; (atheistic) though K. professes to receive revelation.

Its object is to remedy the pains of existence by final freedom from individuality; (Káriká, I; and Wilson, p. 178.)

(3.) *Method*. Observation of phenomena, induction, revelation.

(4.) *Principle*, a doctrine of development.

A dualism of mind and matter exists, but both are from *prakriti*, nature, eternal matter, productive, not a production. *Moula prakriti* is inferred, by induction, from its effects; it is the material cause of all, and there is no need of any other cause. It precedes *buddhi* (mind), the *anima mundi*.

Buddhi is the source of the three manifestations of god, Brahmá, Vishnu, and Siva, or of the three qualities, goodness, foulness, and darkness. Brahmá is only the instrumental cause of things created. Substance becomes perceptible according to its inherent powers.

Cause and effect are one in nature. (Wilson's Káriká, pp. 33 seq.)

The third of Kapila's twenty-four principles is consciousness, or egoism; the last is *âtman*, individual, immaterial, multitudinous souls.

Many of the Puránâs are based on this Sankhya, and in some of them nature is *Maya* (illusion.) "You must conceive mountains, oceans, etc., as the illusions of the apprehension. When knowledge is pure, (real, universal, etc.) then the varieties of substance cease to exist in matter. . . . For what is substance? Where is the thing that is devoid of beginning, middle, and end, of one uniform nature? How can reality be predicated of that which is subject to change, and reassumes no more its original character? (*e. g.* a jar made of clay, broken and reduced to dust.) (Vish.-Pur. ii. 12.)

(5.) *Tendency.* Sensualism, materialism, atheism. K. denies an *Iswara*, a ruler of the world. There is no proof of his existence.

(*a.*) Not perceived by the senses;

(*b.*) Not inferrible by induction;

(*c.*) Nor revealed.

K.'s *à priori* refutation of theism is,

(*a.*) Unaffected by consciousness he could have no inducement to create;

(*b.*) If fettered by Nature, he would not be capable of creation.

Hence *Buddhism* (600–1000 B. C.)

(1.) *Founder* is Sákhya, or Bouddha Mouni; a reformer and propagandist.

(2.) B. contains various systems of philosophy under the common anthropomorphic polytheism, but all aim at the Nirvána, loss of individuality; with some it appears to be Nihilism.

C. *Sánkhya*, of *Patandjali.*

(1.) The *Founder* is Patandjali, an eclectic, stoic, mystic; there are four books of *Yoga-Soutras,* (union precepts); (*a*) On contemplation; (*b*) How to arrive at it; (*c*) The exercise of higher powers; (*d*) ecstasy.

(2.) *Principle*, mysticism. The Védas are useless when their source is attained.

"Quot usibus inservit puteus, aquis undique confluentibus, tot usibus praestant universi libri sacri theologo prudenti."

(3.) *Psychology:* above sense is soul; above soul, intelligence; above that, pure being. Hence,

(4.) *Ethics*, of contemplation, inaction.

"Naturæ qualitatibus peraguntur omni modo opera." (cf. Spinoza.) "Mente devotus in hoc ævo utraque dimittit, bene et male facta." (See Bhag.-Gita § 4, on forsaking works; i. e., religious duties). "The worship of spiritual wisdom is far better than the worship with the offering of things." "Be thou free from a three-fold nature; (the three qualities: vid. supra.)—When thy understanding, brought by study to maturity shall be fixed immoveably in contemplation, then shall it obtain true wisdom; (Krishna); a man is confirmed in wisdom when he forsaketh every desire which entereth into his heart. He is called a *Mouni*—in all things he is without affection. (Bhag.-Gita § 2). The *Yogui* constantly exerciseth the spirit in private. He is recluse, of a subdued mind and spirit, free from hope, free from perception. He planteth his seat firmly on a spot that is undefiled, neither too high nor too low, and sitteth upon the sacred grass covered with a skin and a cloth. There he whose business is the restraining of his passions should sit, with his mind fixed on one object alone, in the exercise of his devotion, for the purification of his soul, keeping his head, his neck, his body, steady without motion, his eyes fixed on the point of his nose, looking at no other place around . . . When he hath abandoned any desire that ariseth from the imagination, and subdued with his mind any inclination of the senses, he may, by degrees, find rest; and having, by a steady resolution, fixed his mind within himself, he should think of nothing else. He is united with Brahm the supreme. He looketh on all things alike. He beholdeth the supreme soul in all things, and all things in the supreme soul." (Bhag.-Gita. § 6.)

"The *Yogui* seeks for wisdom, the supreme condition of Vishnu, which requires no exercise, not to be taught, internally diffused, unmodified by accidents of happiness, etc., not to be defined, void of passion, unagitated by thoughts of duality, pure (*i. e.*, not sensuous, nor logical), etc." "The Yogui who attains Brahm returns not to life again—then he is freed from the distinctions of vice and virtue," etc. (Vish.-Pur. i., 22.) (For development of Pantheism, see Krishna's account of himself in Bhag.-Gita, quoted in Cousin, Hist. Phil.)

D. *Nyaya* (reasoning.) (See Müller's App. to Thomson's Laws of Thought.)

(1.) The *Founder* is Gotama, whose dialectics, in the form of Soutras, should be compared with those of the Peripatetic school, and give proof of the high culture of his age. (Cousin, *in loc.*)

(2.) *Method*, is chiefly logical. The syllogism is explained by G. in a precise and severe way, but he views principles concretely. Like Kanáda, (vid. inf.) he distinguishes the categories. The inductive process also is fully developed.

(3.) *Analysis of ratiocination.* For demonstration (rhetorical) there are five steps:

(*a*) The proposition; *e. g.*, "This mountain is hot;"

(*b*) The reason; "for it smokes;"

(*c*) The major premise, with example; "What smokes is hot; *e. g.*, The fire in the kitchen;"

(*d*) The application; "this is true of the mountain;"

(*e*) The conclusion; "Therefore, etc."

(4.) *Principle*, Spiritualism. Substance is the intimate cause of an aggregated result or product. (cf. Leibnitz.)

The soul is distinct from the body, infinite in principle; a special substance different in each individual, with determined attributes, as knowledge and will, which do not belong to other substances.

(5.) *End,* as in other schools, by science to obtain deliverance from evils, emancipation of the soul from the body, etc.

E. *Vaiseschika.*

(1.) The *Founder* is Kanáda, who treats of logic and physics (see Müller, ubi supr., and cf. Ionic schools.)

(2.) *Method,* induction : there are only two sources of knowledge, perception and inference.

K. distinguishes six or seven predicamenta; (cf. Aristotle's ten,) viz., substance, quality, action, genus, individuality, relation, privation.

(3.) *Principle;* atoms compose the universe, both spiritual and material. There are nine substances, eternal as atoms, transient as aggregates.

(4.) *Conclusion;* materialism, atheism.

(5.) *End;* as with other schools, Nirvána, though, possibly, in a different sense, profound calm, perfect apathy or ecstasy.

(On Nirvána, see Müller's Chips., etc., i. 11.)

CHAPTER III.

GREEK PHILOSOPHY BEFORE SOCRATES.

1. INTRODUCTION. 2. IONIC SCHOOL. 3. DORIAN SCHOOL. 4. ELEATIC SCHOOL. 5. THE SOPHISTS.

[*References* :—Diog. Laert. de Vit., etc. (traditional); Arist. Met., i. 1-8; Ritter, iii.-vi.; Ueberweg, i., §§ 7-33; Enfield, ii. cc. 1-3; Archer Butler, i. (1st Ser.) 4-6; Lewes, i. 1st-3rd Ep.; Blakey, i. cc. 2-6; Cousin, Hist. Gen. Phil. (Ed. 1863) Lect. iii.; Cudworth, Int. Syst. v. 1; For special ref. vid. infra.]

1. INTRODUCTION.

A. *Character.* The first philosophic thought of the Aryan race in Europe, anticipating the latest questions of the nineteenth century; the Greeks the most restless, intellectually active and curious of nations.

The purely religious period very short; and, unlike India, religion of very little permanent influence on philosophy. The former soon becomes anthropomorphic, artistic, not symbolic; the latter, (*e. g.*, Xenophanes) indifferent to popular religion or deriding it. (Ritter, ii. 3.) There is no religious caste; each tribe or city has its own worship.

Sacred books also, (*e. g.*, Orphic Hymns, Hesiod's Theogony) of little influence on phil.; (note Homer's Anthropomorphism.)

(Query ; Influence of Egypt ? Of the mysteries ?) Early Phil. in Greece is eminently practical; its philosophers are statesmen, lawgivers ; *e. g.*, the "seven wise men." See their ethical gnomes.

B. *Date and Place.* The sixth cent. B.C. is a brilliant intellectual period of most rapid development. (Cf. the fine arts, and consider the influence of phil. upon them : Kugler, i. 2.2 ; and note that Greek art does not confirm the "positive" theory of progress ; there is no fetichism in Homer.)

Philosophy appears first in the Greek colonies, Asia M., Mag. Græcia, and Sicily : why ? The consequence is isolation of the different schools.

Their subsequent meeting is at Athens ; then came a migration to Alexandria and Rome ; then revival at Athens, and final closing of the school by Justinian (A. D. 529.)

C. *Subjects and Schools.* All schools study nature rather than man ; for the objective precedes the subjective. All are cosmological, devoted to physics and metaphysics, not to psychology.

There are four schools, each crude but consistent, independently working, and embracing the principal directions of human thought in all ages.

(1.) Ionian ; based on phenomena; devoted to physical science.

(2.) Dorian ; based on relations ; devoted to mathematics and ethics.

(3.) Eleatic ; based on pure being ; devoted to metaphysics and dialectics.

(4.) Sophistical ; antiphilosophical or sceptical, and devoted to the practical or subjective.

2. THE IONIAN SCHOOL.

[*References.*—Arist. de Animâ, i. 2-5; Physics, i. 2-6; Ritter makes this school a special study.]

A. *Character and Divisions.*

(1.) The *Ionians* were a sensuous, lively and impressible race; (authors of history and the *epos*). In politics, they show a marked democratic tendency.

(2.) Their *Method* is inductive, in rude attempts to generalize phenomena.

(3.) *Principle*, in early phil. is *Hylozoizm*, the inseparable connection of matter and life.

Later philosophers add to their materialism, from the Eleatic School, the immutability of being, but affirm its plurality, and explain apparent changes by the combination and separation of immutable primitive elements.

(4.) *Two views of nature.* (*a.*) Dynamical; (*b.*) mechanical.

(*a.*) The spontaneous development and alteration of primitive matter.

(*b.*) Permanent elements, moved from without or self-moving, separating and combining.

(5.) *Philosophical Order.* (Ritter.)

(*a.*) Dynamical.	(*b.*) Mechanical.
Thales,	
Anaximenes,	Anaximander,
Diogenes of Apollonia,	Anaxagoras,
Heraclitus (b. before Diog. but not so purely Ionian.)	Empedocles, (Eleatic.)
(Some would add,)	
Democritus, (with sophistical tendency.)	

B. *Dynamical School.*

(1.) *Thales.*

(*a.*) *Life.* *b.* at Miletus, (circ. 640 B. C).; said to have been contemporary with Crœsus and Solon; to have travelled in Egypt; to have predicted an eclipse; a practical mathèmatician and statesman. There are no authentic remains, and, perhaps, he wrote nothing.

(*b.*) *Principle* is inductive hylozoism. From water all things are derived, but water full of vital energy. (Arist. Met. i. 3.)

Hence the later view of his teaching (as in Cic. Nat. De. i. 10) that " God is the Intelligence who, from water, formed all things." (Anaxagoras.) This dualism is inconsistent with the earlier Hylozoism.

(2.) *Anaximenes,* (*a.*) of Miletus; date uncertain; (flourished 556,–529, B, C.) is said to have discovered the obliquity of the ecliptic.

(*b.*) By induction A. infers that air is the primary infinite substance, manifest through the qualities which it assumes. The cause of sensible, finite forms is the eternal motion of air in condensation and rarefaction. (Arist. Met. i. 3; Cic. de Nat. De. i. 10; Quæst. Acad. iv. 37.)

Diogenes, (*a.*) of Apollonia in Crete; (flour. circ. 550 B. C.) He taught first at Miletus, then at Athens; author of a work "*Περὶ φύσεως.*"

(*b.*) All things are one in essence, otherwise there could be no reciprocal action of things, (Simplicius in Ritter, iii. 5). The principle of life and being is air; individual beings are special manifestations of the universal being.

D. may have been more pantheistic than (1) and (2); he says that the primary air has intelligence.

(4.) *Heraclitus,* (*a.*) of Ephesus; (flour. circ. 500 B. C.)

the "weeping philosopher," ὀχλολοίδορος, he renounced political life. Fragments of his works remain, but he is exceedingly obscure, "ὁ σκοτεινός."

(*b.*) H. is less empirical than his predecessors; induction is less strictly adhered to, and he shows the greatest advance of his school towards spiritualism, yet still is Ionian in holding to the validity of a rational use of the senses.

He sees the universal in the individual and variable, and the individual in a universal and unchangeable principle, viz. *fire.* From fire, πῦρ ἀεὶ ζῶον, in perpetual movement, an intelligent principle, proceed all things. It is the principle even of thought. (Berkeley's Siris, §. 175, seq.) It has illimitable force, universal life; eternal motion is an inherent tendency in this primal fire; "The demiurgos sports in making worlds."

Plurality proceeds from unity, the fire, and is absorbed into it again, and so all things return to the primal fire; (anticipates the Stoics.)

All is composed of contraries; "The strife of all, [perpetual flux and reflux] is the parent of all;" "πάντα χωρεῖ καὶ οὐδὲν μένει." "In idem flumen bis descendimus et non descendimus;" (Sen. Ep. 58,) (cf. Hegel.)

(*c.*) *Psychology*; reason in man, common to all, is a higher emanation of the infinite fire, which becomes conscious in man. The senses are deceptive and earthly, and earth is the primal fire's lowest degradation.

(*d.*) *Ethics.* H. is more ethical than his predecessors, (Arist. Nic. Eth. vii. 3), though he seems to terminate in pantheism; "enter, for here too are gods." (Plato, Theæt. p. 179 seq.; Crat. p. 401. Arist. Met. iii. 7; Phys. 1, i; Nic. Eth. viii. 1, 2.)

(5.) *Democritus*, (*a.*) of Abdera, (490–460, B. C.) "the

laughing philosopher," was a man of wealth, and travelled extensively. He was the author of voluminous works (most not extant) on ethics, physics, and various branches of natural science.

(*b.*) By reflection on induction, D. is a thorough materialist. The only true is something extended in space. Its units are of unchangeable figure, and indivisible; hence, "atoms." They are manifold, of various forms, separated *in vacuo.* Their phenomena, *i. e.* bodily forms, are infinite; therefore, in variety and number they are infinite.

Their only property is motion or force; sensations are subjective.

Bodies are generated and destroyed by the aggregation and separation of these atoms; they are moveable by force from without, but D. does not assign a first cause of their motion. (Arist. Met. i. 4; iii. 4, 5; viii. 2; Phys. iv. 6.)

(*c.*) The soul is a combination of atoms of a finer sort, spherical, like fire. (Arist. De An. i. 2, 3, 5.) It is set in motion from without; effluxes, ἀπορροίαι, εἴδωλα, sent off from objects, enter it through the organs of sense, but give only obscure, imperfect knowledge of the objects. The gods are visions, εἴδωλα; (cf. the Sánkhya of Kapila.)

(*d.*) His *ethics* consist of good, practical precepts, based on a prudential egoism. True pleasure is not corporeal, but mental; even the latter, however, is to be regulated by moderation; (Epicurus.) As the *eidola* are the causes of desires, etc., a man's moral character depends on them.

D. has no place for any theory of God. (Cic. de Nat. De. i. 12, 43.)

With this Ionic school, compare scientific conclusions in the 19th cent., and see Tyndall's Address before Brit. Assoc. 1874; "I discern in matter—the promise and potency of every form and quality of life." Reprinted Littell, Liv. Age, 1581.

C. *Mechanical School.*

(1.) *Anaximander,* (*a*) of Miletus; *b.* circ. 610. B. C.; author of a work περὶ φύσεως. He is said to have invented the gnomon or to have introduced it among the Greeks.

(*b.*) The perpetual movement, naturally inherent, of primary material elements produces all. A. recognizes no GOD, but simply undefined, undetermined (ἄπειρον) matter. All bodies are undergoing continual transmutations through their inherent energy; *i. e.* from the mixture of elements, by separation, bodies are perpetually formed; dissolving to be formed anew. (Ritter, iii. 7; Arist. Phys. i. 4; iii. 4; S. Aug. De Civ. Dei, viii. 2.)

(2.) *Anaxagoras,* (*a*) of Clazomenae, *b.* circ. 500 B. C.; devoted much attention to mathematics and astronomy; at Athens, æt. 45, the friend of Pericles, Euripides, etc., was accused of impiety, imprisoned, exiled.

A. was a profound and cautious thinker, and, though an Ionian, not satisfied with empirical induction or materialism. (Plato. Apol. p. 26; Crat. p. 409.)

(*b*) *Principle,* a dualism of matter and intelligence, of elements of various kinds and GOD, (νοῦς); the first recorded philosophical theist of Greece, πάντα ἔγνω νοῦς. (Arist. Met. i. 3).

By a sort of chemical theory, A. sets out from a chaos of various elements; the universe is a *plenum* of *homœomeria,* different material particles; (Lucretius, i. 834, seq.; 875, seq.). Intelligence is not the cause of them, though they must have it to guide them; it arranges and disposes them by motion. (Ritter iii. 8; Arist. Met. i. 3, 4; iii. 7; x. 6; xi. 6; Cic. Acad. Quaest. i. 12; ii. 31; Plato's Phaed. p. 97, seq.)

(3.) *Empedocles*, (*a*) of Agrigentum, (circ. 444 B. C.) travelled in Italy and Sicily, a physician, priest, thaumaturgist. His life is traditional, full of fables and marvels.

Like the Eleatics, he stated his doctrine in the form of an epic poem, περὶ φύσεως.

(*b*) Apparently, E. was a syncretist, and is differently placed by different historians of phil.; (in Ritter, an Eleatic.)

There are four elements: fire, air, earth and water; but the "sphere" is the original of things containing the four elements, and two coequal forces, love and hate; love unites the elements, hate separates them; birth and death are a mingling and a separation of the elements. Love seems to be identical with the unity of the Eleatics, and is the source of all beings. (Arist. Met. i. 4; ii. 1, 4; De An. i. 4, 5.)

Aristotle's objections to the Ionian physicists.

(*a.*) They have recognized the existence of bodies only, not of incorporeals.

(*b.*) Merely giving elements, they have neglected the formal cause, or the essence of things.

(*c.*) If they took one element, *e. g.* water, they did not show how the other elements could come from it.

(*d.*) Even by Anaxagoras, no account is rendered of the *why*, or final cause. (Cf. Plato's Phaed. p. 98)

3. Italic or Dorian School.

The Dorians were a deeper, more quiet, more conservative race than the Ionians; hence the ethical and speculative character of their phil., inquiring into the "wherefore" of nature, and its inward meaning, unity and moral ends.

Note.—The term φιλοσοφία is referred to this school by Plato, (Phaed. p. 22; Crat. p. 400.)

A school of great influence, but with no prominent names, except *Pythagoras.*

(Porphyrii Vit. Pyth.; Jamblichi Vit. Pyth.; Plato, de Rep. x. p. 600.)

A. *Life.* P. was born in Samos, (circ. 582, B. C.) Little is known of his life, though many remarkable legends are connected with it.

A contemporary of Thales, he travelled in Egypt, perhaps in India; (did he thence derive metempsychosis?); he settled in Crotona, circ. 529, B. C., and founded a secret institute, religious, scientific, moral and political, with common morals, customs, symbolical aphorisms, etc. Esoteric teaching distinguishes his school, which was soon bitterly persecuted. (Enfield, ii. xii. i.)

P. was a man of great and varied attainments, a scientific mathematician, etc. (Cic. de Nat. De. iii. 36.)

Neither he nor his first disciples left any writings; his school was eminently mathematical; symbolic in its exoteric teaching. (Comte. Pos. Phil. tr. Martineau; i. p. 42.)

B. *Method,* is not empirical, but a pure rationalism.

C. *Principle.* Of his philosophy little is known, but he evidently founds the concrete upon the abstract, and is, so far, ideal. Instead of things, their relations appear to be investigated, *i. e. number,* which is applied to music, astronomy, even to morals. "Number is the essence (οὐσία) or first principle (ἀρχή) of all things." "τοὺς ἀριθμοὺς αἰτίους εἶναι τῆς οὐσίας;" "μιμήσει εἶναι τὰ ὄντα τῶν ἀριθμῶν."

(Arist. Met. i. 5, 6; xiii. 6. Nic. Eth. i. 6; Phys. iii. 5; iv. 6. Cf. Wisdom of S. xi. 20, and S. Aug. Civ. Dei, xii. 18.)

D. *Cosmology* (Κόσμος) is a term due to this school, expressing the harmony of contraries in the universe. The primary elements of nature are arranged in a table of contraries. (Arist. ubi sup.) Even corporeal magnitude is reduced to the ideal, the limit or unit, with the unlimited, or interval.

The earth moves; a proposition which shows independence of sensation.

E. *Psychology.* The soul is immortal; a self-moving monad of two parts, (1) rational, νοῦς, and (2) irrational, θυμός; (Cic. Tusc. Quaest. iv. 5.); νοῦς is a portion of the universal soul. (Cic. de Senect. xxi. 78; De Nat. De. i. 11.)

Metempsychosis. At death the soul passes to the regions of the dead, and thence to some other body; thus it is gradually purified, till fit to return to its eternal source. (Ovid Metam. xv. 3; Horace, Carm. i. 28.)

F. *Ethics.* A highly moral system; (see the life of Archytas); GOD is unity; "all is from the original one"= GOD. Good is unity and harmony, evil is diversity or duality, τὸ ἄπειρον, the unlimited, or want of harmony.

4. ELEATIC SCHOOL.

An idealistic pantheism, (cf. Indian Phil., and see Cousin, Fragm. Phil. v. i.) a metaphysical school, wholly disregarding the sensible, preëminently dialectic, *e. g.*

Zeno, (Euseb. Praep. Ev., quoted in Ritter v. i; Plato, Soph., p. 242 seq.; Arist. Met. i, 5.)

A. *Xenophanes*, (1.) *of Elea*; b. 617-556 B. C., at Colophon; expelled; after travelling, settled at Elea, an Ionian colony; but X. is very unlike an Ionian in phil. He transports Ionian physics to Magna Græcia, and unites them with Pythag. idealism. A poet, he wrote a poem περὶ φύσεως. His phil. is theological in form.

(2.) God is unity, infinity, intelligence, all-powerful, all-good. "One sole God, superior to gods and men, and who resembles not mortals in form or mind;" "unwearied, he directs all by the power of intelligence."

He attacks polytheism and the popular anthropomorphism.

The true existence is eternal, immutable.

Experience gives only appearances.

Evil is diversity.

(Arist. Rhet. ii. 23; Ueberweg, v. i, p. 52, Am. Ed.)

B. *Parmenides*, (1.) b. at Elea, (510-532, B. C.;) was a disciple of X.; he also wrote a poem περὶ φύσεως.

(2.) He renders the system of X. metaphysical. He begins with the idea of pure being. Thought and being are necessarily connected; τὸ αὐτὸ νοεῖν τε καὶ εἶναι. Becoming and decay are non-existence; the truly existent is one, eternal, complete, like a sphere. (Arist. Met. i. 5; iv. 5; Plato, Sophist, p. 242 seq.; Ueberweg, § 19.) (Cf. language; *e. g.* εἶναι, γίγνεσθαι; werden, sein; is, be, etc.)

P. neglects plurality, which is a change in appearance, and thinks only of unity.

Reason gives true knowledge; the senses, only apparent. The world of sense is only phenomenal, *non-ens; i. e.*, he distinguishes sensuous presentations from rational cognitions.

C. *Zeno, of Elea,* (1.) b. at Elea, (505-490 B. C.,) is said to have taught at Athens, æt. 40, but he devoted himself chiefly to politics at Elea, and was put to death (?) for conspiracy against the tyrant of Elea. Z. was the first Eleatic who employed prose for his written teachings.

(2.) Z. reduced the Eleatic system to dialectic forms, proving it, negatively, by showing the contradictions involved in the theory of plurality. (See (*a*) argument concerning motion; (*b*) Achilles and the tortoise; (Arist. Phys. vi. 9;) (*c*) the sound of a measure of falling grain; cf. answer in Arist. Phys. vi. 2, attacked by Bayle, Hist. Dict., Zeno.)

Z. probably used many subtle distinctions to confound his adversaries; (Arist. Phys. vii. 5; Plato, Parmen. p. 127-9; Phaedr. p. 261.)

The senses, he said, do not represent truth; and Z. according denies the reality of existence in space and time, and of motion; the ancients thought he denied the existence of the world.

On the hypothesis of multiplicity, each individual is both finite and infinite, in motion and at rest, like and unlike itself, etc. He probably held all things to be mere phenomena. (Kant Crit. P. Reason, Transc. Dial. of Reason, ii. ii. § 7.)

Finally, the Eleatics denied matter and the world, and offered, in the 5th cent., a pantheistic opposition to the atheism and materialism of the Ionians.

(Cousin, Fragm. Philos. v. i.; Ueberweg, § 20.)

5.—The Sophists.

[*References:*—Grote's Hist. Greece, v. viii., c. xlvii.; Plato, Gorgias, Protagoras; Aristoph. Clouds, v. 886, seq.]

The meeting of different schools at Athens, through the rise of that city in power, civilization and the arts, (Anaxagoras, Parmenides, Zeno, etc.), led to doubt of all schools.

The sophists began, indeed, the work of abandoning the objective, and considering the subjective, perception, opinion, desire, will, and of aiming at universal culture, but with a ruling individualism which soon terminated in sophisms and frivolity. (See Callicles' contempt of phil. in Plato's Gorgias.)

They were great in logical sophisms, and the art of persuasion, and reputed to excel in oratory. *Τὸν ἥττονα λόγον κρείττονα ποιεῖν* was the boast of Protag.

They were sceptical in phil., though of various characters and principles; skilled in rhetoric, dialectics, politics, as a class they were without earnestness or moral convictions.

Nothing was true, nothing false; (Pl. Euthyd. p 285, seq.), nothing good or evil, for the just and base were not by nature, but by convention. (Pl. Gorg. p. 482, seq.; De Leg. x. p. 889; Theæt. p. 167, 172; Rep. vi., p. 492, seq.; Arist. Rhet. ii., 24.)

A. *Gorgias*, (1) born at Leontini, was envoy to Athens, for aid against Syracuse, (427, B. C.) A disciple of Empedocles, he became famous for rhetoric and oratory; the art of persuasion was regarded by him as the highest of all arts.

(2.) He sophistically applied Eleatic doctrine to show (*a*) nothing truly is, neither negatively nor positively, nor both at once; nothing can be shown to be derived, nothing to be eternal.

(*b*) Even if anything is, it cannot be the object of thought. If thought is real, what is not real cannot be thought; therefore, everything that is thought is equally real: if thoughts are not real, then the real cannot be in thought.

(*c*) If anything is real and cognizable, it cannot be imparted to others. Thoughts are expressed in words, and words represent different things to different men. (Pl. Gorg. passim; Meno, pp. 70–6; Phileb. p. 58; Phædr. p. 261.)

B. *Protagoras*, (1.) circ. 490, taught rhetoric in Sicily and Greece. He calls himself a Sophist. (Meno, p. 91.) At Athens he was accused of impiety, being unable to say whether there be any gods or not, and expelled from the city.

(2.) P. sophistically develops the "flux" of Heraclitus. All objects of knowledge are relative; objective existence, if there be such a thing, cannot be represented in thought: "ἐστὶ μὲν γὰρ οὐδέποτ᾽ οὐδὲν, ἀεὶ δὲ γίγνεται." (See thorough discussion in Theæt. p. 151, seq., though it is questionable how far Plato strictly follows Protag.)

No position therefore can be contradicted; (Euthyd. p. 286); "πάντων χρημάτων μέτρον εἶναι ἄνθρωπον." Thought is identical with sensation, and knowledge is individual.

The soul is the sum of the different moments of thinking.

See, particularly, Arist.'s careful refutation, (Met. x. 6), who regards Protag. as a disciple of the physicists:

(*a*) His stand point involves the truth of contradictories.

(*b*) Though sensations are subjective, the subject, the *ego*, is permanent.

(*c*) The ego has power to distinguish dreams from the objectively real, etc.

Distinguish also αἴσθησις from φρόνησις.

(Protag. passim; Hipp. Maj. p. 28; Meno, p. 91; Crat. p. 383 seq.; Arist. Met. ii. 2; iii. 8.)

C. Other Sophists of the first period are Hippias of Elis, (Hipp. Maj. and Min.); Prodicus of Ceos, (Crat. p. 383) a lecturer on grammar and language, (see the Choice of Hercules; Xen. Mem.); Critias, the most able of the Thirty Tyrants, an opponent of Socrates, who based religion on political considerations; the soul is material and resides in the blood.

CHAPTER IV.

SOCRATES; PLATO; ARISTOTLE.

1. SOCRATES. 2. PLATO. 3. ARISTOTLE.

1. SOCRATES.

[*Reference* :—Plato; Xenophon; Aristophanes. Distinguish the historical Soc. from P.'s dialectics under the name of his master.]

A. *Life.* S. was born, 469, B. C., the son of Sophroniscus a sculptor and Phaenarete a midwife; a soldier at Potidaea, etc.; he resisted the Thirty Tyrants and the democracy. (Xen. Mem. I. i. 18; iv. 4. 1, etc.; Plato's Apol.)

His personal appearance is described by Alcibiades, in the *Symposium*, of Plato, ugly as Silenus or a satyr.

S. was constantly in public, conversing with all classes in the agora or gymnasia; (Mem. I. i. 10) and at first was confounded with the Sophists; (Aristoph. Clouds.) For the astonishing power of his words, note the language of Alcib. in the Sympos., who also bears testimony to his prudence, temperance, fortitude and self-control.

His condemnation, inscribed in the temple of Cybele: "Soc., Son of Sophron., is guilty of not recognizing the gods whom the state recognizes, and of introducing unknown divinities. He is guilty also of corrupting the youth. Penalty, death."

A change of thirty (three ?) votes would have acquitted him. (Apol.) He might perhaps have escaped from prison, but was too loyal to do so. (Crito.)

"Either death is a sleep, and so not to be feared; or it is life, and so to be desired." "But it is now time to depart; for me to die, for you to live; but which of us is going to a better state is unknown to any one but GOD."

Examine his injunction to sacrifice, when at the point of death. (Phaed.) S. died 399 B. C.

B. *Mission of Socrates;* (1) to establish the objective reality of truth, goodness and beauty against the subjectivity of the Sophists, who made man the measure of all things.

(2.) To add to the "Nous" of Anaxagoras the doctrine of final causes. (Phaed. p. 97; Mem. i. 4, 6; iv. 3, 3., etc.)

(3.) "*Maieutic,*" to lead men to know their ignorance, and search for truth.

"I am wiser than this man; for neither of us appears to know anything great and good; but he fancies that he knows something, although he knows nothing; whereas, I, as I do not know anything, so I do not fancy that I do." (Apol. p. 21.)

(4.) To turn thought from unpractical speculation to self-knowledge, the "*γνῶθι σεαυτόν.*" (Mem. I., i, 11-16; III. ix.) The sciences of nature are of little value in comparison with this. (Mem. iv. 7; Rep. vii. p. 529.)

C. *Method.* (1.) Erotetic, undogmatic, leading to confession of ignorance. Note a skeptical tendency in some of his school.

(2.) If Plato give the historical Soc., by induction, division and definition. (Arist. Met. xii. 4.)

(3.) With the same qualification, the true founder of a scientific method, investigating the connection between the thought and the reality, even in the most trivial things, and seeking for the scientific ground of harmony of ideas in accurate definitions of the essence of things. (e. g. Phaedr. p. 237; Mem. iv. v. 12; i. 1, 16; and cf. def. of science in Dr. Porter's Human Intellect, p. 438.)

D. *Principles ;* are ethical.

(1.) There is a GOD, (Mem. iv. 3), an immortal soul, a future responsibility (Crito; Phaed. p. 80 seq., p. 113 seq.) and an absolute good. (Phaed.)

(2.) Virtue and happiness are one, τὸ καλαγαθον. Virtue is founded on wisdom and knowledge, for no one wilfully injures himself. (Mem. iv. vi, 6.) Happiness, εὐδαιμονία, is not pleasure, but right views of all things carried out in the life. (Philebus.) Pleasure is not the good; for the good is one, and pleasures are manifold, and contrary to one another.

The study of physics is worthless, unless we find the spiritual basis of all science. (Mem. iv. 7; Phaed. p. 97.)

Note S's δάιμων; how to be explained?

2. PLATO.

[*References*:—Jowett's and Stallbaum's Notes; Aristotle; Diog. Laert., Cicero.]

A. *Life.* P. was born at Ægina, 430, B. C.; (d. 349, B. C.) He was of illustrious descent, by his father from Cadmus, by his mother from Solon. His *Nomen* was Aristocles; he was called Plato from his personal appearance. Wealthy, of superior education, a poet, etc., when twenty years of age he became a disciple of Socrates. After the death of his master he travelled in Italy, Cyrene, and Egypt. He then established his school at Athens, the *Academy*. He visited Sicily twice, called thither to give political counsels to Dionysius; but he incurred the tyrant's displeasure, and by some, is said to have been sold as a slave.

B. *Difficulty* in the study of his system. His works are dialogue in form, dialectic in method, often figurative, *mythical* in expression, and frequently undogmatic.

P. also is many-sided, the "myriad-minded" Shakspeare of Phil.; "Deus ille noster." (Cic.) Socrates may be his best representative.

Various classifications of the dialogues; (see Diog. Laert. de Vit. etc., c. 48.) Theaet. may be a serviceable introduction to his principles in opposition to the relativity of Protag.

(On the value of P. in mental training, see J. S. Mill's Autob. p. 21.)

C. *Method.* (See Socrates' method; (2,) (3.)

(1.) Not empirical like the Ionians; this only applicable to phenomena.

(2.) Nor the moderate realism of Aristotle, founding the ideal on the concrete, the universal on the individual; but,

(3.) Basing absolute truth on the cognitions of pure reason. (Rep. vi. p, 508; vii. p. 517, 533.) The *à priori* method, but to be tested by experience.

(4.) Dialectic, (note his development of dialectics), apprehending ideas by rising to the universal, *i.e.*, division and definition, or finding the essence, and then returning from the universal to the particular, (Phaedr. pp. 265, 6: Euthyph. p. 6.)

D. *Divisions of knowledge.* Fourfold, corresponding

with the four faculties of the soul, and based on the fundamental antithesis of the senses and the intelligible, pure being and the becoming, the universal and the particular.

(1.) Εικασία, the sensuous perception of phenomena as mere shadows, by αἴσθησις, the faculty adapted to the perpetually changing κόσμος αἰσθητὸς.

(2.) πίστις, the imperfect knowledge of bodies obtained through sense-perception.

(1.) and (2.) Δόξα, opinion based on the collected results of experience, but not true knowledge.

(3.) Διάνοια, the discursive reason, the understanding, making use of sensible representations, εἴδωλα, hypotheses, etc., as in mathematics.

(4.) Νοῦς, pure reason, gives true knowledge, ἐπιστήμη, of pure ideas, ἰδέαι, of principles, seen intuitively in their eternal source. (Rep. vi. ad. fin.; vii. pp. 507–534. Crat. 440; Tim. p. 27.) On this is based the division of all knowledge.

(1.) Dialectics; (2.) Physics; (3.) Ethics.

E. *Dialectics*, in the narrowest sense, the instruments of investigation, analytics, logic; but used by P. in a wider sense, the art of reducing the manifold to unity of concept, of arranging concepts, by analysis or synthesis, by division and definition. (Phaedr. p. 265, seq.; Rep. vii. 533.)

(1.) *Theory of ideas.* These are the only real existences, perfect, unchangeable, eternal; seen by pure reason, they are its concepts. Distinguish them from εἴδωλα, changeable, and having only a resemblance to true being; the former are ἄρχαι, παραδείγματα, eternal types impressed by the eternal Architect on crude matter, ἀρχέτυπον κόσμου αἰσθήτου, and recognized by reason in all concrete forms, actions, words, etc.

Endless being, then, the only reality, apprehended by νοῦς, must, always and in all things, be clearly distinguished from the becoming, which is the object of sense and opinion. (Tim. p. 28–30, p. 51. Phaed. p. 65.)

The sensible world, on the other hand, is the region of the imperfect, the changeable, the becoming, the subject to time. The individual is what it is, by partaking of the ideal; (Phaed. p. 101 seq.) Proper being, and the difference of individuals, are through and in the ideas. This is equally true of the good and the beautiful. Sensible things are only imperfect εἴδωλα of true being; they are limited by matter, by their changefulness.

(2.) *Theosophy.* God is the one, absolute, infinite, the *good.* This idea is transcendent, "above essence;" (Rep. vi. p. 508; vii. p. 517 etc.); as the sun, it lends to all other ideas, being, essence, even the power of being known by pure reason. P. seems to regard God as Ὁ Λόγος the source and seat of ideas; as νοῦς, perfect intelligence, omniscient, omnipresent, willing good to all.

But notice the different view of his phil. in Aristotle, the figurative style, the uncertain and, possibly, the varying views of Plato. (Tim. p. 37, 68; Rep. ii. 379 seq.; x. 597; Phil. p. 30.)

Aristotle's objections (Met. i. 9.)

(*a*) Ideas are not causes;

(*b*) What is their source and unity?

Note also the influence of the Platonic idea on subsequent thought. (See S. Aug. quoted in Ueberweg, i. p. 340; Roman de la Rose, l. 17, 644; Spenser's Hymn of Beauty; Davies, Nosce Teipsum, etc., etc.,

F. *Physics.* (1.) *Cosmology.* Distinguish the κόσμος νοητός from κόσμος αἰσθητός; the latter is the object of belief, πίστις, not knowledge, the "shadows in the cave" of unseen realities. (Rep. vii.; Tim. p. 28). The ever-existing, ungenerated, is apprehended by νοῦς. Three principles are needed to explain the world;

(*a*) ever-existing matter, in itself undefined, orderless chaos, blind ἀνάγκη;

(*b*) GOD, the Demiurgos, who gave order, goodness, and beauty to this primitive chaos, as the good making all things good, and, as far as possible, after his similitude;

(*c*.) The ideal world the pattern of whatever is generated, and in a state of becoming, γένεσις, in the material world. The order of origin was, (*a*) the world-soul, communicated by Himself from that which could be communicated: (*b*) the bodily cosmos, a perfect sphere, of the four material elements. From these premises follows,

(*a*) The world is not eternal; as it had a beginning, so will it also have an end. Time is a creation, and that which is, is not subject to time.

(*b*) This world is the only possible, and the best possible world. Its limitation is in matter. In this latter is found the ground of evil. From GOD comes only the good, but matter opposes itself, the principle of disorder.

(2) *Psychology.* The soul is not a mere "harmony" of the body. It is a simple, spiritual essence.

(*a*) This *rational soul* is, (α) νοῦς, the seat of ideas, and seeks for the true, the beautiful, the good, *i. e.*, GOD. It is placed in the head.

(β) διάνοια, discursive reason, understanding, arguing from hypotheses, sensible representations, etc.

(γ) αἴσθησις, giving perceptions of the sensible world, but these sensuous cognitions suggest the ideas which they resemble.

This rational soul is the governing principle; the governed, the irrational is, (*b*) θυμός, the seat of emotions, situated in the breast, found also in beasts, it mediates between (*a*) and

(*c*) τὸ ἐπιθυμητικόν, the seat of appetites, the desire of what preserves and continues the perpetually changing body. Its seat is the belly; is found also in plants. (*b*) and (*c*) perish with the body; but the rational soul simply uses the body as its temporary organ by which it is brought into relation with the world of the *becoming*, of sensuous phenomena.

Proof of (*a*), (*b*), (*c*), as distinct divisions of the soul is the conflict of (*a*) and (*c*), (*b*) siding with the former though itself irrational, seen in children and brutes, and sometimes overmastering reason.

(Phaedr. p. 246; Rep. iv. 436, seq.)

Immortality of the soul; i. e., of the rational soul.

Proofs, (1) knowledge is reminiscence of ideas possessed before the soul's union with the body: the existence of the former, therefore, does not depend on the latter. (Phaed., p. 72 seq.)

(2.) From the *idea* of the soul, a self-moving, self-subsisting essence, to which, as such, life is essential. A dead soul is a contradiction.

(Phaed., p. 65, seq. Phaedr., p. 245 seq.)

(3.) An essence can only be destroyed by some ill necessarily attending it, in this case, moral ill. This is impossible. (Rep. x., p. 608 seq.)

Metempsychosis. To search and learn is the recalling of ideas which the soul brings with it into the body. After death, it will migrate into other bodies, according to its life here, whether of subjection to corporeal appetites, or of philosophical emancipation, as far as possible, from the body.

(Meno, p. 81 seq.; Phaedr., p. 247-9; Phaed., p. 81, seq.)

Note. The world cycle of ten thousand years; but in this whole subject, it is difficult to separate P.'s scientific thought from poetic speculation.

Plato distinguishes (*a*) the representative faculty, imagination, bringing up former impressions of objects, (Phileb., p. 33, seq.); (*b*) μνήμη, preservation of sensations; (*c*) ἀνάμνησις, recollection, which, independently of sensation, recalls ideas or cognitions.

G. *Ethics.* (1) *Pleasure.* P. takes an intermediate position between Hedonism and Cynicism; distinguishes between true and false pleasures, the pure and the impure, those which are of the rational nature, and those which are of the irrational. Pleasures, then, are not the highest good, nor its test or measure, since they are various and contrary to one another. (Phil. passim.)

(2.) *Summum bonum;* is the idea of the good, *i. e.*, GOD, towards which as ultimate end the aims of the wise will be directed in all things. But this idea, which cannot be embraced in its unity, will be sought in the manifold, in science, ἐπιστήμη, in truth and reason, in beauty, in virtue. (Rep. vi. p. 505 seq.)

(3.) Ἐυδαιμονία, subjectively, man's highest good, is found in resemblance to GOD; as the phenomenal and becoming are to be conformed to the divine and eternal; (Theaet., p. 176; Rep., x. p. 613.) The soul then possesses truth and goodness. Other goods are *relative, e. g.*, special sciences and arts, health, riches, sensual pleasures.

(4.) *Virtue*, then, is harmony of soul; so far as possible, it is attained by aiming at the Sum. Bon. (1st. Alc.)

It is identified with wisdom, with reason, as the essence of the soul. Whatever is in conflict with this is alien to the soul; and vice, therefore, is founded in ignorance, for no one is willingly and consciously evil. All aim at some seeming good, agreeable because it seems a good, though many err involuntarily. (Meno, p. 77, seq.; Gorg., p. 466, seq.; Protag., p. 360; Tim., p. 86.)

(5.) *Divisions.* Virtue is in essence one; four-fold according to the three parts of the soul.

(*a*) *Φρόνησις*, wisdom, prudence, is the virtue of the reason;

(*b*) *'Ανδρεία*, courage, is that of the *θυμός*, the spirit, the passions, when reason directs them;

(*c*) *Σωφροσύνη*, temperance, moderation, is that of the appetites, when reason controls them;

(*d*) *Δικαιοσύνη*, justice, is the harmony or due regulation and mutual adjustment of all.

These are the four "cardinal virtues" of Christian Phil. (S. Aug. Civ. Dei., iv. 20.)

(Note. This, like the rest of Phil. for the few. (Sympos. p. 204; Rep., vi. p. 500; Protag., p. 352; Phaed., p. 82.) Evil is grounded in the corporeal or becoming, faintly accounted for, and remediless.)

(6) *Politics.* The *state* is founded on nature, not on compact; it is ethical, its rule is the welfare of the whole as a unit, and the idea of the good, which does not depend on actual, positive laws. (Leg., vii. p. 817.)

The *ideal state* is found in the Republic, after the analogy of man's soul.

(*a*) Reason=the wise, philosophers; for the right of governing is not in man as man, but in the wise and good. The state will not be freed from its evils, until philosophers be kings, or its kings be philosophers. (Rep., v. 473.)

(*b*) Passions=the army, for defence, and execution of laws.

(*c*) The appetites=laborers and tradesmen, who are in absolute subjection.

Socialism. Under the direction of (*a*) a communism in all things is established, property, children, women ; children are the wards of the commonwealth from their birth ; the State educates them. (See De Quincey on the Rep., and cf. the ideal of the Cath. Ch.)

In the Laws, a less theoretical, more practical view of the State. But from these principles results that monarchy, if founded on reason, or aristocracy under the same conditions, is preferable to a democracy, for justice will assign honor and power to each in proportion to his merit. (Laws, iv. p. 711, seq.; Polit, p. 300, seq. ; Rep., viii. init.)

H. *Æsthetics.* (1) *Beauty* is one, subsisting in itself, *i. e.*, the good. Objects are beautiful through their participating in this. It is seen on earth by the reason, through the senses, in types and changeable forms which suggest it. If the types are ravishing, how much more the reality. (Sympos., p. 210–2.)

(2.) *Love* is the soul's longing for union with the beautiful. "They that are followers of Zeus, seek for some one who resembles Z. in his soul to be the object of love." (Phaedr., p. 250.)

(3.) Beauty is (*a*) spiritual ; therefore (*b*) in truth, derived to (*c*) the soul, (*d*) the body, (*e*) arts, (*f*) sciences.

In Hippias Major (Platonic) beauty is not ;

(*a*) The becoming, which is relative, phenomenal ;

(*b*) The useful, which may be turned to evil ;

(*c*) The advantageous, which produces the good, but is not the good ;

(*d*) The pleasurable, for pleasures are manifold, and subjective.

(4) *Art,* when it copies the phenomenal is the lowest ; the highest seeks to embody the spiritual. (See art topics in Rep., ii. p. 376 to middle of iii. ; and trace the influence of P.'s æsthetics in art and literature, *e. g.*, in the Eliz. age.)

I. *Mathematics,* in special sciences, are intermediate between the sensual and the ideal ; they are not philosophy, because they begin with hypotheses, and employ visible figures, etc. ; (hence διάνοια.) These, however, are not the true objects of investigation, but that which is seen by intellect alone. They are a guide to higher phil. (οὐδεὶς ἀγεωμετρήτος εἰσίτω shows the spirit of this school.) (Rep., v., 475, seq. ; vi. 510, seq. ; vii., p. 523, seq.)

The ideal numbers may be seen by higher reason, in the harmony of the universe. (Tim., p. 53, etc.)

2. Aristotle.

[*References:*—Diog. Laert., Ritter, Grote, etc. Reviews, Edin., Oct., 1872 ; Br. Quarterly., Ap., 1873.]

A. *Life.* A. was born at Stagira, 384, B.C. ; his father was Nicomachus, a physician, and his son bears the same name : he was a disciple of Plato, æt. 17–37. By Philip he was made Alexander's tutor, and was afterwards aided by the latter in his scientific researches. In Alex.'s absence he taught at the Lyceum ; and from the shady walks, περίπατοι, his school was named Peripatetic. He taught thirteen years, was accused of impiety, (?) and retired to Eubœa, where he died 322, B.C.

Pure intellect and analysis were never carried further; he seeks absolute precision of conclusions, but is most unspiritual, unsympathetic, wanting the intuition of genius and the ability to unite the multiplicity of experiences.

Works.—He is universally learned. Variation of style, how accounted for? Often condensed to obscurity, abrupt and wanting in connection. (Acroamatic?)

Singular history of his works; bequeathed to Theophrastus, they were finally concealed under ground to hide them from the King of Pergamos, and so damaged: finally Sylla obtained them. When edited, the lacunæ conjecturally filled?

(1.) Dialectics: (*a*) Treatise on the "prima philosophia," τὰ μετὰ τὰ φυσικά.

(*b*.) Organon, collected logical treatises; (1.) Categories; (2.) περὶ ἑρμηνείας; (3.) Prior and Posterior Analytics; (4.) Topics; (5.) Sophistical Elenchi.

(2.) Physics: (*a*) φυσικὴ ἀκρόασις; (*b*) Περὶ οὐρανοῦ; (*c*) Μετεωρολογικά; (*d*) Natural History of Animals, etc., etc.

Physiology: (*a*) Περὶ ψυχῆς; (*b*) On sensation and the sensible; (*c*) Περὶ μνήμης καὶ ἀναμνήσεως; (*d*) on sleep; (*e*) on divination, etc., etc.

(3.) Ethics: (*a*) Nicomachean Ethics; (*b*) Eudemian; (*c*) Magna Moralia; (*d*) Politics; (*e*) Economics (incomplete), etc., (*f*) Poetics (incomplete), (*g*.) Rhetoric.

(B.) *Method, and Theory of knowledge.* (1.) A.'s method always is *à posteriori*, to begin with the sensible, the individual, the many, in order to proceed to the intelligible, the one; from τὰ καθ' ἕκαστα to τὰ καθόλου.

He agrees with Plato in the principle that there is no

science except of the general, but insists that that is found only in the individual; but he is averse to the ideal, and he continually denies the existence of ideas apart from actual things. (Met. i. 9: xii. 4, 7.)

The universal is that which is common to many, and can be predicated of them all; it is not objectively real.

(2.) All *knowledge* is grounded on sensuous perception, but this is the foundation for higher knowledge, of which intellect only is cognizable. But this does not exist in and by itself; without sensation no one could know anything. (De An. iii. 8.)

All concepts are derived from, accompanied by, definite images, without which the soul does not think. (De An. iii. 7.)

The *order* is (*a*) sensation (of individuals); (*b*) sensuous presentation; (*c*) Memory; (*d*) comparison; (*e*) distinction; (*f*) experience; (*g*) knowledge. (Post. An. ii. 19.) But the last is obtained by, and is in, the νοῦς only. Experience tells us "that it is," not *why* anything is.

The universal, according to its nature, is prior and better known; but, for us, the individual is such. (Phys. i., 2, 3.)

(3.) *Active and Passive Intellect.* The sensible is contingent phenomena, but being is known by intellect alone, though it exists only in the sensible, and is known at the same time. (Post. An. i. 31.)

(*a.*) The reason in man, the seat of ideas, is at first as a writing-tablet on which nothing is written; ideas exist in it only potentially, ἐν δυνάμει; this (like matter, ὕλη, in beings), is the passive intellect.

(*b.*) The active intellect, τὸ αἴτιον καὶ ποιητικὸν,

an eternal activity, incorporeal, simple, passionless, awakens, enlightens the other, and ideas pass into actuality, ἐνεργεία, ἐντελέχεια.

(4.) *Truth* is the correspondence of the combination of mental representations, with a combination of things. (Met. v., 4.) Sensation is always true; error, if any, is in the judgment. (De. An. iii. 3.)

Phil. may be *divided*, as (*a*) theoretical; (*b*) practical, ethics.

(*a*) is (α) theology; (β) physics; (γ) mathematics (pure); (*a*) is (i) Analytics; (ii.) *Phil. prima.*

(C.) *Principle.* (1) Substance is that which is in no other, but in which all other is; it can be predicated of no other, but all other is predicated of it. This, individual, is οὐσία πρώτη; species is a "second essence," the quiddity, τὸ τὶ ἦν εἶναι, common to many individuals.

(2.) The two constitutive principles are (*a*) matter, ὕλη, (*b*) form, εἶδος, μόρφη; (*a*) is the principle of potentiality, of individuality, the determined, the ὑποκείμενον; (*b*) is the determining, the idea, seen by the mind only, the essence whereby the individual is what it is; abstracted from the individual, it is the universal, predicable of many individuals.

There is no truth apart from the individual; yet three classes of truth are to be distinguished:

(*a*) Particular, obtained empirically, by induction. (Post. An. i., 1-31; Topics i., 1.)

(*b*) Deductive, obtained by demonstration;

(*c*) Principles of pure reason, ἀρχαί, intuitive; when their terms are understood, the basis of demonstration. (Nic. Eth. vi. 6.) A. fails, however, to give unity to his system by an analysis of these.

(D.) *Analytics:* the forms of thought, of science.

(1.) The *concept* is the essence, οὐσία, of the individual abstracted; it is expressed in the definition. Distinguish in the concept the universal, the *species*, common to many invividuals, and the limiting, the *differentia*, related as matter and form. These specific concepts are again, by abstraction, *subsumed* under higher concepts, the generic; thus by continued abstraction we reach

(2.) The *Categories*, modes of being and thought, the various species of mental representations, of concepts, of predicamenta; they are (Categ. 4; arbitrarily) ten; (*a*) essence, τὸ τὶ ἦν εἶναι; (*b*) quantity; (*c*) quality; (*d*) relation; (*e*) the where; (*f*) the when; (*g*) position; (*h*) habit; (*i*) action; (*k*) passion.

(3.) *Propositions*, λόγοι. Truth or falsehood is possible in these only; the principle of contradiction is the ground of demonstration. A. distinguishes contingent from necessary truths, not separating forms of being from forms of thought; the former are based on the possible; the contradictory of which is not the possible-not-to-be, but the impossible; as the necessary is contradicted by the not-necessary. (De Interp. xii.) The necessary is that which is in actuality; the possible, that which may be moved in opposite directions.

(4.) *Syllogism*, is "a discourse in which from certain propositions another necessarily results by means of those laid down." (Top. i., 1.)

The three figures are pointed out, but only the Categ. Syll. discussed.

(*a*) The *demonstrative* syll., deductive, by means of the middle concept, connecting the higher with the lower, sets out from some general principle, prior in its nature, better known in itself.

(*b*) The inductive, ἐξ ἐπαγωγῆς, proceeds from the lower, from particulars, better known to us as more nearly allied to sensation. (Pr. An. ii. 23; Post. An. i, 12.)

(5.) *Proof* is by means of the syllogism; (*a*) apodeictic from a necessarily true principle;

(*b*) Dialectic, from a probable principle to a probable conclusion;

(*c*) Eristic, fallacy.

Hence, science is knowing phenom. in their ground and causes; it unites experience of phenom. with knowledge of the principles of pure reason, (*e. g.* the principle of contradiction, Met. iv.): it has for its object the necessary and unchangeable; *scientia est de necessariis.*

(E.) *Metaphysics*, the "first philosophy," the principles and ultimate causes of all being. (Met. ii. 2.)

The Four principles of being, ἀρχαί, αἴτιαι, are (1) matter, ὕλη; (2) form, μόρφη, εἶδος; (3) efficient cause, τὸ κινητικόν, (4) end, final cause, τὸ οὗ ἕνεκα. (Met. i. 3.)

(1.) *Matter* is the indeterminate, the becoming, potentially, ἐν δυνάμει, whatever is produced, in itself unknowable, without predicates, underlying all change or becoming, *materia prima;* (Met. vi. 10; De An. iii. 4.)

Purely passive, an eternal principle of necessity limits the essences formed of it; thus God, though not limited in Himself, is so in His relation to what is produced; for He does not give the potentiality, which is eternal as He.

(2.) *Form*, the inner, immanent principle of determination, constitutes the actuality, ἐνεργεία, the essence of the thing, inseparable from matter; τοῦ δυνάμει ὄντος λόγος ἡ ἐντελέχεια: (Met. vi. 10; vii. 2, etc.; De An. ii. 1; Phys. ii. 1.)

(3.) *Substance* is the unity of matter and form, which

are always co-existent, the one potentially, the other actually, ἐνεργείᾳ.

Matter is the ground of multiplicity; form is limited by it; different forms are actualized in different matters. The ground-matter exists, as opposed to form, as privation, στέρησις, which may make a third principle of substance.

The one, then, not existing apart from the many, is present in the many. (Ueberweg, § 48.)

(4.) *Motion*, in general, is the combining of form and matter, the transition from the potential to the actual. Its ground is not in matter, for it is an ἐνεργεία, though imperfect. (Met. x. 9.) Form or actuality is prior to matter, at least in thought. But, on the other hand, matter is an eternal principle of things, and motion is eternal. (Met. xi. 7.)

(5.) *Final cause*, is the good, the end of motion, τὸ οὗ ἕνεκα; every becoming has a design, and this is the first cause, and knowledge of it is the highest aim of phil. It is, at least in generation, the form, a perfect ἐντελέχεια, (Met. vii, 6), having its end and completion in itself. Divide ends, however, into energies and works. (Nic. Eth. i. 1.)

Essence and end, then, are the same; and often, also, the moving cause, since like begets like, and the form is one, though the individuals are many. Matter is the contrary of these, a necessary means, on which acts the moving force already existing in some other matter.

(6.) God is the first moving cause, πρῶτον κινοῦν ἀκίνητον, acting on the *materia prima*. (Phys. viii. 5.) He is one, devoid of matter the ground of multiplicity, an eternal entelechy, not in time or space, pure reason, perfect and happy. He is at once efficient cause, end, and form of the world, *anima mundi.* The object of thought in Him is identified with the thought itself, intelligence and the intelligible; τῆς νοήσεως νόησις. (Met. x. 7.)

A. does not recognize a special Providence, nor moral attributes in God, (Nic. Eth. x, 8); He is not cognizant of the world.

A. does not distinguish the infinite from the indeterminate, τὸ ἄπειρον; it is that beyond which something more may always be taken. (Phys. iii, 7.)

(F.) *Physics* are concerned with that which has motion or change; they proceed from phenomena to probable conclusions. (Met. vi. 1; x. 7; Post. An. i. 33.)

(1.) *Cosmology.* The world is an eternally self-moving, limited, sphere, possessing an *anima mundi,* its form; it has continuous, uniform, circular, motion, proceeding from the imperishable heaven, which is moved by the First Cause as its end.

Nature, then, a living being, consists of matter and form, (Phys. ii. 1), both eternal. The former is the ground of imperfection. The distinction between the natural and the rational is that the latter has choice of determinations, while the former is determined to one definite activity. (Met. ix. 2) All phenomena are produced by the living force in nature which works towards this one end, the perfect form of things; but not consciously, ἡ γὰρ φύσις δαιμονία, ἀλλ' οὐ θεία; and this energy, from imperfect matter, may produce monsters and abortions.

Local Motion, being the transition from the potential to the actual, and, consequently, continuous, presupposes (*a*) *space* and (*b*) *time.*

(*a*) is relative, the limit of the containing body so far as the contained body is capable of local motion. All things, then, are in heaven, which is not in space, and space does not exist without contents, (denies a vacuum.) (*a*) is infinitely divisible potentially; i. e., all that has magnitude is capable of infinite division; it is, potentially, infinite in extent; actually, the world's limit; (*b*) is an accident of motion, the number of motion, (Phys. iv. 10-13), and would not be if there were not a soul. *Now* is the principle of its continuity, as the point in space; (*b*) is, potentially, not actually, divisible to infinity.

Of the four changes, μεταβόλαι, (first, generation and decay) the three motions in (α) magnitude, (β) quality, (γ) place, are founded in (γ) local motion, which also precedes generation and decay (non-being to being, being to non-being.)

The *earth*, in the centre, far removed from the prime mover, is exposed to generation and decay.

The elements, fire, air, earth, and water, (matter warm and moist, or the contraries,)—are not permanent. The fifth element, ether, of the heavens, is perfect, permanent.

(2.) *Psychology.* All things being animated, there is a continuous progression from the lowest up to man.

(*a*) The *Soul* is ἐντελέχεια ἡ πρώτη σώματος φυσικοῦ δυνάμει ζωὴν ἔχοντος; (de An. ii. 1); it is the end, the essence of the body, its formal, final, moving cause; it is the "vital principle," and the organic body is essential to its existence. It has not extension, and is not moved in space; the man is moved, not his soul. It has its end in itself, while each bodily organ is for some soul function.

It is (α) θρεπτικόν, as in plants, the principle of generation, nutriment, growth and decay.

(β) αἰσθητικόν, with pleasure and pain; affected by the sensible, the particular, the phenomenal, by which the soul is impressed with sensible forms, as the wax of a seal. In the more perfect animal are five possible senses, with a *communis sensus* combining them.

Memory is part of the communis sensus, but joins to the sensuous representation, the perception of time, (distinguish ἀνάμνησις, voluntary, peculiar to man.)

Imagination, φαντασία, is a weaker, continued sensation.

(γ) ὀρεκτικόν, desire following pleasure, and aversion shunning pain, as motions of the soul; these two are irrational, found with(α)in brutes; in man to be ruled by reason, and, with relation to it, passive.

(δ) κινητικόν, locomotion in the higher animals, resulting from (γ). The higher soul is evolved from the lower; its seat, the heart.

(ε) διανοητικόν, the rational soul, in man only, containing the other four as powers, of which (α) only is not subject to the rational.

(*b*) *Reason*, νοῦς, is related to the soul, ψυχὴ, as GOD to nature; it distinguishes man.

(α) νοῦς παθητικός, the potentiality, capacity of receiving concepts through sensible forms. (Trendelenburg.)

(β) νοῦς ποιητικός, discerns universal principles, necessary truths, eternal, imperishable, the universal reason, GOD; (Nic. Eth. vi, 6); it makes sensible objects, through abstraction, intelligible. (εἴδη νοήτα.)

A. distinguishes (α) the practical reason, deliberate preference, intelligent will, from irrational desire, but not clearly; reason is related to desire, as sensation is; both presenting the object, the good.

(β) Theoretical, speculative; here distinguish διάνοια,

ratiocination, dealing with contingent principles, with particulars, in prudence, deliberation, etc., (Nic. Eth. vi.) it proceeds from principles by deduction.

(G) *Ethics.* A. prefers the general name of *politics*: (Greek thought.)

Its divisions are (1) Ethics; (2) Economics; (3) Politics (modern).

(1.) *Principle*; not the absolute good (God), but the good for man (Nic. Eth. i. 6); he is by nature a ζῶον πολιτικόν, and morals are grounded on his nature and end, which is his highest good.

The good, in particular, is, (*a*) moral, τὸ κάλον; (*b*) the convenient, τὸ συμφέρον; (*c*) the agreeable, τὸ ἡδύ.

(2.) *Virtue*, since nature always tends to the highest good, is grounded in (*a*) natural sentiments, πάθη; its seat may be in the sensitive and appetitive souls, *e. g.* ἀνδρεία and σωφροσύνη, though rationality makes these good in man. Πάθη, in themselves not moral, become so in their rational government.

(*b*) habits, ἕξεις, dispositions of passions whose result is ἦθος, moral character; (Nic. Eth. ii, 1, 5) hence arise

(*a*) Moral virtues, ἠθικαί, acquired by acts, which form habits; (A. opposes the Socratic union of science with virtue; (Nic. Eth. vii. 3); their seat is in the appetitive soul, (ὄρεξις);

(*b*) Intellectual virtues, διανοητικαί, founded on (*a*) and perfecting them. (Nic. Eth. vi. 3-13; Pol. vii. 13). These are (*α*) practical, viz. (I.) art, and (II.) prudence; (*β*) speculative, viz. (I.) science, ἐπιστήμη; (II.) intelligence, νοῦς, intuition of principles; (III.) wisdom, right view of things to be done, embracing (I.) and (II.) is the perfect activity of the most perfect part of the soul, the chief end, the highest felicity.

(3.) *Summum Bonum*, is pursued not as a means but as an end; it is *happiness*. What is that? "a perfect, practical activity of soul in a perfect life." (Nic. Eth. i., x. 6-8; Mag. Mor. i.) The highest is θεώρια; yet it is partially dependent also on (*a*) the body; (*b*) external things, as wealth, friends, etc., (man's end limited to an earthly existence.)

Pleasure, as such, is neither good nor evil; it follows all energies; on the good follow good pleasures; on the evil, evil pleasures. (Nic. Eth. x. 1-5.)

(4.) *Practical ethics*, of moderation. Virtue, being the habit of good actions, is a mean between extremes in action and the conduct of passions; "in medio tutissimus ibis." (Nic. Eth. ii. 6.)

Rashness—Courage—Cowardice.

Intemperance—Temperance.———

Extravagance—Liberality—Meanness, etc.

(An arbitrary law; who shall determine τὸ μέσον? A. makes virtue relative, and limited by the imperfections of nature; *e.g.*, woman and the slave.)

(5.) *Politics*. (*a*) The state exists by nature, since man is ζῶον πολιτικόν; it arises from love and natural needs, (Pol. i. 2; iii. 1, 9); apart from it man is a savage, ἀφρήστωρ, ἀθεμίστιος, ἀνέστιος. (Hom. Il. ix. 62.) Utility is its rule, for necessaries, good order, and virtue; and the inquiry must be, not the absolutely good, but what is attainable. Hence the moral standard is for the most part, based on the latter, and on positive law. By disposition of nature, some are to think and govern, others to do manual labor and be governed. Slavery therefore justified, and, in some cases, tyranny. (Pol. i. 2, 5, etc.)

(*b*) Virtue in a state is *justice*, the highest political virtue, a habit having relation to others in the commonwealth, leading to acts according to law, whose object is common good. It gives to every one his own.

It is (a) *distributive*, dividing honors and property according to merit, in geometrical proportion; A's merit: B's merit: : A's share: B's share.

(β) *Retributive*, commutative, equality in exchange, correcting encroachments of one upon another, in arithmetical proportion.

This is also corrective in involuntary transactions between man and man (criminal offences.) (Nic. Eth. v. 1. 4.)

Political justice is (α) *jus*, natural, valid everywhere, independent of positive law; (β) legal, the naturally indifferent when enacted by the state. (v. 7).

(*c*.) *Divisions*. The number of free, equal citizens is, necessarily, limited; sovereign authority is in three forms; (α) monarchy; (β) aristocracy; (γ) republic, πολιτεία; when the rulers consult their own interest, caprice, or passions, we have (α) tyranny; (β) oligarchy; (γ) democracy; (Pol. iii. 6, 7); (α) is the best or the worst; and next (β), as tending, under proper limitations, to the supremacy of the wisest and best, but (γ) to the rule of military force. (Pol. iii. 7.) But the character and circumstances of the people must be considered.

A. distinguishes in the state three powers, (α) deliberative; (β) elective to office; (γ) judiciary.

A.'s ethics, as a whole, are eminently unspiritual; he knows no conscience in which the Divine law testifies to duty, no remorse, no reconciliation with that law; (cf. the

Beatitudes, and Buddhism, B. St. Hilaire, Buddha, p. 173), but he has supplied the forms of thought in ethics, as in higher phil., to the thinkers of the world.

(6.) *Aesthetics.* Art is imitation , *μίμησις*; but it reaches after the essence of things, idealizing; its aim is both pleasure and moral benefit; *κάθαρσις τῶν παθημάτων.*

CHAPTER V.

SOCRATIC, PLATONIC, AND ARISTOTELIAN SCHOOLS.

1. Socratic Schools. 2. The Academy. 3. Peripatetic School.

1. Socratic Schools.

There are two special influences in Socrates; (1) questioning, dialectic, eristic; (2) moral, practical; each was developed by those who but partially followed the master, into (1) Megaric, (2) Cynic, (3) Cyrenaic Schools.

A. *Megaric School.* (1) *Euclid* of Megara, (distinguish from Euclid Alex.) was present at Socrates' death; retiring to Megara, was followed by many of his fellow-disciples.

He united S.'s conceptions of the good with the Eleatic *one.* The good is the only being under many names, God, wisdom, νοῦς, etc. The opposite of the good is non-being. Plurality and diversity are denied. (Cic. Acad. Qu. ii. 42.)

This school is *eristic,* famous for refutation, showing the contradictions involved in any empirical theory of knowledge. (See their many curious sophisms.)

(2.) *Stilpo* of Megara, a lofty character, united Megaric thought with (practical) cynicism, teaching ἀπάθεια, so leading towards the Stoics.

B. *Cynic School.* (1) *Antisthenes,* b. 444, B. C., was a pupil of Socrates. He taught in the gymnasium "Cynosarges." (Diog. Laert.)

He opposes the ideology of Plato, but tries to grasp the ethical in S.'s teaching. Virtue, *i.e.,* self control, is the only good; and the "*summum bonum*" is "a life according to virtue." Pleasure, sought as an end, is evil. What lies between good and evil, riches, honors, etc., is ἀδιάφορον. Knowledge and virtue are one.

"The wise does not trouble himself with the laws of the state, but only with those of virtue." He despises high birth, glory, etc. Nothing is foreign to him; he is a cosmopolite. (Note the decline of Greek national life.)

(2.) *Diogenes* of Sinope, "Σωκράτης μαινόμενος," "the dog," despised culture; cynicism became antiphilosophic, till the Stoics elevated it. (Sen. Ep. i. 5.)

C. *Cyrenaic School; Hedonism.*

(1.) *Aristippus,* of Cyrene, b. circ. 435, B. C., was a disciple of Socrates. (Diog. Laert.)

He takes the *eudaemonism* of S. in extremely one-sided view. Pleasure is the end of life, which he identifies with pleasure of the moment, a gentle emotion according to nature.

Pleasures are to be valued according to their degree and duration, but morally they are equal. None are in themselves evil, though evil causes may produce an inferior pleasure; (note inconsistency.)

Two form of hedonism are found in the Cyrenaic School. Some later disciples present *altruism* instead of egoism. (Plat. Phileb. p. 66.)

Wisdom and virtue are good as means to an end,

for they lead to the highest pleasure ; they teach us to govern pleasure, not to be governed by it. (Hor. Ep. i., i. l. 18 ; i. 17. l. 17.)

All knowledge is derived from sensation, subjective and objective, but the latter is (x). (Protagorism.)

This school soon developes into Epicureanism.

2. The Academy.

Distinguish the A. as (1) the Old, (2) the Middle, (3) the New. Plato's disciples showed little comprehension of his principles ; they learned, chiefly, to question the empirical.

(1.) Culture takes the place of a true philosophic spirit.

(2.) Controversy of schools tends to general skepticism.

(3.) The Greek States decline towards their fall.

(1.) *The Old Academy*, the direct followers of Plato, unite P.'s ideology with the Pythagorean theory of numbers; *e. g.*, Speusippus, Xenocrates, etc. Already appears a skeptical tendency with reference to absolute good and truth.

(2.) *The Middle Academy*, becomes more and more sceptical. *Arcesilaus*, (b. 315, B. C.,) opposes the dogmatism of the Stoics ; (that the sensuous φάνтασμα can be known to be conformed to its object. Note the variations of the former, and see Hume's argument therefrom.) No certain knowledge is possible; hence, ἐποχή. (Cic. Acad. Qu. i. 12; de Orat. iii. 18.)

The wise will never assert any dogma, but probability is sufficient for rational practice.

(3.) *The New Academy*, is, essentially, one with the Middle, but more fully developed.

Carneades (*a*) (214–129, B. C.,) of high repute as a rhetorician, was embassador to Rome with the Stoic Diogenes, (155, B. C.,) where his teaching gave great offence and led to speedy dismissal. (Diog. Laert.; Cic. Qu. Acad. ii. 45; Plutarch, vit. Cat. Maj.)

(*b.*) What is the *criterion* of the true? (a question coming into more prominence.)

(α) Not reason, for that must have concepts.

(β) Not conception, for that must be preceded by (irrational) sensation.

(γ) Not sensation, for it needs a criterion by which to distinguish the true from the false.

(*c.*) C. develops *probabilism*. He distinguishes in sensation, the objective and the subjective; in the latter relation, sensation is probable, πιθανὴ φανταςία, or improbable. The sensuous presentation is repeated, and being found to agree with the preceding, produces assent, while contrary presentations have the opposite effect: C. distinguishes degrees of probability.

(α) Changes of relations in the subject do not weaken the assent;

(β) The sensuous presentation may harmonize with others and be contradicted by none;

(γ) It may be thoroughly investigated in all its parts and connections, without being destroyed thereby.

(*d.*) *Ethics*, are more skeptical than those of Arcesilaus; with the latter, good exists though not certainly known; with the former it seems to rest on, and vary with, civil institutions. (Cic. de Rep. iii. 1, etc.)

3. Peripatetic School.

Beside comments on Aristotle, this school was given to scientific research, but soon reached its limit; and, though in some points developing A.'s principles, it had little influence of its own. *Theophrastus*, author of the "Characters," is reputed successor of the Master. *Aristoxenus* makes the soul a sort of musical vibration of the body; *Dicæarchus*, the life or force diffused through all bodies, and inseparable from them. There is no immortal intelligence. *Strato* holds the world to be a pure mechanism; there is a force in nature, devoid of all consciousness, which will explain all change, all production. Nature is matter having the potentiality of forming creatures, life, soul, intelligence. (cf. Prof. Tyndall.)

So also, in man there is no νοῦς apart from the body; what is called reason is in a bodily organ; and the sensible is the ground of all knowledge. (Cic. Tusc. Disp. i. 10, etc.; Acad. Qu. ii. 38; De Nat. Deor. i. 13.)

CHAPTER VI.

DECLINE OF ANCIENT PHILOSOPHY.

1. STOICISM. 2. EPICUREANISM. 3. PYRRHONISM. 4. NEO-PLATONISM.

1. THE STOIC SCHOOL.

So distinct a school and phase of human thought, owing little to individual genius, little marked by the influence of any one man, yet distinguished, at least in its later period, and in Rome, by its disciples, seems to call for a different mode of study from the preceding.

A. *The Stoics:* 1. *The Greek*, protesting against and resisting the corruptions and decline of their age, are

(1.) *Zeno,* (b. circ. 340, B. C.; d. circ. 260, B. C.,) a native of Cyprus, a merchant, shipwrecked, losing all, betook himself to philosophy. At first a disciple of the Cynic Crates, then of Stilpo of Megara, then of the Academy. He is said to have taught in the Στοὰ Ποικίλη, for fifty-eight years; hence, "The Porch." He committed suicide in old age. His writings are extant only in fragments and show no well digested system. (Diog. Laert.)

(2.) *Cleanthes,* successor of Zeno in the Stoa, author of the well known (pantheistic) hymn to Zeus, also did little to systematize Stoicism. He, too, ended his life by suicide. (Sen. Ep. 107.)

(3.) *Chrysippus,* (d. 208, B. C.) was a very voluminous writer, the second founder of the school, as a systematizer of it, and an earnest opponent of Academic skepticism, and of Epicureanism. With other Stoics, he founded the science of Grammar; none of his (705 ?) works remain.

(4.) *Panaetius,* (180–111, B. C.), had for disciples P. Scipio Afr., Lælius, etc. His περὶ τοῦ καθήκοντος was the foundation of Cic. De Off. (iii. 2). With him begin Stoical decline from a strictly philosophical stand-point to practical ethics relaxed from the primitive severity, to rhetoric, and an inclination to eclecticism.

(5.) *Posidonius,* a disciple of Panaetius, born in Syria, taught at Rhodes, where Pompey and Cicero were disciples; was, also, a rhetorician and an eclectic. (Tusc. Quæst. ii, 25.)

II. The *Romans,* practical, eclectic, originate no independent thought, (cf. their art and literature) do not firmly grasp the principles of any school, but are, morally, divided between Stoicism and Epicureanism, the former being the protest of the best against the corruptions of the empire, and the expression of their contempt of their age, while hopeless of its reform. (Cato, Brutus, Lucan, Juvenal, Persius, etc.; "Summum crede nefas, etc."; "Victrix causa Diis, etc." See also Sen. Ep. 14.)

(1.) *Cicero,* (106–43, B. C.) produced *De Rep.* and *De Leg.* during the first triumvirate; *De Fin. Bon. et Mal., De Offic., Tusc. Quæst.* (Lib. 5), *De Nat. Deorum.* (Lib. 3) *Acad., Quæst.,* etc., during Cæsar's dictatorship. Averse to dogmatism, an elegant scholar, especially in Greek learning, he is essentially eclectic, inclining to the Middle

Academy. (Acad. Qu. ii. 21; De. Nat. De. i. 5.) Yet he sometimes seems to recognize primary truths. (See Whewell's Hist. Moral Phil., Pt. ii. Lect. vii.) In morals, however, C. inclines towards the Stoics, (De. Off. ii. 14; Qu. Tusc.. iv. 17; v. 1) but only as a probable theory. He is most positive in his opposition to Epicureanism. (De Fin. ii. 22; v. 11; De Leg. i. 7.) By making the "*honestum*" equivalent to the "*bonum*," and both to the becoming, *decorum*, he introduces a relative standard of virtue. (De Off. i. 27, 28, 35; De. Fin. v. 22, 24.)

In physics he wavers between different schools; *e. g.*, concerning the immortality of the soul, relation of the Universe to GOD, etc.

Yet the elegance of his style made him influential on Roman thought, the western Fathers, the middle ages.

(2.) *Seneca*, of Corduba, (A. D. 3–65), the tutor of Nero, memorable for the splendor of his fortune, and unhappy end, shows the contrast of a weak and inconsistent life, with his eloquent and brilliant statements of Stoical principles. His works, *De Brev. Vitæ*, *De Providentiâ*, *De Vitâ Beatâ*, etc., and the *Ep. ad Lucil.* are remarkable for their pointed antitheses, and elaborate and overloaded ornament; he exaggerates Stoical morals, and we may call him a Stoical rhetorician. Yet, with higher views of Deity than many of his predecessors, Fate becomes providence. (De. Prov.; Ep. 73. On immortality, see Ep. 102.) He deviates widely from the old Stoics in metaphysics and physics, with the practical Roman mind turning rather to ethics.

(3.) *Epictetus*, the Phrygian slave, set free, taught phil. at Rome, till driven thence by Domitian, (A. D. 94); then taught in Epirus; the poor and lame Stoic gave, until an advanced age, the model of a wise and heroic life. For his principles see his Enchiridion, from his pupil Arrian, remarkable for its simple purity and grandeur of sentiment. He adopts, with great earnestness, the moral side of Socrates' and Plato's teaching against Epicurus and the new Academy. There is in man an innate principle, ἔμφυτος ἔννοια, of the good; when he errs, it is through ignorance of its application to particular cases. Hence, compassion and forgiveness; but, withal, there is the selfishness of the Cynic, and hopelessness towards moral evils, which are irremediable. (Ench. 12, 16).

The practical tendency of later Stoicism brings forward more prominently the relation of man's will to nature and his life. What is in man's power, his opinions, impulses, desires and aversions, is his own work; what is not, his body, fortunes, reputation, power, is not his work. God himself would not control man's will.

E. lays special stress on man's relations to God; man was made to behold and understand God and His works; his humble spirit and dependence on God, are a remarkable contrast to Stoical pride. (Ench. 22).

Reason has control of man's φαντασίαι, of nothing more. Govern then your thoughts according to nature, for this is the good; it is within you; what is without is for you nothing but your opinion of it. (Ench. 6.)

Hence, self-denial, mortification of the irrational part of man. (Ench. 13, 29, 34, 48.)

Let man remember his relation to the world of which he forms a part; this will be a foundation for relative duties. (See Pascal, Pensées, p. 122 seq.; Farrar's Seekers after God.)

(4.) *M. Aur. Antoninus.* His Meditations present the

religious side of Stoicism, tending to mystic self-contemplation; the "demon," the god within us, is the centre of his thought. He is largely indebted to Epictetus, and shows the same spirit of religious humility, the same aversion to science, and the same seeking after self-knowledge. (Med. ii. 13 ; xii. 26.)

In general, the spirit of the later Stoics seems the result of their age, resignation and passive courage ; τὰ ανθρώπινα καπνὸς καὶ τὸ μηδέν. Consider the possible influence, reciprocally, of Christianity and Stoicism, on the former in its early philosophy, and their sympathy in aversion to atheism, polytheism, skepticism, and to the speculative as distinguished from the practical; and see Soirées de St. Petersburg, ii. pp. 119–133. (cf. Kugler, on the Roman art of the period.)

B. *Stoicism.* (1) *Principle.* The practical, as an end, outweighs the theoretical. The strife after virtue is the one worthy object. and on it is founded man's happiness.

The division of phil. is threefold, but all parts are referred to the practical; Logic, Physics, Ethics. (Sen. Ep. 89.)

(2.) *Logic.* (*a.*) *Theory of Knowledge.* Stoicism is a system of dogmatic empiricism, which may be compared with the nominalism or conceptualism of the Middle Ages; The universal is only in thought.

All cognitions, φαντασίαι, come from the sensuous perceptions, αἰσθήσεις. The soul is originally a *tabula rasa*, and "nihil in intellectu, quod non prius in sensu," is a fundamental axiom. Sensuous presentations, often repeated, acting on the soul, their passive recipient, as a stamp on wax, by the aid of memory, produce ἐμπειρία. The successive steps are

(*a.*) αἰσθήσεις, of the individual;

(β.) προλήψεις, natural, spontaneous notions of the universal, produced by (α.);

(γ.) ἔννοιαι, are (β.) corrected by experience and reflection; in forming these the mind becomes active. The Platonic theory of ideas is, of course, rejected.

The Stoics aimed especially at

(*b.*) *A Criterion of Truth.* This seems to be distinctness in the sensuous presentation, when the φαντασία shows itself and what produces it. (Cic. Acad. Qu. i. 11; ii. 47.) This leads to a voluntary but firm conviction of truth; this is a φαν. καταληπτική.

(*c.*) *Categories.* Every true substance being corporeal, ideas, ἔννοιαι, existing only in our minds, the general being identical with what is conceivable, the name signifying, not the thing in itself, but the concept in the mind, the genus is a union of several concepts, and the categories are the highest genera.

(α.) Substance, τὸ ὑποκείμενον;

(β.) Quality, attributes, properties, τὸ ποιόν;

(γ.) The relative, τὸ πῶς ἔχον, which is based on the nature of the thing, as sweet and bitter;

(δ.) Particular, accidental relation, τὸ πρός τι ἔχον, the correlative; *e. g.*, the right side. (cf. the noun, adjective, verb, and conjunction.)

Through concepts come judgments and inferences. The Stoics developed the hypothetical syllogism.

(3.) *Physics*, are materialistic, tending to pantheism; whatever is real, is material. (Sen. Ep. 106.)

(*a.*) *Cosmology.* Matter, the passive, and force, the active, are the two ultimate principles; (Plut.; Diog. Laert. vii. 132, seq.; Sen. Ep. 89;) both are reduced to body, as that which acts, or is acted upon. Force, intelligent and omnipotent, is inseparably joined with matter, giving it form. Nature is GOD. GOD is *in* the world, the *anima mundi*; (Hymn of Cleanthes.) The world as a whole is one, finite, beautiful, (in symmetry and proportion of endlessly varied parts,) ordered, conscious, and that consciousness is the world-reason, Deity. (Cic. de. N. D. ii, 5–8, 22.)

Fate, necessity, εἱμαρμένη, arises from the fact that force has set immutable laws on matter; GOD, the world-soul, acts from necessity of nature; hence also are developed in passive matter, oppositions, conflict of forces, moral evils.

Providence, πρόνοια, is due to GOD, the world-intelligence, conducting all things to their end with unity and wisdom, looking to individuals, rewarding and punishing, perfect, happy. (Cic. de. N. D. i. 14; ii. 65; Diog. Laert. vii. 147; Plut.)

The Heraclitean flux. GOD, the principle of life is the vital heat, a form of force; (Cic. de N. D. ii. 9, 10.) Earth and water are the passive elements, issuing from the world-fire, the primal πῦρ τεχνικόν, and they will return to it again. At the end of a cosmical period is a general conflagration when all things are absorbed into deity, followed by a new evolution, for GOD is the σπερματικὸς λόγος of the world, (Cic. de N. D. ii. 22, 32; Plut. adv. Stoic. 36; Diog. Laert, vii. 136.)

Moral evil. Though the world as a whole is perfect, yet moral evils, in parts, have necessary relation to the perfection of the whole (vid. et supr. and cf. Hymn of Clean.).

(b.) *Psychology*, applies the same principles; there is a ruling active force in the mind, and a passive matter; the soul is corporeal, a vital fire or air, and the union of soul and body is a κρᾶσις of two bodies, like that in the world.

Immortality is variously held; with some, e. g. Cleanthes, the soul endures till the world-fire, for it is a spark of Deity. (Sen. Ep. 63 ad fin.; 92; 120. M. Aur. Ant., Med. ii. 4; vii. 9. 18; xii. 25, etc.)

The soul is one, a unity of force, from which, a ruling, rational principle, ἡγεμονικόν, issue the irrational senses and instinct, ὁρμή, seven in number. Appetites and passions are a corrupt reason. (Cic. Quæst. Tusc. iv. 7, 11.)

Free will: The mind is controlled, not by external circumstances, but by its own nature, along with the general laws of the world. Chrysippus distinguishes the relative freedom of individual acts from the collective character of humanity controlled by law.

(4.) *Ethics.* (*a*) Man is the highest product of nature, and mankind a commonwealth with the gods; all things beside are for the common sake of these. (Epict. Disc. i. 3.)

(*b*) *Virtue*, is an end, a good in itself, the *summum bonum*, the only true good, the only source of happiness. Other things are ἀδιάφορα.

(α.) Yet certain of these have a relative value, τὰ προηγμένα, (health preferable to sickness, etc.,) and hence arise τὰ καθήκοντα or imperfect duties, as the care of health, etc. (Cic. De Fin. iii. 10, 15, 16.)

(β.) Other indifferent things are absolutely so.

(γ.) Others are to be rejected, avoided.

Pleasure is neither moral, nor an end of life.

Virtue is *one;* the four cardinal virtues are different manifestations of it, but he who has one, has all.

There is no mean between virtue and vice, the good man and the bad; all good actions are equally good; all evil, equally bad, by reason of their source. (Diog. Laert. VII. 120.)

(*c*) The *rule* of virtue is not founded on prudence, results, positive law, notions of individuals or nations, but on the law of nature, "to live according to reason,"="to live according to nature," which is reasonable, governed by law, etc. (Diog. Laert. vii. 87; Cic. de Fin. iii. 9; Sen. Ep. 76, 89). This, however, must be understood of universal nature; if that of the individual be considered, the Stoical rule relaxes. (Cic. De Fin. iii. 5.)

Politics are less regarded than in earlier Greek phil. The sage is a cosmopolite, and all the wise are his fellows.

(*d*) The *wise* is he who possesses virtue, all other things are to him indifferent; hence, his ἀπάθεια. He is master of himself, the only rich, free, or lord. He is a god in all but immortality.

His virtue,=wisdom, he can never lose; without this man is a fool. (Diog. Laert. vii. 123; Epict. Encheir. 19.,

(*e*) *Passions*, the corrupt reason, opposing law, are to be eradicated; they are false opinions. Affairs do not trouble men, but their opinions about affairs; ἀνέχου καὶ ἀπέχου.

Troubles, so called, are part of the system of the world. Pain and pleasure, being neither conformed to law nor opposed to it, are ἀδιάφορα.

Remember always that duty, and, therefore, happiness, lie in that which is in our own power; not so, health, wealth, reputation; (Sen. Ep. 50, 85, 116.)

(5.) *Moral defects of Stoicism.*

(*a*) Arrogant sense of human *independence.*

"Non sunt ista bona quæ in te isti volunt congeri, unum bonum est quod beatæ vitæ causa et firmamentum est, sibi fidere." "Quod votis opus est? fac te ipsum felicem." (Sen. Ep. 31, 73.)

(*b*) *Apathy*, and condemnation of human passions; impossible, if desirable; undesirable, if possible. (Sen. Ep. 74, 85.)

(*c*) *Immoral* tendency; the wise cannot do wrong, for all his actions spring from the inward virtue. An impracticable standard ends in practical license, so long as the motive is not self-interested or voluptuous; e. g., lying for gain, prostitution, etc.

(*d*) Defence of suicide. ("*καπνός ἐστί, ἀπέρχομαι.*") (Cic. de Fin. iii. 18; Diog. Laert. vii. 130; Plut. adv. Stoic. 33; Sen. Ep. 17, 58, 70, 77.)

2. Epicureanism.

This system offers no great names, except Lucretius. (See Br. Quarterly, Oct. 1875.) (Note, the condition of Greece at the period of its origin.)

Epicurus (A.) *Life.* (342–271 B. C.) At an early age a student of Democritus, in his 36th year he opened a school at Athens, his followers making a social league or fraternity. His life was considered blameless. He wrote voluminously (works not extant,) and composed short formulas for his disciples, which remain in Diog. Laert. x.

(B.) *Divisions.* Canonics, physics, and ethics; but his logic is principally criteria of truth, and his physics are with reference to ethics, their aim being to free man from superstitious fears of nature and the gods. (Lucret. de. Rer. Nat. i. 62 seq.)

(C.) *Principle* is pure sensualism, a union of the atomic system of Democritus with the hedonism (modified) of Aristippus. Phil., as with the Stoics, has for its end the practical; its object is happiness, the removal of disturbing causes. Its chief obstacle is ignorance, (1) of the laws of nature, which produces false hopes and fears, the remedy being physics; (Rer. Nat. ii. 59.) (2) of the nature of man; hence the need of canonics and ethics.

(D.) *Canonics.* (1.) *Theory of knowledge*, is purely sensualistic. External objects, bodies, produce (*a*) sensations, αἰσθήσεις; material images, εἴδωλα, from bodies, perpetually emanate from their surface, ἀπόῤῥοιαι, and enter the organs of sense; (Rer. Nat. iv. 26 seq.)

(*b*) προλήψεις, mental representations, permanent images in the memory, are the collected result of several sensuous impressions, when the εἴδωλα reach the mind, which is their passive recipient. (Cic. de Fin. i. 6.)

(2.) *Criterion* is (*a*) the sensuous perception, which as such is true; reason cannot oppose, for its concepts and judgments are based only on this;

(*b*) The concepts, then, are equally true; error is found in our generalizations, in assumptions which sensation does not confirm; (verification;)

(*c*) The feelings, πάθη, agreeable and disagreeable, which, duly considered, are a guide for practical conduct.

(E.) *Physics.* (1) *Cosmology*, is that of Democritus, developed. Atoms and movement explain the universe. Nothing exists but body and vacuum, all beside is property or accident.

(*a*) *Atoms*, are sensible entities, so small as to escape the sense; they are the indivisible elements of bodies, infinite and eternal; their properties are size, form, weight. There is a vacuum in which they move, which is also infinite in extent. (Rer. Nat. i. 329.) By their weight, perpetually moving downwards, yet deviating from a parallel course, their collisions produce ever-changing bodies, continually generated and destroyed.

"De nihilo nihil fit;" and nothing is destroyed. (Rer. Nat. i. 155, seq.; 951 seq.; ii. 61, seq.; 294 seq.)

(On the inconsistency of the atomic theory with sensualistic principles, see Ritter, x. ii. Physics of Ep.)

(*b*) *The gods*, probably exist, since they produce images as in dreams. They are immortal bodies, in a happy life, and trouble not themselves about human affairs. They are formed of the finest atoms; they are not to be supplicated or adored. (Rer. Nat. ii. 646, seq.; 1090, seq.)

There is neither teleology nor fate in nature.

(2.) *Psychology*. The soul is atoms of the finest kind; for, otherwise, it would not affect bodies, nor be affected by them. These atoms are scattered at death. (Diog. Laert. x. 63–67; Lucret. de Rer. Nat. iii. 161, seq.; 830, seq.)

Sensations, varying according to the atoms of the images, and the state of the bodily organs, are agreeable or disagreeable, and thus produce the passions. (Rer. Nat. iv. 633, seq.)

Man is developed from the brute state. (Rer. Nat. v. 925, seq.)

(F.) *Ethics*. The *summum bonum* is happiness,=pleasure; brutes seek it instinctively; let men do so rationally, using wise calculation to avoid the disagreeable, to gain the agreeable. (Diog. Laert. x. 129.)

(1.) *Pleasure*, is of two kinds; (*a*), in action, ἐν κινήσει; (*b*) in rest, ἀπονία, ἀταραξία; the former is most vivid, (passions), but brief and mixed; the latter is true happiness, the repose of the soul.

Pleasures differ among themselves in vivacity and duration; e. g., of the body, and of the soul; the latter are higher, for the soul remembers and anticipates. (Diog. Laert. x. 136.)

(2.) *Virtue* is wisdom, φρόνησις, right judgment; for present pleasure may bring lasting pain; present pain, lasting pleasure; and the higher pleasures are to be preferred by the wise, viz., those of virtue.

True repose, freedom from passion, is either through perfect freedom from needs and desires, which is impossible, or through limiting them to such measure as can always be satisfied; and this is the practical rule, independence of the pleasures of luxury and idle opinion, *e. g.*, public honors. (Diog. Laert. x. 130.)

Domestic affection, patriotism, disturb the soul's quiet.

(3.) *Divisions.* The four cardinal virtues are the four great *means* of happiness.

(*a*) *Prudence*, (a) escaping superstitious fear of gods and their vengeance, and of death;

(β) regulating pleasures with reference to the future, etc.

(*b*) *Moderation*, restricting desires to our power of satisfying them.

(*c*) *Courage*, keeping off troublesome emotions; bearing temporary pain for ultimate happiness, and taking leave of life when it is wholly disagreeable.

(*d*) *Justice:* There is a compact among men not to injure one another, and he who observes it is happy in friendship, in fearing no strife, in being protected in his pleasures by law, etc.

(4.) *Politics*, are based on utility and a compact, men having been originally savages; a system of natural rights. The interest of the moment may not be permanent, and therefore the need of mutual sacrifice. (Rer. Nat. v. 1105, seq.; cf. Rousseau, Condillac, and see Calderwood, Mor. Phil. c. ii.)

III. PYRRHONISM.

Note the change, political, social, moral, artistic, at once a cause and a result of philosophical decline, of skepticism. (Ritter x., iv. 1.)

The skeptics confine themselves to a refutation of dogmatic principles, especially Stoical. Happiness implies a renunciation of dogmatism, and of search into the nature of things. There are three schools:

(1.) Pyrrho and his followers.

(2.) The New Academy (vid. sup.)

(3.) Aenesidemus and his school.

(A.) *Pyrrho's School.* (1.) *Pyrrho,* of Elis (circ. 360-270 B. C.), was, partly, a follower of the Megarians, but specially devoted to Democritus; (Diog. Laert. ix, 61, etc.,) he is chiefly known through

(2.) *Timon,* (B. C. 325-235), a disciple first of Stilpo, and then of Pyrrho. (Diog. Laert. ix.) Sense and intellect are equally deceptive; owing to the instability of our impressions, perceptions and representations can neither be called true nor false; (the subjective not yet denied, but the objective certainty). "That a thing is sweet I do not affirm, but only admit that it appears so." (Diog. Laert. ix. 105.)

The supra-sensible is an unknown (*x*); of two contradictories one is not more to be affirmed than the other. Hence, practically,

No dogmas, οὐδὲν μᾶλλον, but suspension of judgment, ἐποχή, for real things are unattainable, (ἀκαταληψία).

The beautiful, the ugly, the just, the unjust, rest on human statutes and customs; and true happiness is found in freedom from dogmas concerning them, ἀταραξία.

(B.) *Aenesidemus' School.* (1.) *Aenesidemus*, (1st cent. B. C.).

All principles, so called, are reducible to hypotheses. Imputed to him are ten τρόποι, or ways of justifying doubt;

(*a*) Different classes of beings are differently constituted; whose sensations are true?

(*b*) Different men are differently constituted;

(*c*) The several organs of sense give different impressions from what is called the same thing;

(*d*) Our own physical and mental states vary, and representations of things vary with them;

(*e*) Position, distance, etc., alter the appearance of things;

(*f*) All experiences of things are affected by other things, and by the subject himself; (a subjective element in knowledge);

(*g*) The object, changing quantity, structure, etc., produces various appearances;

(*h*) Sensations always appear in various combinations and associations, and relations to ourselves; (relativity of knowledge);

(*i*) Notions vary as objects are perceived more or less frequently;

(*k*) Opinions, customs, theories, differ.

(See Berkeley's Hylas and Phil., Dial. i., against the absolute existence of matter.)

Aen. especially attacked the principle of causality.

(*a*) Only body can act on body, and even then contact is necessary, but impossible;

(*b*) Two things are mutually conditioned, and which is cause, and which is effect, cannot be determined; for,

(*c*) The cause, so-called, must either be synchronous

with, or precede, or follow the effect; and each of these is absurd.

(2.) *Agrippa*, (2d cent. after Christ,) reduced these ten commonplaces to five;

(*a*) The discordance of opinion;

(*b*) All knowledge is relative;

(*c*) Every proof requires proof, *ad inf.*;

(*d*) All systems are based on hypotheses, and in these is disagreement;

(*e*) Demonstration moves in a circle.

(See Kingsley's Hypatia, c. v.)

(3.) *Sextus Empiricus*, a Greek physician, (circ. 200 A. D.) wrote *Adv. Math.*, etc., which are extant. He reduces the common-places to three.

Neither body nor soul can be known, for how can the thinker know himself? Experience is nothing but association of phenomena. Thought is modified sensation.

Experience is our only moral guide, for by nature nothing is either good or evil, and conduct depends on the circumstances and conditions of life.

He denies the existence of God.

(*a*) He can be neither body nor soul;

(*b*) There is evil, which he either cannot, or will not remove, and either alternative is contrary to what men mean by the term God. Phil. is an irrational delusion.

(C.) *Criticism of Pyrrhonism.*

(1.) In being dogmatic, which it cannot avoid, it is suicidal. It asserts doubt, at least as a mental state.

(2.) The ten common-places are directed and valid against Epicurean sensualism; they do not touch the intuitions of pure reason, *e. g.*, the principle of contradiction, which the Pyrrhonists often assumed. So, also, the argument against the syllogism, because its major is itself an induction from particulars, and therefore contains the conclusion.

(3.) Such a school has no permanence; it is the temporary result of controversy, or of indifference, resigning man's noblest work. It is easier to doubt, than to investigate.

(4.) It rests on an irrational demand for proof of the validity of that which it, in common with mankind, is compelled to assume, and which is its own voucher.

4.—Neo-Platonism.

A. *Introduction.* Alexander brought Greece into con tact with the East. His successors, Attalus at Pergamus, the Seleucidæ in Syria, the Ptolemies in Egypt, spread abroad Greek literature, phil., and art; Alexandria, especially, became a new centre of commerce, science and the arts. (Note the Museum of Ptol. Lagus, its universal library, the "Septuagint" under Ptol. Phil.) At Rhodes, also, was a school (rhetorical) of the Stoics.

While scientific culture attempted an *eclecticism* of all Greek schools, we find in Alex. also a *Syncretism* of Greek ideas of all phil. systems, with Oriental religions, leading to deification of individuals, an attempted unifying of all religions, ascetic mysticism. (Note the language of the Athenians to Demetrius.)

An opposite extreme from materialistic and practical Stoicism and Epicureanism, from the scepticism of the Academy, it found refuge in mystic contemplation and direct intuition of truth in its source.

An attempted reform of popular religion, modified by Oriental ideas, all-embracing, rested on primeval religious tradition. When all other schools were dead it still struggled against the Christian faith, but it ended in *theurgy*.

Its *first principle* was a mystic theosophy; union with GOD was the beginning and end of wisdom. Pythagoreanism and Platonism were most accordant with the aim, but Peripatetic and Stoic ideas were added. Oriental *emanation*, through a decreasing series of entities (GOD himself inaccessible to man) at last terminated in matter and evil, remote from GOD. Therefore in sciences the *transcendental* was sought, and, in a contemplative and spiritual life, a refuge from the evils of action in the world of nature.

B. *Helleno-Judaic Philosophy*. *Philo*, (1) (b. 25 B.C.) "*Judæus*," of a distinguished family, pleaded the cause of the Jews before Caligula: a very voluminous writer.

(2) *Principle*, an inconsistent Syncretism, is largely borrowed from Platonism. Perception is of the individual, the corporeal, which is unreal, and the sciences only end in knowledge of our ignorance, or, at best, in the probable; their only value is in purifying the soul from error, and preparing for a higher knowledge. This is, in the *Nous*, of imperishable ideas, through the Logos.

Hebrew Revelation is indeed a source of truth, but under the form of images; its histories are allegorical, while Greek phil. presents the truth under the forms of reason. Interpret the former by the latter.

(3.) *Theosophy*. GOD is above all predicates, even the good and the beautiful; we can only name Him τὸ ὄν; from His works we know that He is, not what He is. The S. Ss. give anthropomorphic, allegorical notions of Him.

(4.) *The Logos*, is intermediate between Him and the world, His Σοφία, εἰκὼν θεοῦ. He is the seat of Ideas, the archetype of the sensible world, the Organon of the Unnameable One in its production, the κόσμος νοητός.

This Logos, the second god, the first-begotten, reveals Himself in the sensible world. (Λόγος ἐνδιάθετος and Λ. προφορικός.)

True knowledge is knowing GOD through the L.; in that we know all ideas.

From the L. proceed a series of emanations, or energies, down to man and the material world, which in itself is mere passivity, non-being. (See Am. Ch. Quarterly, Oct., 1875.)

(5.) *Ethics.* The four cardinal virtues are active, needed in human society, and, like the sciences, preparatory; higher are the contemplative virtues;

(*a*) The *purifying*, emancipating from evil, *i. e.*, the sensuous; faith, hope, piety, penitence;

(*b*) The *unifying*, wisdom, contemplating God, given by the grace of the Logos, who is the only light of man's *Nous*. Let man silence sense in the ascetic life, and rise above his discursive reason to oneness with God.

Man is then free from the bondage of sense, of matter, so far as is possible. He has the intuition of God; and outward perception, active will and judgment, are abandoned (ecstasy). God alone works in him.

P. speaks of his own exaltation above himself and surrounding circumstances; he became full of ideas and thoughts not his own: ("genius").

(Cf. the Gnostics, the Jewish cabala, and the Alex. fathers.)

Passing by Apollonius of Tyana, the wonder-worker,

and Plutarch, the eclectic Neo-Platonist, (who places evil in the soul), we come to

C. *Plotinus.*

(1.) An Egyptian (205–270 A. D.), taught at Rome, æt. 40; he had, six times, the "Vision of God." Porphyry wrote his life, and collected his writings in six Enneads (extant).

(2.) *Theosophy.* The first principle we can only name the One,=the Good. But no properties can be predicated of it; it is unutterable. It is not *τὸ ὄν*, nor *οὐσία*, beauty, goodness, nor *Nous;* it is over all these; for even "the good," the first cause, *ἀρχή*, are relative words. "The One" is most convenient, though imperfect; (Enn. vi. 9, 3; 9, 6, Ritter).

All common conceptions of God are anthropomorphic, and even thought, being, unity determine Him.

(Note; the real and the determined are synonymous; the finite rather than the infinite is determined; but cf. *ἄπειρον* in Gr. The attempt is the impossible concept of the Absolute First apart from all relations.)

Mythology becomes symbolism.

(3.) The *Nous* with the *νοητόν* makes a duality; therefore it is not the First, but an emanation and an *εἴκων* of the One. Turning back to its source, it becomes conscious. It is the second God, God's Son, the one World-Reason. Radiation of light from the unchangeable sun is a frequent illustration (Enn. v. 1, 7).

Ideas, τὸ νοητόν, are immanent in the *Nous*, which is the unity of all intelligible essences; these, the object, are identified with *Nous,* the subject. Thus the all, or the many, emanates from the one, for the good communicates itself.

(4) The *Soul.* The multiplicity of ideas is the active, efficient principle of the phenomenal world, but does not act directly upon (passive) matter.

Intermediate is the third principle, the *World-Soul,* the third God, emanating from the World-Nous, its Logos, its thought, its εἴκων, which produces, in matter, the multiplicity of finite souls.

(5) *Matter,* is the terminus of the emanations, a shadow of the real, by itself without form, quantity, quality, a mere negation. In itself, also, it is the evil; which, however, is a mere negation of good.

The sensible world, then, is from two principles, the World-Soul, which gives form, and formless matter. In itself it is not real, for its qualities are mental concepts, and take these away, not-being remains. What is, is ideal (Idealism).

(6) *Psychology.* ψύχην γεννᾳ νοῦς. The soul is related both to the αἰσθητόν and the νοητόν, (Enn. iv., 8, 8.) The body is in the soul, not the soul in the body. It depends on the body only so far as it is the principle of life and sensation; otherwise, it is free. The World-Soul suffers degradation through matter, sinking still lower in the brute and vegetable creation. The true man is soul only, or rather reason, using matter as its tool (Enn. 1, i., 10) But the fall is not total, for the individual soul can turn back to its origin.

The Divine *Nous,* therefore, immanent in the World-Soul, is united with individual souls, their rationality.

Knowledge is of five kinds:

(*a*) Sensuous, which is only a dream;

(*b*) Of the operations of the soul;

(*c*) From analysis and synthesis; but for true knowledge the soul must turn back to the *Nous*, to *à priori* principles;

(*d*) Of primary virtues or principles, not objective, but a development from the soul itself;

(*e*) The highest is *ecstatic*, the contemplation of the One, σοφία ἐν θεωρίᾳ, which gives a supernatural light above intelligence or love; (we love a person).

(7.) *Ethics.* The soul, in begetting the corporeal, having descended, must turn back. Matter is evil, and the soul has well nigh forgotten its divine origin. (Enn. v. 9, 10). Reason alone is free.

There are three kinds of virtues:

(*a*) *Civil*, the four cardinal virtues.

(*b*) *Purifying*, ascetic, delivering from sin, which is the bondage of matter. The body's desires must be destroyed.

(*c*) *Contemplative*, unifying, producing union, ἕνωσις, with GOD, accomplished not by thought, which is action, κίνησις, but by rest, ecstasy. This is man's *summum bonum*; "οὐχ ἔξω ἁμαρτίας εἶναι ἀλλὰ θεὸν εἶναι."

Some men are naturally sensuous, pleasure-seekers; others practically virtuous; others, by the ascetic life, attain the "Vision of God."

(See also Olympiodorus in Cousin, Fragm. Philos. I. p. 477.)

D. *Subsequent History of Neo-Platonism.*

(1.) *Porphyry*, a disciple of Plot., b. in Syria, (233 A. D.,) taught with great success at Rome, made evocations and worked miracles, had the "Vision of GOD," d. 304 A. D.

He systematized and extended the doctrine of his master, made it more ascetic, (himself a "vegetarian"), defended necromancy, opposed christianity.

(2.) After Por., N-P. became, as in Jamblichus, chiefly theurgic; *Julian* tried to support it as an antagonist to Christianity.

(3.) *Proclus,* b. at Constant. (412 A. D.), was a pupil of Plutarch and Syrian at Athens, taught and died there (487 A. D.) He had apparitions, and worked many miracles. P. was a man of genius and vast erudition; honoring the gods of all nations, he was what he describes the philosopher as being, "the hierophant of all nations."

Many gods are emanations from the One; below them are demons; man ascends to the highest through these media. This is the object of faith and love, viz., the divine goodness and beauty.

Justinian closed the school at Athens, 529 A. D., and the surviving teachers went to Chosroes, hoping to find a congenial air in Persia. Disappointed, they returned to neglect and contempt; *this was the end of Anc. Phil.*

CHAPTER VI.

RISE OF CHRISTIAN PHILOSOPHY.

1. INTRODUCTION. 2. OPPONENTS. 3. APOLOGISTS. 4. ANTE-NICENE PATRISTIC PHILOSOPHY. 5. POST-NICENE PATRISTIC PHILOSOPHY.

1. INTRODUCTION.

Christian Rev. was a new and fertile element in thought. Virtue, which had been a philos. theory, was taught as a life, as a supernatural perfection, attainable by all through the Holy Ghost.

Reason was elevated by familiarity with highest truths, received, at first, as a faith. Previously, there had been no permanence of principles; supernatural truths now became not only the guide, but the object of reason; *i. e.*, speculative phil. was allied with speculative theology.

There are three eras: (1) Patristic; (2) Scholastic; (3) Modern. The first laid the foundation for Christian phil. in Christian dogmas formulated, systematized, especially the doctrine of the Logos Incarnate; while, for ethics, were established their spirituality, and their root in love.

In the first era are two periods: (1.) Ante-Nicene (to 325 A. D.), essentially unphilosophic, phil. being only employed for defence,

(*a*) In philos. terms applied to statements of Christian truths;

(*b*) For the "præambula fidei;" *e. g.*, monotheism justified to reason.

(2.) Post-Nicene, to Charlemagne, (A.D. 800), phil. applied to, and co-operating in, the development of Christian dogmas.

2. Opponents of Christian Dogma.

A. *Gnosticism:* the first attempt of pre-existing phil. to accommodate itself to Christian facts and dogmas. This reconciliation was founded on esoteric teachings of Christ; hence the γνῶσις, a direct knowledge of the One, the First Cause. Its forms are excessively fantastic, but in general agreement concerning emanations, the *Aeons*. (See Mosheim, First Three Cent., etc.)

(1.) *Cerinthus*, against whom is the Gospel of S. John. The world was not made by the supreme God; He caused the Aeon Christ to descend on Jesus at His baptism, withdrawn before His death.

(2.) *Saturninus*, of Antioch, in Hadrian's reign. The Unknowable God originated angels, etc.; they, the world and man. The God of the Jews was only an angel. The flesh is from the evil principle. The Unknown Father sent His Son, Christ, who took only the appearance of a human form. (Docetism.)

(3.) *Basilides*, of Alex., also taught a series of emanations from the eternal Father. One of the lower, the God of the Jews, formed the world. The First-born, Nous, is

Christ, who was not, in reality, crucified. The body is not immortal.

B., with most of the Gnostics, found two souls in man; the one, divine, rational, pre-existent, for its offences sent down to an earthly body; the other, from the soul of matter, sensuous, brutal.

(4.) *Valentinus,* (B. and V. both in the first half of the 2d cent.) of Egypt, taught, in Rome and Cyprus, that a succession of aeons in sum constitutes the *pleroma.* Jesus is its common fruit. Highest among the (30) Aeons is an Ogdoad; lowest, is Wisdom; from her "Achamoth," the spirit of formless matter, and from her is the Demiurgos, from whom the Law and the Prophets. The Son of Mary was not made by him, for the body of the former was psychical, or spiritual. He came to attack the tyranny of the Founder of this world; (common Gnostic theory.)

(5.) *Carpocrates,* of Alex., taught a universalistic rationalism. Pythag., Plato, Jesus, had the true gnosis. He asserted the pre-existence of souls; the world is from the lower angels.

(6) *Marcion,* of Pontus, taught at Rome. There are two eternal principles, one of good, the other of evil, darkness, matter. Between them is the Demiurgos, the opponent of the good GOD, who is just, indeed, but the maker of the world and the cause of physical evils, bloodthirsty, changeable, and full of contradictions. Jesus, sent by the Father, in the appearance of a man, against him and the Prince of darkness, was assaulted, not really slain by him. Hence, extreme asceticism, abstinence from flesh, etc., against the evil of matter.

B. *Manicheism,* is best known through its disciple and opponent, S. Aug. It is a combination of Gnosticism with (Zoroastrian) dualism; the element of the latter in Gnost., being here completely developed, but emanations added from the former.

Manes, a Parsee, of the Magian race, at the court of Sapor (A.D. 280), was put to death by the Magi. (For revival of Persian dualism, and political life, see Gibbon, i. 8.)

There are two eternal worlds, of light, and of darkness, and two eternal laws or principles,—good and evil, (J. S. Mill); the latter, with the spirits of darkness, dwelling in chaotic matter, the world of darkness. The O. Test. is from the spirit of darkness. The world-soul, the third emanation from the Good, is Christ. GOD, of course, is of limited power, etc. The two worlds are mingled in this present earth of ours.

Man has two souls; one, the life of the body, is from the evil principle, the other is a part of the world-soul; hence extreme asceticism, or licentiousness.

C. *Monarchianism*, the opposite of the Gnostic poly theism, was a modified Ebionitism.

(1.) *Praxeas* (circ. 150, A.D.), *Noetus*, (circ. 230 A.D.) taught that the Deity appears in various relations to men; in Christ, as the Son.

(2.) *Sabellius*, of Libya, at Alex. and Rome, (257 A.D.) "ἡ μονὰς πλατυνθεῖσα γέγονε τριάς." The Logos is the power of GOD.

(3.) *Paul of Samosata*, bishop of Antioch (260, A.D.); Christ was made divine by His ethical perfection. GOD dwelt in Him, strengthening His reason and will.

D. *Arianism*, was a union of Monarchianism and Gnosticism, based on Philo; as Gnostic, it held that GOD cannot directly unite Himself with corporeal matter, but only through a medium. A created Logos, the medium by which GOD made and governs the world, joined to itself a human body, not a soul (Apollinarianism.) There was no inward conflict in Christ, because there was no *Nous*.

3. APOLOGISTS.

A. *Against the Heathen.* Justin M., Tatian, Athenagoras, and Theophilus Antioch., distinguish a threefold birth of the Logos; (1) immanent, eternal, as a Divine Person; (*Λογ.* ἐνδιάθετος of Philo.)

(2.) emanent, at the creation of the world; (*Λογ.* *προφορικός*);

(3.) Incarnate, in human body, soul, and spirit.

They also give teleological proof of the resurrection.

B. *Against heretics.* S. Irenæus, (140–200, A.D.) Hippolytus, Tertullian, teach an eternal Deity, in a threefold Divine "economy."

Evil has its ground in the misuse of human freedom. The "traducian" theory of the origin of human souls is employed in explaining the (inherent) evil of humanity. The (Gnostic) threefold division of human nature is opposed. Man consists (Stoical) of body and soul, *ψυχή*. Spirit, *πνεῦμα*, is a supernatural gift, god-likeness, (S. Iren.) Reason, *νοῦς*, is a power of the soul. (Tertull.)

4. ANTE-NICENE PATRISTIC PHILOSOPHY.

Independent Christian Phil. appeared first in the east, at the catechetical school of Alex.; *e.g.*, S. Clement Alex. (from 189 A.D.), Origen, S. Gregory Nyss. In the West, we find Minucius Felix, Arnobius, Lactantius.

A. *S. Clement Alex.*, recognizes partial truths in Greek phil., highest in Plato, the gift of the Divine Logos who is the Image, εἰκών, of the Father, the unity of ideas, the antitype of the world. (See Mosheim, Cent. II, §§ 25–6.)

B. *Origen*, (A.D. 185–254) (1) b., at Alex., disciple of S. Clem. Alex., at eighteen lay-catechist of the school. Controversy with his bishop led to his retirement to Palestine. He wrote περὶ ἀρχῶν. Christian faith is the *norm* of right thinking about divine and human things, but Philonism and Neo-Platonism in him are very prominent.

(2.) *God* is incomprehensible, higher than truth, wisdom, or being, μονάς or ἑνάς, known only in and through His works.

The *Logos* is the (personal) Divine Wisdom, ἰδέα τῶν ἰδεῶν; through Him all things were made, and all things become and remain through Him. He is the universal revealer, the source of human reason, of all truths seen by it.

World-Aeons, in perpetual succession, are without beginning, for GOD is eternally mighty and good; hence, always creator.

(3.) There are two worlds, of matter, and of spirit; the former differs only in concept from the sum of its qualities.

Spiritual beings, on the other hand, are essentially alike; differences arise only from (free) choice of good or evil; for spirits are not, essentially, one or the other.

In the *pre-existence* of souls, some have always kept their loyalty to GOD, while others have fallen away in different degrees; most of all, demons; less, in various degrees, those now united with human bodies and a sensuous, corrupting soul.

Created souls cannot exist, save in concept, apart from

body, (understood as above,) and death is not the parting from all body, but only from the earthly or fleshly, veiled by which is another. (Swedenborg.)

(4.) *Freedom of will* is necessary to good or evil, but for the former is needed Divine help; the latter is simply privation, or falling away from GOD. The rational soul, in order to rise, must emancipate itself from the bondage of the material, and of the sentient soul, and be joined to the Son of GOD.

(5.) *Eschatology.* Through the redemption by the Logos, souls will be gradually purified, in this world, or after death by fire, until at last all, and, finally, Satan, will be restored to their first estate.

The world-aeons end in the resurrection of bodies, in the elevation of the material world to its first condition, in the unity and perfection of the whole creation.

C. *Lactantius,* (d. 325, A.D.) was tutor of Constantine's son, Crispus. His *Instit. Divinæ* are marked by Ciceronian purity of style.

Matter is created; if it were eternal, it would be unchangeable, and a world-formation impossible.

Each soul is immediately created by GOD. He distinguishes *animus* from *anima.*

The *summum bonum* belongs to the soul not to the body, and can neither be increased nor diminished; *i.e.,* it is everlasting life in GOD, attainable, not by reason, phil., but by religion; man is *animal religiosum.*

Virtue consists, not in destroying, but in rightly regulating the emotions.

5. POST-NICENE PATRISTIC PHILOSOPHY.

A. *S. Athanasius,* the Great, (296–373, A.D.) (Life

given at length in Gibbon ;) "*Contra Gentes*," and "*De Incarnatione Verbi*," have special relations to phil.

(1.) *God's* unity is known from the order and harmony of the world, as our soul in us, from the organic unity of many parts in the body. But he who raises himself above the sensual, and is inwardly purified from sin, needs no such proof; in the mirror of his soul he will recognize the Logos, and the Father through Him.

To deny God is to deny the soul, and conversely.

God is infinite, and cannot be comprehended by the soul; He is known only through His works, *i. e.*, the Logos is known, the revealer of the Father; but we rather know what God is not, than what He is.

(2.) The soul is essentially different from the body for it knows what sense does not reveal; it rises above the empirical; it thinks and loves the unchangeable and immortal; therefore it is such itself.

(3.) Only because of soul, is man subject to a law of doing good and avoiding evil. Will is free; and herein is the ground of good and evil. The latter is not being, but privation. The good consists in man's knowing and loving God; if he turn away to the sensual, this privation of knowing and loving God is evil.

B. Many thinkers in the East, following Origen tried to unite Neo-Platonism with the Catholic faith; *e.g.*, S. Gregory Nyss., Synesius of Cyrene, a disciple of Hypatia, and, most influential,—*Dionysius Areopagitica*, in "*Theologia Mystica*," '*De Cælesti et Eccles. Hierarchia. etc.*," (Circ. 490, A. D.) After Scotus Erig. translated these, they exerted a great influence on the middle ages, especially on the mystics.

Dion. Ar. gives a complete mystic theology christianized, a "positive" and a "negative" theology.

(1.) *God* is infinitely above all good, all being. No predicates are applicable to Him, as applied to created things. He is above all names, all concepts, the unutterable; but He is the cause of all being, and so embraces in Himself all their predicates. Through these He is not known as He is in Himself, but we draw nearer to Him.

(2.) In Him are all created things, προορισμόι; but these are not only ideas but active powers; through these, then, come from God all things that are. The goodness of God thus sheds itself abroad, as the sun its light, without losing transcendence and unity.

God is all in all; the being of all things is grounded in the transcendent being of God (cf. Emanations of Neo-P.) All things, also, strive to attain to the transcendent unity from which they came; God, because of His goodness, draws them back. He is the end, as well as the cause, of all.

If man would pass by the various circles of the mystic hierarchy, ((*a*) the unpurified, (*b*) the holy, (*c*) the perfect, (monks) etc., the central point being Christ) he must pass beyond sense and the super-sensual, beyond all activity of sense and reason, and, in this holy silence, lose himself in Deity; the deification of man.

C. *S. Augustine*, the highest, clearest, most comprehensive of Christian philos., has left a permanent mark on Christendom and the world; the Plato of Christendom. (See Sir Wm. Hamilton's Met. xxxii.) He demands special study as marking the union of reason and phil. with the new faith; an epoch in the history of thought and phil.

(1.) *Life;* b. 353, A. D., in Numidia, was a rhetorician, a Manichean, at Carthage, Rome, Milan. He turned first to the scepticism of the New Academy, then rose to the lofty idealism of Plato. Converted under the preaching of S. Ambrose, (always followed by the prayers of his mother Monica) in 395, A. D., was bishop of Hippo, in Africa; d. 430, A. D.

His first works were philosophical; *e.g.*, "*Contra Academicos;*" "*de Vit. beata;*" "*de Ord.;*" "*de Immort. An;*" and works against the Manichees. Later, and of special philosophical value, the Confessions, and "*De Civ. Dei.*" His literary labors were immense.

(2.) *Theory of knowledge.* In point of time authority precedes scientific knowledge; "tempore auctoritas, re autem ratio prior est," (Ord. ii. 9.) Knowledge cannot go so far as faith, for Rev. gives truths which cannot be perfectly grasped by reason. Knowledge contains two factors, subject and object: the latter is twofold, the sensible, and the supra-sensible; the subject therefore has two powers, empirical and rational. (Ord. ii. 11.) Certainty is possible, for the probable is like the true, and has the latter for its measure. (Contra Ac. ii. 7.) Even where no proposition is dogmatically affirmed, the disjunction of contradictories is known. Even in doubt, is knowledge of existence, and of the doubt, etc., for consciousness attests that we think, will, remember, etc. Neither happiness nor wisdom is possible unless truth can be found. (c. Acad. iii. 4, 10, 13; Beat. Vit. c. ii.)

Sense-perception reveals an outward world, and does not deceive; deception is due to careless, prejudiced inference, etc.

There are two *modes* of knowledge of the intelligible;

(*a*) Proceeding from the sensible to its cause;

(*b*) Inward knowledge, in the reason, the more excellent; but man must purify his soul from the deceits of sin. (Solil, i. 6; Verâ Rel. c. 39.)

The ground of intellectual knowledge is in the Absolute truth, *i. e.*, GOD. The proof is Platonic.

(*a*) There must be a *norm* of the true, beautiful, and good, by which to distinguish it. That norm must be unchangeable, always present, over-ruling our spirit. Such is GOD only.

(*b*) Suppose a human teacher offer us proof; we must have in ourselves a measure of that proof, viz. absosolute truth, *i. e.*, GOD's eternal Word, revealing it to us, with clearness and evidence, according to our moral state. (De Magis. c. 11.) The outward teacher only sends us to Him, and is not properly the teacher; *i. e.*, he may excite belief; he does not give knowledge.

Our spirit, then, is united mysteriously with the unchangeable truth. "In GOD's light we see light, and He sheds it on all, so that all see intelligible truth according to their moral state." (De Ord. ii. 16.) "Divina non jam credenda solum, verum etiam contemplanda, intelligenda, atque retinenda."

From this is our knowledge of created things. The Divine Word embraces in Himself the *rationes*, the type-forms of all things, after which they are made. We know the essence of things, thus, "in rationibus æternis." So we arrive at the knowledge of GOD as the Light showing all intelligible things, the ground of all knowledge.

The sensible world, as in Plato, is made after the image of the intelligible, has verisimilitude, and is the object of opinion.

(3.) *Theosophy and Cosmology.* GOD is proved to be from our concept of the true and good.

(*a*) We know the true, but it is such only through a participation in the absolute truth. We only know a thing as true by reference to that which is unchangeable, seen by all alike, and not dependent on any; this is GOD. (Lib. Arb. ii. 12.)

(*b*) We strive after the good, for we would be happy; but changeable goods are not the good in itself, but are good through participation in the absolute and unchangeable, *i. e.*, GOD.

GOD is above all the categories, even that of substance. Essence or being is the most suitable predicate; but He is incomprehensible. This is truest knowledge of GOD; "Deus melius scitur nesciendo." (De Ord. ii. 16.)

He is absolute unity; whatever properties, wisdom, goodness, etc., may be attributed to Him, are one and the same, His absolute, infinite essence. He *is* goodness, wisdom, etc., absolutely unchangeable, absolute Intelligence, Will, Spirit. As such, He is the Trinity. The Logos is His eternally-begotten Thought; the Holy Spirit, the personal Love of these. GOD, in the Logos, expresses, causes all created things. (cf. Neo-Pl. and Conf. vii. 9).

GOD is omniscient; we know things because and as they are; but they are, because and as GOD knows them. Almighty, but also unchangeable, He can do all that contradicts not His nature and essence.

Creation. Needing nothing, He created with absolute freedom. He needed no pre-existing matter, nor from His essence proceeds the world; then it were like Him; but He created from nothing, after the eternal ideas whose seat is the Logos.

Creation is the revelation of GOD's goodness, but GOD is perfect without the world.

The created is not eternal, for it is changeable and transitory, limited by time and space.

Time is the measure of motion and originates with it, the law of successive thought in created beings. (Conf. xi. *ad fin.*) The world is not *in* time and space, but time and space are in and with the world.

Theodicea. The evil is by GOD's permission, against His will, *i. e.*, His holiness. He wills in permitting its existence, but makes it contribute to greater good than if it did not exist. It is included in the order of creation, for nothing is outside of that order. As darkness sets out light, so the justice of GOD were not, if all were good. (De Ord. i. 6, 7; ii. 4.)

(4.) *Psychology.* The soul is simple, spiritual, immortal. The categories of quantity and place are not applicable to it. The proof is

(*a*) If body, it is known to itself as a body of certain qualities; but this is not so.

(*b*) From sense-presentation. Body could not have such a mass of sensuous images, much less intellectual cognitions which reach the immaterial and supra-sensual; *e. g.*, in geometry. This shows the nature of soul. (Quant. An. cc. v., xiii.)

(*c*) We penetrate into truth more perfectly, the further we withdraw from the merely sensual. This were impossible, if the soul were merely a harmony of the body. (Quant. An. c. xiii; Immort. An. c. x.)

(*d*) The body is mutable, reason immutable; therefore soul is not a harmony of the body. (Immort. An. cc. ii. iii.)

(*e*) The soul's sensuous experiences, in its whole *ego*, are complete at every part of the body; therefore it is simple, incorporeal. (See Bishop Butler, on Personal Identity.)

From the soul's simplicity and spirituality result,

(*a*) *Individuality; i. e.*, not one universal soul, but to each his own;

(*b*) The absurdity of transmigration;

(*c*) Community with the angels, also embodied, but immortal. Between them and the beasts is man, *animal rationale mortale.*

The first human soul was created for union with a body. This union is not the ground of evil. Traducianism and Creationism both seem to present insuperable difficulties. (Retract. ii).

The soul has (*a*) an inferior part, vegetative and sensitive powers, sensuous experience and activity: these are essentially united with bodily organs;

(*b*) A higher part, reason, will, and memory, not conditioned by bodily organs.

But the distinction of these two is relative only.

The soul is what gives its specific character to the body; "tradit speciem anima corpori, ut sit corpus, in quantum est." (Immort. An. c. xv).

Man is neither body nor soul, but a third, single nature, the unity of the two. The relation of the two is a mystery. In the sensitive soul, beside the five senses for sensuous knowledge, is the common sense, their unity, the presentative faculty. (Lib. Arb. ii. 3.)

The soul, as spirit, has three faculties, (*a*) *intelligentia*, (*b*) *voluntas*, (*c*) *memoria*.

Intelligentia is (*a*) contemplative; (*mens, ratio*; "ratio est aspectus animi quo per seipsum, non per corpus, verum intuetur:" Immort. An. c. vi).

(β) discursive, (*ratiocinatio*).

All these are relative distinctions in one essence.

The spirit is the image of God the Trinity in its threefold unity, form, and order; or, being, intelligence, and will; or, towards God, memory, thought, and love. (Conf. xii. 11).

Immortality of the Soul. The proof is Platonic.

(*a*) If that which is in a subject is unchangeable, then the subject is. Truth is in the soul, so far as it recognizes it and knows it.

(*b*) The soul is inseparable from reason; the contents of reason, viz. truth, are unchangeable, therefore reason is immortal; therefore so is the soul, for reason can be only in a living subject.

(*c*) The soul is life, not an animated subject; therefore it cannot cease to be; annihilation is impossible.

(*d*) Being has no contrary which can destroy it; *e. g.*, elements of body are not destroyed in death; being remains. The being of soul, also, has no opposite; its life is truth.

(5) *Ethics.* (*a*) *Free-will*, is the subjective ground of ethics; This concept has a two-fold sense; (α) ability, capacity, of choice; (β) Freedom, from evil and to the good; (super-natural.) (α) is an essential property; it is a freedom from physical necessity. The power to choose, to determine, is what constitutes will. Will not self-determined would be a contradiction in thought. This is the most evident fact in consciousness; without it, no moral good nor evil; no moral laws; no well-desert, nor ill desert; no reward nor punishment; no praise nor blame;

no remorse nor self-approval. (See Cousin on The Good.)

(β) is dependent on Divine grace, which only can free from evil and preserve the power to (super-natural) good. (Conf. vii. ad fin.)

(α) *Liberum arbitrium*, cannot be lost, but (β) can be forfeited through our own fault.

Divine foreknowledge affects not the former, for GOD foresees actions as free. Man does not act because GOD foresees; but GOD foresees because man wills and acts. (Lib. Arb. iii. 3.) Man's free power is more certain, so to speak, because He foreknows it.

(*b*) *Summum bonum.* The good admits of a twofold distinction; (α) *bon. beatificum;* "eo fruendo quisquis beatus est, propter quod cætera vult habere, cum illud jam non propter aliud, sed propter ipsum diligatur." (Ep. cxviii. iii. 13.)

The *Sum. bon.* must (α) make us perfectly happy; (β) be not amissible; (γ) be the ground of our perfection. Therefore it is not sensuous pleasure, nor even virtues, which are but means; it is GOD, the Vision and the Love of GOD. (De Beat. Vit. §§ 10, 11, 34; Civ. Dei, viii. 8; Lib. Arb. ii. 19.)

(*c*) *Divine Law* is the way to this; in following this norm consists moral good, and the fulfilment of life's work. Hence comes the obligation to strive after virtue, for this is the means to the *sum. bon.* Apart from this, action is no more virtue, but only vice.

Virtue is "animi habitus, naturæ modo et rationi consentaneus"; "ars bene recteque vivendi." It is aptness and disposition of will, strength and constancy in accomplishing the good. It is not ἀπάθεια, but the ruling of the passions according to the moral law.

Love comprises all other laws; (α) of GOD, referring what we have, are, and do, to Him; From this, (β) True self-love, willing our true *sum. bon.* (vid. supra.) (γ) of our neighbor, willing his *sum. bon.* also.

This also comprehends all virtues;

(α) Prudence, distinguishing what hinders love from what it demands;

(β) justice, the service of the loved:

(γ) courage, to endure all for what is loved;

(δ) moderation, love keeping itself unstained for what is loved.

(*d*) *Evil*, is no substance; all that is, is good. It is negation, privation of the good, and only possible through the good. A being purely evil is simply non-being. (Confess. vii. 12.) Evil is against nature, robbing it of part of its good, a corruption of nature. It is two-fold:

(α) *Malum culpæ*, the moral privation of moral good, man turning from the *sum. bon.* to transitory good. (Lib. Arb. ii. 19.) Man thus inverts the order of things, and in this lies evil conduct. He thus violates the Divine law which marks out the only way to the *sum. bon.;* and so this *mal. culpæ* is "dictum, factum, vel concupitum contra legem Dei."

(β) *Malum pænæ*, is caused by (α). It is the actual privation of the *sum. bon.;* Intellectual blindness, moral hardness, misery, not now complete, for transitory goods offer some satisfaction; but that this come to an end, is of Divine justice; and this retribution is good, because it is just. It is only evil to the evil men who produce it.

The good is positive, not only in act, but in aim ; the evil, positive in act, is negative in aim, *i. e.*, it has a *causa deficiens*. (Lib. Arb. ii. 20.)

D. After S. Aug. philosophical progress ceased. The barbarians extinguished all light, except in the monasteries, and those only preserved it for better days.

(1.) *Boethius*, (470–526, A. D.) a Roman Senator, under Theodoric long imprisoned, translated Aristotle's Categories, and De Interp., with the Isagoge of Porphyry, and added comments ; he also wrote *De Consol. Phil.*, a Theodicea. (See Gibbon's elegant sketch of his life, c. xxxix.) GOD is the highest good of man ; our life's aim is to strive for happiness in Him, not in earthly things ; these are means which GOD uses, to lead us to Him. Earthly evils are thus made tolerable.

(2) *Cassiodorus*, a Senator, (458–575, A. D.) discussed the *trivium* (Gram., Dial., Rhet.) and the *quadrivium*, (Mus., Astron., Geom., Arithm.) He wrote *De Artibus ac Disciplinis Artium Liberalium*, which became a sort of text-book. His *De Anima* proves the immateriality of the soul. It is made in GOD's image, and its predicates do not belong to the categories of body, *e. g.*, quantity.

(3) *Isidore*, Hispaliensis, bishop of Seville, did much to civilize the Visigoths. His *Originum* is an encyclopedia.

(4) *Beda*, Ven., (674-735 A.D.) a voluminous writer, chiefly borrowed, and made compendia. *De Nat. Rerum* is from Isidore.

CHAPTER VIII.

SCHOLASTICISM.

1. INTRODUCTION. 2. PERIOD OF GROWTH. 3. FULL DEVELOPMENT. 4. DECLINE.

[*References*:—Milman's Lat. Christ. v. iii. viii. 5; v. vi. xiv.3; Cousin Phil. Mod.; Stöckl.]

---

1. INTRODUCTION.

Two new elements now enter phil.; (1) the Christian Revelation, (2) the barbarian races emerging into civilization under its influence and that of the Eastern and Western empires: (at a later period Saracenic and Judaic influence.)

Phil., at first subordinate to theology, emerges into an independent career, though guided or ruled by Christian thought; it is the development of patristic phil. into systems. (On influence of Cath. Ch., cf. Comte, Pos. Phil. trans. Martineau, v. ii, p. 262 seq.)

Predominating influences are (1) Cicero, (2) S. Augustine, (3) Aristotle, although, until the 12th cent. were known only part of his logical treatises, with the Isag. of Porph. In 1128 A.D. were added the Analytics and Topics, through the Arabs.

Phil. had a two fold development;

(1) *Scholastic*, speculative, by the aid of the trivium and quadriv., in the cloister-schools founded by Charlemagne, himself, at the age of forty, a pupil of Alcuin, etc.

(2) *Mystic*, contemplative, allegorizing S. Ss., following Dionys. Areop. (see S. Theresa in Southey's Notes to Joan d'Arc, 18; Gibbon, c. lxiii.)

Nominalism and realism are the general key to philos. questions in the Mid. Ages. (Cousin, Fragm. Philos., ii p. 100.) The question was started by Porphyry, through Boethius; "of genera and species, whether they subsist, or exist only in the mind, whether separate from sensibles, or in sensibles, I decline to speak; it is a profound subject, and demands deeper investigation."

Of universals, then, *sc.* the five "*predicamenta*," are three views:

(1) *Realism.* Universal concepts are objectively real, the only realities; individuals are not proper substances, but manifestations of true being; "*universalia ante rem.*" (Erigena.)

Moderate realism, as in Aristotle, finds "*universalia in re*," distinguishing, as A. did, the contents of the universal and the form of universality. The individual is the proper substance; the universal form, "*prædicabile de omnibus*," is given by abstraction. The universal has objective reality, as to its content, *in* individuals.

(2) *Nominalism.* Universals have no objective reality, are products only of our thought. Similar things are indifferently expressed under common names; "*univ-post rem.*"

Extreme nominalism makes genera mere words for individuals, "*flatus vocis.*"

(3.) *Conceptualism*, moderate nominalism, makes genera subjective concepts expressing the totality of manifold, but homogeneous, things ; the matter is similar in individuals of the species, the form is different ; *e. g.*, humanity in Socrates and Plato. So also in species of the same genus ; *e. g.* man and beast ; (the matter, animal.)

This is the perpetual question of phil., pervading science, politics, morals, religion. (Cousin. Frag. Phil. M. Age, p. 62.)

Note that this is, still, a question of the day. See Max Müller, in Littell's Liv Age, No. 1578 ; Mivart. Gen. of species, p. 289 ; Agassiz' "Type-forms." "If species do not exist at all, as the supporters of the transmutation theory maintain, how can they vary ? And if individuals alone exist, how can the differences which may be observed among them prove the variability of species ?" See also Cont. Rev., Nov. 1875.

There are three periods ; (1) of Growth, (600–1200 A. D.,) (2) of full development in the 13th cent., (3) decline, in the conflict of mutually destructive systems.

2. Period of Growth.

A. *Alcuin*, at the head, first, of the "Schola Palatina," then at Tours, where he was abbot, wrote treatises on the *trivium*, and *De Animæ ratione*, based on S. Aug.

B. *John Scotus Erigena.* (1) b. in Ireland (circ. 800 A.D.,) was at Paris, (Schola Palat.) under Charles the Bald, (A.D. 843); he wrote *De Divisione Naturæ*, translated and followed Dionys. Areop.; was also a follower of Basil, Greg. Naz., Greg. Nyss., and Origen. He was an Alexandrian Neo-Plat. ; "*vera philos. est vera religio*" and conversely.

(2) God is the essence of all things ; He only has

essential subsistence; negative theology denies of GOD all predicates, even substance, or essence. He is *transcendent* Being, Goodness, Power, etc. "Affirmative" theol. uses these predicates symbolically, for He is their cause in created things.

(3) GOD is the source of primordial causes, archetypes, ideas, contained in the Divine Wisdom. Creation is the eternal procession of GOD, through these into the world of creatures, (emanation,) the "second nature," "*quæ creatur et creat;*" the invisible making Himself visible, etc.; "*theophania.*" The sensible world is the "third nature," "*quæ creatur, non creat,*" the product of the ideal world, all things that appear in space and time. The "fourth nature," "*quæ non creatur et non creat,*" is also GOD, as the end of all things, for to GOD all will again return; "*unum, individuum atque immutabile manebunt.*"

Erig. is an extreme realist. GOD, as unity, evolves the generic; then species, etc. The species is the proper being of the individual; otherwise, the latter is merely the assemblage of accidents: hence the appearance of diversity, which is the result of the Fall, all things, in reality, being one essence, the second nature; (Pantheistic emanation).

(4.) He is a *mystic.* Reason finally looks, without any medium, directly at the highest truth, or rather, that truth beholds itself in man. Man finds not GOD, but GOD finds himself in man.

(C.) *Roscellin,* (1) of Compiègne, b. in Brittany, studied at Soissons and Rheims, taught at Tours and Compiègne. His letter to Abélard alone is extant; (Vid. Anselm and Abélard; Cousin, Fragm. Philos. M. Age.); he was, life-long, persecuted for applying nominalism to the Cath. faith.

(2) R. was an extreme nominalist; not the originator of the system, but its clearest exponent and sharpest defender in the 11th cent. Universals are merely universal names, "*flatus vocis*," for the totality of things.

This he applied to the doctrine of the Trinity, in the form of tritheism. There are three divine essences or substances, like one another; for only individuals have a real existence.

(D.) *William*, of Champeaux, (1070-1121, A. D.) a scholar and lecturer at Paris, founder of the famous school of S. Victor, a friend of S. Bernard, wrote "*De Origine Animæ*."

W. is an extreme realist. The universal is wholly in each individual; individuals, in essence, are one, differing only in their accidents. This view was afterwards softened down in order to meet the objection that "then Socrates would be Plato."

(E.) *S. Anselm*, (1.) b. in Piedmont (1034, A. D.), Abbot of Bec in Normandy, archbishop of Canterbury (1093 A. D.), d. 1109 A. D.; wrote "*Dialogus de Veritate*," (opposes nominalism); "*Monologium*," means of arriving reasonably at the faith, etc.; "*Proslogium*," faith seeking understanding.

(2.) *Principle;* faith is the pre-requisite and the regulator of knowledge, but leads to it; "*non quæro intelligere ut credam, sed credo ut intelligam.*" (Pros. c. i.)

(3.) *Theosophy*. God can be known through reason. A. attempts ontological, *à priori*, proof, from the concept to the objective existence. That than which a greater cannot be conceived, cannot exist in intellect alone; for then a greater can be conceived, *sc.* that which exists not only *in intellectu sed in re.* (Ueberweg, § 93.)

(A. was opposed by the monk Gaunilo, apparently with success.)

A adds *à posteriori* proof ; (Monol.) the ideal of goodness, power, etc., must exist, since it is the necessary form of whatever is. The universal exists independently of individuals, which are good, etc., through participating in one absolute good, etc. The imperfect supposes a perfect; the relative, an absolute. (cf. Fénélon, "De L'Existence de Dieu ;" Bossuet, "De La Conn. de Dieu," etc.)

There must be a first cause for things which begin to exist; if many causes, they also have a first cause, GOD. There are gradations of good, etc., and the scale cannot be infinite.

Deductions from the concept are, (*a*) Divine perfections must be predicated, not qualitatively, but "quidditatively ;" GOD's justice, *e. g.*, is Himself, not a quality; (*b*) He is absolute unity; for, in the compound the parts are, in a sense, higher than the whole which is derived from them ; but GOD is absolutely the highest Being.

Similarly A. deduces eternity, unchangeableness, etc.

(3.) *Cosmology*. The same line of argument is applied to creation. If finite substances are from the Divine Substance, then it is subject to change and corruption. But created substances are, in idea, eternal in the Divine mind. The Divine ideas are the immanent Word of God, eternal, and not the mere collected ideas of a created world : God Himself is the object as well as the subject.

(4.) *Psychology*. In freedom of the will, distinguish *voluntas justi* from *vol. commodi ;* the latter is not free but necessitated ; the former, *rectitudo voluntatis*, chooses the good for its own sake.

Evil has its origin in free will ; the rational creature

can will to forsake righteousness; actions, etc., are only evil in the evil will.

(F.) *Abélard, Petrus, "Palatinus Peripateticus."* (1) b. in Brittany (1079 A.D.), a pupil of Roscellinus, then of William of Champeaux, he soon became the most renowned lecturer and dialectician of his age. Until 1121 A.D., he taught at Paris in the Cathedral School (foundation of the Univ. of Paris,) etc. Crowds from all parts of Europe attended his lectures. His writings being condemned by the Council of Soissons, he retired to the oratory of the Paraclete. Crowds of pupils followed him. In 1136 A.D., we find him again at Paris, but his rationalism was opposed by S. Bernard, and condemned by the Council of Sens (1140, A.D.) He appealed to Rome; but, on his way, stopped at Clugny, where, having recanted, and been reconciled to S. Bernard, he died, professing the Cath. faith. (1142, A.D.)

(2.) *Principle.* Opposing his masters, he aimed to establish a new school over realism and nominalism, and laid the foundation of "conceptualism." Inspired by Aristotle, he taught a moderate nominalism, that nothing exists apart from the individual, and in it the individual only.

Genera are formed by the mind; a group of similar objects, on the ground of their similarity, being embraced in one common concept, which can then be predicated of them all.

In his free interpretation of S. Ss. etc. ("*Sic et Non*") A. is the founder of modern Christian rationalism.

(3.) *Ethics.* Christian ethics are a reformation of the natural. Moral good and evil reside not in the act, but in the intention; actions, as such, are indifferent; (laying stress on the subjective side of morals.)

(G.) *Christian Mystics*, of the twelfth cent. Two special principles may be distinguished:

(1.) The mystic route to truth is by supernatural grace.

(2.) In place of the pure myst. of the Neo-P., the contemplative life is founded in love.

(1.) *S. Bernard*, of Clairvaux, (1091-1153, A.D.) "*Doctor Mellifluus*," was a man of renowned activity in the church life of his age, and of widest influence. The route to illumination is (*a*) inward humility; (*b*) love of GOD. Beholding the truth in his own spirit, man is raised above himself (ecstasy), an anticipation of the future life, when, not losing individual substance or personality, man will be "lost in GOD."

(2.) *Hugo, of St. Victor*, being teacher there, was a man of great eloquence, and attractive beauty of thought. (1097-1141, A.D.)

There is a threefold power of knowledge; (*a*) *cogitatio*; (*b*) *meditatio*; (*c*) *contemplatio*, corresponding with the threefold powers of the soul; (*a*) directed to the sensible world; (*b*) discursive reason; (*c*) direct intuition of the ideal.

The means to (*c*) are moral perfection in Christian love and withdrawal from the sensual. Through Divine grace, the soul then free and untrammelled, beholds Divine truth.

Sin obscures (*b*) and blinds (*c*).

3. FULL DEVELOPMENT OF SCHOLASTICISM.

(A.) *Character and Causes.* From the 13th to the 15th cent. is the golden age of Scholasticism; the great universities were founded; the religious orders marked the energy of religious life ; architecture, poetry, etc., showed the power of a new, inventive, creative genius. (cf. Kugler, Hist. Sc., vol. II.)

Three periods may be distinguished; (1) Conflict of nominalism and realism ; (2) triumph of realism ; (3) revival of nominalism. (Note the relations of these to politics, art, etc.)

The *characteristics* are (1) a strictly scientific and logical method giving (*a*) the question ; (*b*) arguments *cont. and pro ;* (*c*) solution categorical and syllogistic ; (*d*) answers to arguments against the solution.

(2) *Aristotelian* forms of thought are universal, his logic, his analytical method, applied to all subjects whatsoever.

(3) *Platonism*, of S. Aug. and the earlier patristic writers in the background, yet modifying Aristotelian concepts.

In addition to the advance of christendom in civilization, order, etc., etc., the *special causes* of this era, productive and modifying, are

(1) The physical, ethical, and metaphysical treatises of *Aristotle*, introduced through the Arabs, at first confounded with forged works of Neo-Plat. cast, and condemned by the church (circ. 1205, A. D.), were, from 1235, A. D., generally adopted. (Note the influence of S. Thomas Aq.)

(2) Influence of *Arabian* phil. ; the (metaphysical) works of Alfarabi, Avicenna, etc., were translated through the Spanish into Latin ; and though the "Averroists" were opposed by christian philos. and condemned by the church, yet they gave an added impulse to thought. (vid. inf.)

(3) *Judaic* influence ; *e. g.*, the Judaic School at

Cordova, which translated the genuine and spurious works of Arist. and the Peripatetics, from the Arabic into Hebrew and Latin: this led to other translations directly from the Greek; of special influence on Christian phil. is Avicebron's "*Fons Vitæ*," (circ. 1050 A. D.)

(B) *Arabian Philosophy*, was based on Aristotle, at first with Neo-Pl. elements, but later, it became more purely Aristotelian. A.'s physics were applied to medicine, (the chief Arab philos. being physicians,) and his logic developed for science, though opposed by the orthodox.

A. was introduced through Syrian Christians under the Abassidae, (circ. 750 A. D.) along with the Timæus, Rep. and Laws of Plato, and Proclus.

(1) *Alfarabi*, taught at Bagdad (the chief school of the East) and at Damascus. (d. 950, A. D.)

He proves the existence of God, from the principle that all change implies a cause (Arist. Met. XI. 7), a first cause. He uses Neo-Plat. emanations to explain the world.

He distinguishes in man potential intellect from νοῦς ἐπικτητικός, which is through the operation of the Divine Intelligence.

(2) *Avicenna*, (980-1037, A. D.) taught medicine and phil. at Ispahan. (Note his famed *Canon medicinæ*.) He develops Alfarabi, but follows Aristotle more closely.

(*a*) *Logic*; "*Intellectus in formis agit universalitatem.*" Matter is the principle of the plurality of things; the mind, of universality.

Genera exist, (α) *ante res* in the mind of God; (β) *in rebus*; (γ) *post res*, as conceived by abstraction in the human intellect.

(*b*) *Metaphysics*. There must be a first cause, who is absolute unity, wisdom, life, power, will, etc.; but the world, time, motion, are eternal. (Arist.) The potential as rendered actual, is grounded in God; God and the world are related as cause and effect; neither exists without the other.

God is the perpetual cause, the continual producer of the world, and this, not through will, but through His thought, the first emanation, the "first intelligence," containing actuality and potentiality. From this proceed the world-soul, νοῦς ποιητικός, and human souls, forms of things, potentiality, matter. Evil is the necessary limitation of good in the material sphere.

The object of God's knowledge and providence is not the individual, but the universal.

(*c*) *Psychology*. The soul is the essential form of the body. (Arist.) The νοῦς ποιητικός is the same in all men, an immaterial being, not dependent on the body. By it potential intellect is rendered active, as forms are given to matter. This is through the sensuous presentation. Not all intellectual knowledge, however, is through this means, for the Νοῦς ποιητ. also enlightens the soul without any sensuous medium; "*intellectus infusus*."

Orthodoxy subsequently triumphed in the East, and phil. was transferred to Spain; (12th cent.)

(3) *Averroes*, (*a*) b. at Cordova, (1126-1198, A. D.) was a physician, mathematician, jurisprudent, etc.; persecuted by the Orthodox, he was banished to Morocco.

(*b*) *Principle*. In many points Avicenna's science is of individuals in their universal aspect. Forms, subsequently developed, are *embryonically* contained in matter, and developed by matter's innate power. (cf. Tyndall.) A. differs most from Avicenna in his

(*c*) *Psychology*. *Nous*, not only active, but potential, is one in all men, acting on all individual and passive intellects to develope νοῦς ἐπικτητικός.

Intelligible species are educed from the human soul by the mental power of abstraction. Man's passive understanding receives and prepares the sensuous *phantasma* for the active (common) intellect; men differ only in the greater or less perfection of the passive understanding.

There is no essential difference between the human soul and that of brutes; the former is a developement of the latter in the *vis cogitativa,* the power of distinguishing and comparing individual sensuous presentations.

The individual *nous* exists after death only as an element of the universal, which is an emanation from deity.

Religion is to be supported by philosophy as typical of truth, the latter containing pure truth, the former, truth under an image.

The influence of the Averroists was extended and powerful, maintaining, especially, a GOD of unknown attributes, perhaps a force in matter; hence arose questions similar to those raised through later developements of physical sciences; is there a GOD, apart from nature, who developes it (teleology), or are all its powers in it working blindly? (cf. H. Spencer's Biology, pp. 234-336; Mivart's Gen. of Spec., p. 264.)

Against phil. in the Mussulman world, were the orthodox theologians, "Motekallemin," (teachers of the word), and the mystics; *e. g.* Algazel, (d. 1111, A. D.)

Against the Averroists, argued, with powerful dialectic,

(4) *William* of Auvergne (bishop of Paris, 1248, A. D., d. 1249) in his "*De Universo,*" and "*De Anima,*" based on Aristotle, with ideology from Plato's Tim. and Phæd.

As Aristotle proves a first cause, so W. proves Good

and Being, unconditioned, original, existing, not by participation, but in and of itself.

A world of intelligibles is known through intellect, as a world of sensibles through sense.

The archetype of these is God's Son.

He gives metaphysical proof of the world's beginning, from potentiality and necessity.

The soul is related to body, as the cithern-player to his cithern.

(C.) *Judaic Philosophy.* Three parties may be distinguished among the Mediæval Jews: —

(1) *Cabalistic,* the traditional party, Judaic Gnostics. The esoteric meaning of the O. Test., at first traditional from Moses, was afterwards to be found in the Cabala;

(2) *Neo-Platonic,* developed from the Cabala;

(3) *Aristotelian,* as a foundation for Jewish dogma, finding pure truth in phil., represented by images in religion. This, as among the Mussulmans, created an antagonistic party.

Moses Maimonides, (*a*) b. 1135 A. D., at Cordova; studied Aristotle under Averroes; was opposed by the Jews as heretical; retired to Fez, and then to Cairo, as physician to the Sultan; d. 1204 A. D. He wrote "More Nevochim," *Ductor perplexorum.*

(*b*) He aims to reconcile Aristotle with Judaic dogma. No attributes can be predicated of God. Such predicates either (*a*) indicate His different workings in the world, or (*b*) are purely negative; *e. g.*, wisdom, predicated of Him, asserts that He is not unwise, etc.

M. opposes Aristotle concerning the eternity of matter.

Towards Rev., he shows a rationalizing tendency. M. had almost unlimited influence over Jewish thought, and very great among Arab and Christian philos.

(D.) *Albertus, Magn.*, (1) b. in Swabia, (1193 A. D.); educated at Paris and Padua, he joined the Dom. Order; in 1254 A. D., was Provincial in Germany; he taught at Cologne and Paris; he was bishop of Ratisbon (1260–2, A. D.), but returned to Cologne, and taught with greatest renown; (d. 1280);. "*Doctor Universalis*;" commented on Aristotle; wrote against Averroes, "*De Unitate Intellectus;*" composed *Summa Theologiæ*, applying Aristotle's philos. to Rev.; also, treatises on Nat. Hist. He was popularly reputed to be a magician.

(2) *Principle.* He distinguishes philos. from theology, the former based on reason, the latter on faith; the former speculative, the latter practical. In relation to revealed truth, reason perfects faith, leads to faith, refutes its adversaries.

(3) *Metaphysics.* Potentially, form is in matter, and is developed from it by an efficient cause. The form is the rational thought in matter, the work and the manifestation of Intelligence; as, conversely, through the form, things are intelligible.

The universal exists in the form, not in the matter of things. It exists, then, (*a*) *ante rem*, in the mind of God; (*b*) *in re;* (*c*) *post rem*, as a subjective concept in the human understanding.

Theosophy. God is incomprehensible by intelligence, but not unknown by it, as the First Cause, differing from and exceeding all that is caused. Not only His being, but His essential attributes, may be partially known by reason through His works.

That "GOD is," is also a proposition indirectly proved from the absurd and impossible conclusions resulting from its denial.

(4) *Physics.* (*a*) *Cosmology.* Here he opposes Aristotle; matter is not eternal, for GOD has been proved absolute cause of all being. The formula, "*ex nihilo nihil fit,*" and the proofs offered, have force in physics, are applicable to secondary causes. The world, time, motion, had a beginning.

(*b*) *Psychology.* The spirituality of the soul is proved from its intellectual activity, which is not of a material nature; from the simplicity of thought, from the freedom of the will.

The rational soul is the essential form of the body, differentiating man from the beast. Active and potential intelligence are not separate principles, but its powers. The former abstracts intelligible forms from sensible things, and so renders them intelligible; and thus the latter arrives at knowledge of the essence of these things.

Freedom of the will consists in power of choice, not limited by any necessity.

Conscience is the law of reason, which engages us to act or not to act; "*lex mentis habitus naturalis est quantum ad principia, acquisitus quantum ad scita.*"

A. distinguishes from conscience the moral sense, "*synteresis,*" which is not a habit, but a *potentia.* His philos. principles, however, are more fully developed in

(E.) *S. Thomas Aquinas,* who should be thoroughly studied as a key to Scholasticism. (1) He was born at Acquino, in the kingdom of Naples (1225 A. D.); connected with the Royal house of Hohenstaufen; ed. at Montecassino and Naples ; entered the Dom. Order. He afterwards pursued his studies at Cologne and Paris, under Alb. M. He taught crowds of scholars at Cologne, Paris, Bologna, Naples, etc.; was summoned by Greg. IX. to the Council of Lyons, but died on the way (1274 A. D.); "*Doctor Angelicus* ;" was canonized in 1323 A. D.

His works are: Comment. on Arist., on the Sentences of Petr. Lomb., on S. Ss. ; "*De Veritate*," "*Summa contra Gentiles* ;" "*Summa Theol.*," etc., etc.

S. Thom. A. is the Aristotle of the Middle Ages. Strict analysis was never carried further, and his influence has been permanent in thought, both in theol. and phil.

(2) *Principle.* (*a*) He assumes Aristotle's concepts as sufficient and indispensable in all possible subjects, although slightly modified by Plato through S. Aug.

(*b*) *Reconciliation of reason and faith* is, for the first time, fully attempted, by fixing with precision their respective limits ; and his determination has been permanently accepted by Christian phil. Truth is twofold: (*α*) Natural, discovered and demonstrated by reason ; (*β*) Supernatural, needing Rev. These are not different in essence, much less contradictory; for both are grounded in the Divine Wisdom. If reason find arguments against the faith, they are probable or sophistical. Reason can refute objections to (*β*), and show that it is not opposed to (*α*) or to reason ; it can also establish the credibility of Rev. Reason also offers us analogies, consequences which bring Rev. truth nearer to the speculative reason ; (*e. g.*, the internal word and love in man); but the assent of faith is an act of will. (*Sum. Theol.* I. Qu. I. 8).

(*c*) *Relation of Phil. to Theol.* Rev. assumes, reveals certain natural truths, which, without it, would be discovered only by the few, and after long labor and search, and with liability to error through the limitations of reason itself. (Sum. II. II. Qu. ii. 4.) These truths are *præambula fidei ; "gratia naturam non tollit, sed perficit."* Hence, the distinction between phil. and theol. The former proceeds, *à posteriori*, from the creature to God ; the latter, by deduction, from God to His works.

(3) *Theory of Knowledge.* We begin with individuals. The object produces in the subject an image of itself; so that the subject, in a certain sense, resembles the object. This image, the *species*, is not that which, but that by which, the object is known. It is the formal principle of knowledge: (*a*) of sensuous knowledge (sensible species) ; (*b*) of intellectual (intelligible species) ; (*a*) represents the sensuous phenomenon, (*b*) the intelligible " esse." But "*omnis nostra cognitio intellectualis incipit a sensu*" (Summa I. Qu. I. 9), and "*nihil sine phantasmate intelligit anima.*" Thus, the fact is accounted for, that lesions of a bodily organ [the brain] interfere with intellectual operations, since the former is essential to imagination, etc. (Sum. I. Qu. lxxxiv. 7 ; Cont. Gent. I. 3). There are no innate ideas ; the mind in itself resembles a "*tabula rasa ;*" knowledge of principles is, indeed, a natural " habit ; " but the terms which these principles contain can only be known through intell. spec. received from phantasmata.

The primary object of intellectual knowledge is the intelligible in the sensible ; abstraction is made by the intellect from the phantasmata in three degrees ; (*a*) of *materia signata*, or *individualis*, the principle of individuation, to get the species of a natural thing; *e.g.*, "*these bones*," etc.

(*b*) Of *mat. communis*, or corporeal matter, as in mathematical forms; but not of *mat. intelligibilis*, or substance. The former has sensible qualities, heat, cold, etc.; the latter has quantity. Thus is abstracted *mat. intellig. individualis*.

(*c*.) Of *mat. intell. communis*, as in *ens*, one, power, act.

This is direct knowledge; indirect, is the soul's knowledge of itself in thought and reflection. Finally, the mind raises itself, mediately, to the knowledge of GOD.

Aquinas distinguishes the active from the passive intel lect; the former, by abstraction, produces the intell. spec., the latter thus obtains the concept.

The complement of these is *ratio*, the power of proceeding to new truths through deduction on the basis of principles supplied as above.

We do not see the truth immediately in GOD; He is the last, not the first term of knowledge.

Truth and falsity are primarily in the intelligence when making propositions: the former adds to being (*ens*) its relation to the mind.

(4.) *Metaphysics* (Aristotelian.) Primary substance is the individual; its principles, in corporeals, matter and form. In the concept of matter, (*a*) negation, (*b*) potentiality of determination, of actuality; form is the principle of determ., of actuality.

Forms are (*a*) substantial, constituting the substance in its *esse*; (*b*) accidental, giving outward determination.

Forms also are (*a*) material, or inherent; (*b*) subsistent, which can be actual without matter, are immaterial, spiritual.

Distinguish between *essentia* and *esse:* a determined essence (*substantia*) needs an efficient cause to render it actual; this gives it being. *Esse: essentia::* actuality: potentiality.

Spiritual beings have not matter and form, but essence and being; the concept of these, their determinate being is their form; whereas in material things, the essence is of matter and form, and, since many things have like form and matter, the essence is the universal, the *quidditas* of individuals. The common essence of many individuals is actual in these only so far as it shares their quiddity.

The .principle of *individuation* is the quantitatively limited matter, *materia signata,* with its individual accidents, as opposed to the *materia communis.*

Spiritual beings do not admit of a universal concept.

By abstraction, we can consider the universal alone, which, as such, exists only in the mind; objectively, only in individuals, *in re,* which have a like essence, and of which the univ. can be predicated. (Sum. I. Qu. lxxxv. 2.) It is *ante rem,* in the Divine mind (I. Qu. xv.); *post rem* in the human, through abstraction.

Eternity is life, unlimited, "*tota simul,*" (prior and posterior non-existent), immutable, perfect and complete at once. *Time* is apprehended by number applied to motion. The difference between the two is not *per accidens,* but *per se.*

Theosophy. Intuitive knowledge of God is not possessed in this life; proofs are needed. Rejecting the (Ambrosian) argument from the concept to objective being (Sum. 1. Qu. ii. 1), the only valid arg. is, *à post.* from the works of nature to their First Cause.

(*a*) There must be a first cause of motion; whatever

is moved, is moved by another; for motion is change from potentiality to actuality.

(*b*) Effects such as we see, must have a first efficient cause.

(*c*) The accidental, contingent, conditioned (*possibile*), depends on the necessary, unconditioned.

(*d*) There are grades of perfection in earthly things; this implies an absolutely perfect.

(*e*) Nature is directed towards intelligible ends, while it has not intelligence. (Sum. I. Qu. ii. 3.) But all this gives inadequate concept of GOD: "*sensibilia - - - sunt effectus causæ virtutum non æquantes.*" (Cont. Gen. i. 3.)

In GOD is no composition of matter or form, nor any other. He is *pure* actuality; for potentiality, in any sense, would imply an actuating cause.

In Him essence and being are one.

In Him is no imperfection, because no potentiality; all perfections which earthly things possess, being from Him, are in Him, one and indivisible.

From GOD as Absolute Intelligence follows, necessarily, the concept of GOD as Absolute Will. He wills what is not Himself freely, because it is not necessary to His perfection and beatitude. From this follows His Omnipotence.

His Providence is the ordering of all things, both universal and singular, with reference to an end, (opposes Maimonides and Averroes), for it extends as far as His knowledge and causality.

The casual is with respect to a particular cause, not to the universal.

Ills, corruptions, defects, are permitted in particular things, contributing to the greater good of the whole.

(5.) *Physics. Cosmology.* (*a*) Reason can prove a creation *ex nihilo*, (matter not pre-existent or eternal,) but (*b*) we know only by faith, the limited duration of the world, (*Esse per se subsistens* is one, sc. GOD), though (*c*) it cannot be proved to have had a beginning. (Sum. I. Qu. xlvi. 1, 2.) The proposition (*a*) follows from the principle that GOD is the First Cause of all being, *i. e.*, not only of form but of matter. And since matter is not *in* GOD, it must be His creation. As for (*b*), *ex nihilo* does not necessarily involve "*post nihilum.*" (*c*) is against Aristotle; if, of necessity, the world have no beginning, then of necessity it exists; but in what shall this necessity be grounded? (Vid. Stöckl *in loc.*)

Optimism. The end of creation is the manifestation of GOD's perfection; He is the final cause of all things (Sum. I. Qu. xliv., 4); and hence all things are ordered, with different degrees of good, for the perfect good of the whole.

Evil in parts (deficiency of good), heightens the excellency of the whole.

The world is one, both in correlation of all parts to one another, and in one order relatively to the one efficient cause.

Psychology, is Aristotelian developed:

Genera Potentiarum Animæ. (Note; distinguish in the mind (*a*) faculties, (*b*) habits, (*c*) acts.

(*a*) *Vegetativ.;* (α) nutritiv.; (β) augmentat.; (γ) generativ.

(*b*) *Sensitiv.*; (α) exterior, (five); (β) interior, which has four powers, (I.) *sens. communis*, (II.) imagination, (III.) memory, (IV.) *vis æstimativa*, of particulars as hurtful or beneficial, useful or useless, etc.

(*c*) *Appetitiv.*; (*α*) *sensitiv.*, is (I.) concupiscible, by which the mind pursues the agreeable or useful, and avoids the hurtful; (II.) irascible, by which the mind resists what hinders the one or aids the other, (*e. g.* anger, hope, fear, etc.): its object is difficult good; (*β*) *rationale*, "*actus appetitus intell.*," *Voluntas*; (Love, etc., equivocal terms.) Its object is the good as a known good. Love is the root and ground of all other emotions of its class.

(*d*) *Motivum*, according to place.

(*e*) *Intellectivum*, (souls of this order include the lower genera); (*α*) passive (*possibile*), receiving species of things and retaining them; (*β*) active, abstracting species from images and rendering the potentially intelligible, actually so; cognizing universal forms.

Included in (*β*) are (I.) *intellectus*, "*cognoscens simplici intuitu*," (II.) *ratio*, "*discurrendo de uno in aliud*," though not as separate faculties, *potentiæ*, of the mind.

The intellect requiring phantasmata which are prepared by the sensitive power, which has its organ in the body, the body [brain] is fatigued in thought, *per accidens*.

The soul (sensitive) is the form of the body.

Immortality. The soul, as an intellectual principle, is incorporeal, "*forma per se subsistens*," therefore incorruptible; not so the soul of brutes, which is sensitive, not intellectual. Of its five genera of faculties some are only in it as their subject, these remain after death; others, which are of the compound being man, do not.

Against the Averroists, an intellectual principle is in each individual man.

The sensitive soul is *ex traduce*, not created; proof is, it is not *res subsistens*, but the form of a composite substance, the animal. But the intellectual soul is created by

God, *res subsistens*, for active virtue existing in matter (*in semine*) cannot produce immaterial effects. (Note that man's soul, *one* essence, possesses the lower powers, and becomes the form of the embryo when it is ready to receive it: the veget-sensit. form then disappearing.)

(6.) *Ethics.* (*a*) *Good* and being are identical, *sec. rem*, but differ in thought, for the former contains the concept of the desirable (Sum. I., Qu. v., 1); every being, as being, is good; when called evil, it is so called as wanting something (privation).

The good is (α) *honestum*, (β) *utile*, (γ) *delectabile.*

Moral good in acts, is derived from (α) the genus, what they have of the plenitude of entity, (evil is deficiency). (Sum. II. I., Qu. xviii. 1–4);

(β) The species, the object in its relation to the agent (convenient);

(γ) The circumstances;

(δ) The end, extrinsic.

Only voluntary acts are moral; they are formally good or bad according to their end; materially, according to the outward act. But since the quality of good in the will depends on the object offered to it by reason, (moral light, conscience,) the same goodness depends, secondarily, on reason itself; primarily, on eternal law, which directs reason.

(*b*) *Summum bonum.* All men seek beatitude as their ultimate end, and this cannot consist in any created good. God is its cause or object; its essence is in the speculative intellect. In special sciences is found only a participation of this perfect beatitude; its perfection is in the Vision of God, "*Cognitio perfecta intelligibilis finis.*" Joy is concomitant to this, the rest of the loving in the loved.

In the beatitude of this life (imperfect) a well-ordered body is needful, since speculative intellect makes use of it. Outward goods also are serviceable, as instruments for the works of an active and contemplative life, which perfect this earthly beatitude.

(*c*) *Free will.* GOD'S will is always accomplished; but as First Cause. He makes some second causes necessary, others contingent. He does not will sins to be committed, but wills to permit them.

Man's will is not under necessity of co-action (external compulsion), but is determined to the means which are necessary to its ends; and, by natural necessity, to its end, beatitude; and whatever in general is natural to man. It is determined to the good as good, but not of necessity to this or that good. Freedom of choice (*liberum arbitrium*) is related to will, as *ratio* to *intellectus*; the former viewing various things as means to an end, or obstacles to it; the latter, simply the end. Brutes have not choice, for sensitive appetites determine to one object only.

The voluntary is that whose principle is inward (this need not be the first principle), along with knowledge of the end sought for. The will seeks the good only, or apparent good; the intellect (*int. practicus*) moves the will not as efficient cause, but by presenting to it its object. So also the sensitive appetite moves the will "*ex parte objecti.*" In willing the end, the will moves itself to will the means.

The primary exterior mover of the will is GOD only; yet not by compulsion (contrary to the motion of the will); for then, willing and not willing would be coincident. GOD, as first efficient cause, does not determine it to will this or that. Its moral goodness depends ultimately on its *formal* conformity to the Divine will; it may be good when not *materially* so conformed.

The order of will and action is (α) simple volition (determined) of the end; (β) intuition of the end by certain means; (γ) deliberation (rational) concerning the means; (δ) consent (rational and voluntary) to the means; (ε) choice (rat. and vol.) of some one means; (ζ) use (vol.) of the means; (η) execution; (θ) fruition.

Acts of the will can be directed (*imperati*) by reason; the latter can command itself, and assent or dissent in the case of contingent (not demonstrated) truths. Acts of the sensitive appetite are partly subjected to reason, and partly follow the condition of the bodily organs.

(*d*) *Moral sense* (*synderesis*) is not a special faculty (*potentia*), but a *habitus* of the practical reason, giving intuitive knowledge of primary practical principles (Sum. I., Qu. lxxix). *Conscience* is the act of this habit, by which we practically apply this knowledge. Even erring reason creates obligation; and will at variance with it, is evil, if the *error* is voluntary; otherwise, if it is involuntary. Good will alone does not constitute a good act, but due matter and circumstances, determined by reason.

(*e*) *Virtue* is "good mental habit by which one lives rightly." (See Arist., def. of *habitus*).

The four *cardinal* virtues are grounded in four subjects; in practical reason, (α) prudence, which is distinguished from the other intellectual virtues (not moral), *sapientia, scientia, intellectus,* in having contingent (not necessary) principles, derived from education and experience.

(β) Justice is grounded in the will, a perpetual fixed will to render to all their dues; metaphorically, it is applied, also, to the parts of a man's own nature. (Arist.) The commutative, is of voluntary and involuntary exchanges, as passions and actions; it implies restitution. It includes religion, piety, gratitude, etc. Against it is the vice which injures a neighbor in his person, those joined to him, or his possessions.

(γ) Temperance is in the concupiscible part of the *vis sensit.;* courage, in the irascible. Passions in themselves are not morally good or evil, but only as subject to reason and will, or according as their object is rational or not. These virtues are grounded, not perfected, in man by nature.

The *theological* virtues are divinely infused for a supernatural end, a second beatitude above and beyond man's nature; their object is GOD: (α) faith, for cognition of supernatural truth, perfecting the speculative intellect;

(β) hope, for the willing of this supernatural beatitude;

(γ) charity, for spiritual union with the source of it.

Virtues are also divided (Neo-Plat.) into (α) political, (β) purifying, (γ) exemplary, *i. e.* after the Divine pattern. (II. I. Qu. lxi. 5.)

(*f*) *Evil*, the privation of good, is, in voluntary agents,

(α) *malum pœnæ*, privation in the agent himself;

(β) *malum culpæ*, privation in his actions, either negation or defect of due manner and order. GOD is, *per accidens*, the cause of the former, not of the latter. Hence it follows that there is no

Summum malum, the cause of all evils; (evil, privation, has no terminus). The assumption of two principles arose from considering particular causes of particular effects, without regarding the sum of all being: what was hurtful, *per accidens*, to another, was regarded as hurtful in itself. (J. S. Mill.)

Vice is against the nature of man because it excludes the order of reason. Sins, acts against order, are (α) against God, (β) against self, (γ) against neighbor.

Sin. Man, like everything else, seeks the good; sin is in corruption or disorder of man's principles of action; (α) intellectual, sins of ignorance; (β) *appet. sens.*, of passion; (γ) of will, disordered in loving the less good more than the greater, sins of malice or evil will.

Mortal sin can be in (α) will, (β) reason, (i) not knowing what it can and ought, (ii) not duly governing inferior powers.

Passions cannot directly control the will, but only by distracting or misleading the judgment.

The sinful act as act is from God (material part), the formal part (deficiency) which makes it sin, is not. He is the cause of blindness of reason and hardness of heart, by withdrawing grace.

Good and evil actions justly merit retribution, either from individuals or from society; the same holds good with respect to God, as He is the proper end of all actions, and as He is Ruler of the Universe.

(*g*) *Law* is founded on reason, not on will, for reason is the rule and measure of human acts ordained for a *common* good (since a part is for the whole, and man is a part of society), either by the community or one man "*vicem multitudinis gerens.*" (II. I. Qu. xc. 1, 2, etc.)

In the most general sense, law is

(α) *eternal,* in the Divine Mind, reason governing the universe, the principle of Providence; Will and reason in GOD are one; He *is* reason. Fortuitous things, so called, are under higher law;

(β) *natural*, in us, participating the eternal; by it good and evil are discerned: a natural inclination to due act and end; the primary, self-evident principles of practical reason, that good is to be sought, and evil avoided; *sc.* (i) good of nature in general, law of self-preservation; (ii) of animal nature, as sexual love and care of children; (iii) rational, as that ignorance is to be shunned, not to offend others, etc. This is one law for all nations, in its common, unchangeable principles, not equally known, however, in its remote deductions, and it may be depraved by passion, evil customs, and bad natural dispositions: it is the foundation of all moral positive laws;

(γ) *human*, in particulars, by probable, contingent deductions, from (α) and (β); as determined to special cases the declaration of *jus*; (i) *jus gentium*, direct deductions from the law of nature concerning man as man; (ii) *jus civile*, particular determinations in each state; these are (1) moral or (2) positive, pertaining to Divine *cultus* (ceremonial), or relating to man's neighbors (judicial).

Human laws are to restrain the evil, especially in what injures others: if just, they bind conscience; not so the unjust, except to avoid scandal and tumult, and not at all those which contravene the natural. Authority, divinely given, does not extend to unequal or unjust burdens; the law of common sense is higher, for no human law but has exceptions, and the spirit of it is to be sought for.

(δ) *Divine*, positive, promulgated for man's eternal beatitude as a supernatural end.

The State is best in which, by popular voice, the best are chosen to rule, all having a share in the government by choosing and being eligible; the blending of monarchy, aristocracy, and democracy; for by this, peace and patriotism are best secured. (Note S. Thomas' liberalism.)

The *use* of natural things is, by nature, not in society but in individuals; still they are bound to hold them for the common good: in extreme necessity any one may, without violating natural justice, use another's possessions.

(*h*) *Prayer.* Human affairs are under Div. Prov., not necessity; prayer is not useful to change the Div. Mind, but God has disposed effects, has appointed from what causes, and in what order they shall come; among which causes are human acts—prayers. These, then, are to be used according to Divine command, as other secondary means are, which are ordained by God as conditions of a certain result, in order that man may deserve to receive what God fore-ordained before the world was.

(F.) *S. Bonaventura,* John Fidanza, (1) (1221–1274, A.D.), b. in Tuscany, a Franciscan, studied and taught at Paris, general of his order; wrote besides Comment. on the Sent. Petr. Lomb., "*Speculum Animæ,*" *De Septem Gradibus Contemplationis,* "*Itinerarium mentis ad Deum,*" etc. "*Doctor Seraphicus.*"

(2.) B. is a mystic of the school of the St. Victors; ecstacy is the end of science and virtue, the union of the soul with God, a (supernatural) love which unites the loving with the Infinite, so that the former is lost in the latter.

Plato through S. Aug. is preferred to Aristotle; A.'s doctrine of the ethical mean is only valid in the common life. The way of contemplation is by grace on God's side, on man's by holiness and prayer; the three principal steps are, (*a*) the outer world, which bears the mark (*vestigium*) of God; (*b*) the inner, or the soul, the image of God; (*c*) immediate intuition of God Himself. (Stöckl.)

(G.) *Roger Bacon,* (1) (1214–1294, A.D.), b. in Somersetshire, Eng., a Franciscan, at Univ. of Paris, taught at Oxford; devoted to mathematics, physics, languages; suspected by his order, and forbidden to teach; Clement IV. removed the interdict; Bacon wrote for him, *opus majus, op. minus, op. tertium.* After C.'s death, he was imprisoned, as a sorcerer, in his convent; his works treat of optics, astronomy, mathematics. "*Doctor mirabilis.*"

(2.) Experience, (outward, inward,) is necessary to knowledge; demonstration, without it, gives not certainty, but only connection of premises and conclusion.

(H.) *Duns Scotus,* (1) founder of the Scotists, opponents of the Thomists, b. at Duns, Irel. (1266 A.D.), Franciscan, taught at Oxf., Paris, Cologne; d. there, (1308 A.D.) "*Scotia me genuit, Anglia me suscepit, Gallia me docuit, Colonia me tenet.*" A most subtle dialectician. His philos. is fully presented in Comment. on Sent. Petr. Lomb.; he wrote also comments on Aristotle, "*De Rerum principio,*" etc. "*Doctor subtilis.*"

(2.) Aristotelian, though not so strict a follower, as S. Thomas. His genius is rather critical than constructive; questioning with extreme subtilty, the arguments by which Thomism is sustained.

The verities of faith rest on the will of GOD, and faith on the will of man.

(3.) *Matter* is actuality, being, in the order of nature, prior to form, which simply determines its actuality. All created beings have matter and form, (GOD only being pure form,) the former being unlimited, potential, the latter, the principle of individuation, actuality. The "*primo-prima*" matter (formless) is the same in (created) bodies and spirits; the *2do-1ma*" is subject to generation and decay; the "*3tio-Ima*" is that which is shaped by the artist, having already received its natural form.

The *universal*, then, is not the form of things, but is objectively real, distinct from the individual, though existing only in it, potential existence, the ground of unity among individuals. Positive determinations being added, first specific, then individual, we reach the last (individual) form, *hæccitas;* "*quodcunque ens est in se quid, et habet in se aliquem gradum determinatum in entibus.*" But if this latter constituted the only reality, there would be only singulars, but no unity of nature.

Thus the universal is prior but undetermined, and can be thought (*distinctio rationis,*) as it is, (*a parte rei,*) potential being. The last form is not a thing, *res*, nor a mere concept, it is a formal reality.

God can be known, *á posteriori*, as (*a*) the First cause, (*b*) the Final cause, (*c*) perfect Being, unity.

S. applies his metaphysical principle; (vid. supr.) "*Divinæ perfectiones distinguntur a parte rei, non realiter quidem, sed formaliter.*"

Reason cannot prove that GOD is Almighty; nor,

(4.) the *creation* of the world out of nothing. Free will in GOD is His supreme law. Against S. Thomas, who said that GOD acted conformably to His nature and essential attributes, S. saw in GOD nothing to be a reason for creation, etc. In strict logical consistency is his

Psychology; There is a unity of nature in the universal, as a "formal reality," among souls, as, in the individual soul, in its faculties.

The immortality of the soul cannot be proved; it is of faith.

The *will* is superior to the intellect; its freedom is an

absolute indifferentism, undetermined by its object which is "*naturaliter agens*" i. e. with necessity. The will can direct the intellect to an object, or turn it away. "*Voluntati, etiam quando producit hoc velle, non repugnat oppositum velle;*" "*potentia ad successionem oppositorum.*" Even in perception, the intellect is active under the will.

(5.) Moral law, then, is founded on the will of GOD; the good is good because GOD commands it.

4. DECLINE OF SCHOLASTICISM.

The 14th and 15th centuries made no further progress in phil.; but to the two Schools Thomist and Scotist, "realists" and "formalists," were added, the Nominalist, (revived) and, (by reaction), the Mystic, both wide spread and vigorous, the former tending to empiricism and skepticism, the latter, equally, to rejection of all phil., although at first, starting from scholasticism to reach the people in popular forms: (German Mystics).

Scholastic forms were growing more and more careless or barbarous, stiff or tasteless; unity of thought and aim being lost in subtle distinctions and verbal quibbles, victory over an antagonist being sought instead of truth.

(A.) *Nominalist.* *William of Occam*, may represent the school; (1) b. Surrey, Eng., joined the Franciscans, a disciple of Duns Scotus, taught in Paris under Philip le Bel, and took his side in the controversy with Boniface VIII.; later he sought the protection of the Emp. Louis of Bavaria against the pope; "*tu me defendas gladio, ego te defendam calamo;*" d. at Munich, (1347 A.D.) He wrote *Summa logices*, Questions on Physics, on the Sentences, etc.; wrote also on the Eccles. power; "*Venerabilis inceptor,*" "*Doctor invincibilis.*"

(2.) *Principle, and theory of knowledge.* All knowledge begins with sense-perception: this is intuitive knowledge. The act of abstraction is a spontaneous act following two perceptions, and is knowledge of the same objects in an indeterminate way, the concept being a sign of either of them; but "*Scientia est de rebus singularibus,*" for sensation gives particular objects only. Sensible and intelligible species are equally denied; the object and the sense-perception are sufficient, (cf. Reid), and "*entia non sunt multiplicanda præter necessitatem.*" Image and concept are natural signs of the only realities, particular objects.

Neither Thomism, Scotism, nor conceptualism will bear the canon "*entia non sunt, etc.*" for abstraction does not eliminate a reality, but only generates a sign of it in the thinking mind.

Words. Terms are arbitrary signs of signs, *i. e.*, of concepts. The *universal* is the undetermined concept, "*significans univoce plura singularia,*" the result of abstracting knowledge: as a thought, it is as singular as any other. Genus is a concept applicable to more, species, to fewer, individuals.

(3.) No *theological* dogmas are demonstrable; even GOD's existence and unity are matters of faith. For reason, there may be more than one world, more than one prime mover; finite effects can only conclude, rationally, a finite cause.

We know GOD, not in His existence, but in His attributes, which are concepts or signs, whose difference is not grounded in the nature of His Being: "*eos conceptus prædicamus non pro se, sed pro Deo;*" "*licet enim hi conceptus dicant aliquid Dei, nullus tamen realiter dicit quod est Deus.*"

Ideas in God are the thought of individuals; the imperfect unlimited concept, the universal, can only be known as a product of our thought.

The doctrine of the Trinity is realistic, opposed to reason, rests on faith merely.

(4.) The *Soul* cannot be proved to be an immaterial, incorruptible substance; it is not the only essential form of the body, there is also *forma corporeitatis*. The intellectual and sensitive souls are not one; for the latter has extension, is joined *circumscriptive* with the body; the former has not extension, is joined *diffinitive*. As with bodies, so with the soul, we know not the substance, but (intuitively) qualities, as acts of willing, thinking, pleasures, etc.

(5.) *Good* is simply what God wills: "*adeo ut mutata eâ voluntate, quod sanctum et justum est, possit evadere injustum*. (On O. See Br. Quarterly, July, 1872; Jan. 1874.)

John Buridan, Rector of the Univ. of Paris in 1327, A.D., a pupil of Occam, developed nominalistic logic, and offered a theory of the will (intellectual determinism) in his logical treatises, and Questions on Arist. In the former, he sought a ready means of finding the middle term, "*pons asinorum*." In the latter, the will is determined to the judgment of the higher good; if motives are equally balanced, the will cannot decide to act: (the ass between the bundles of hay). How then is the will free? It is not so in the instant of judgment, but it may be at another when that judgment is not in the mind: or it can turn the judgment from the higher good to the lower; or it can delay its decision of a given case, and the judgment of the mind may change.

Nominalism, strenuously opposed in many quarters,

was forbidden in the Univ. of Paris, (1340 A.D., etc.,) but at the opening of the 15th Cent., Pierre d'Ailly (nominalist) was chancellor. Louis XI. (1473) issued a new decree against it, abrogated in 1483.

The Thomists, *e. g.* Archb. Bradwardine, of Canterbury, maintained the cause of realism, especially in the Dominican Schools, arguing,

(1.) Nature chiefly aims at and preserves species ;

(2.) Human laws recognize the human race as essentially one ;

(3.) The goods we seek are changeable, there is a *sum. bon.*, their unity.

(On the fruits of nominalism in art, in the 15th Cent., see Lubke, Vol. II. *e. g.* Donatello, p. 167: Note the decline of poetry, and architecture.)

(B.) *Mysticism :* Under this head may be arranged a group of thinkers, widely different in character, though united in a ground of extreme realism, and having in common an ever increasing distrust of scholasticism, a despair of reason, a refuge in higher intuitions. (See Br. Quarterly, Oct. 1874).

Earliest, most thoroughly scientific in form, and of wide spread and permanent influence, is

(1.) *Eckhart,* (*a*) (b. at Strasburg? circ. 1250 A. D.) joined the Dominicans, taught and preached through Germany ; was made general Vicar of his order : d. 1329 A.D. ; Twenty-eight theses were condemned in papal bull. (See Ueberweg, v. I.)

(*b*) *Principle,* follows Dionys. Areop. and Erigena, tending (unconsciously) to emanistic pantheism. The inner ground of man's soul is Divine, a "spark" of Deity;

knowledge is a real union of subject and object. The soul's highest power is an immediate intuition of the "Godhead" transcending the determinate.

(*c*) *Theosophy:* The Absolute is impersonal, concealed ever from thought; of the "Godhead" no predicates may be used; It is hidden in eternal darkness. In the act of self-knowledge, God is developed as the Trinity, the form of "Godhead," which beholds itself with love; the subject is the Father, the object is the Son, the love is the S. Sp.

God is the essence of all essences, which are ever in Him; in sending forth His Son, He sends forth all things, (ideal world). In space and time, *natura naturata*, are the Three Persons of the Trinity, eternal as the world is, but in *natura non naturata* is only the "Godhead."

(*d*) *Cosmology:* Apart from God, the world is non-entity; God is in all things, and is all things, for creatures have no essence except God. Yet He is not nature, but above it, for the world of space and time is created out of nothing. The motive of creation is God's goodness, which necessarily extends itself; and, by the same necessity, creation is continuous, eternal. Different from this, as the realizing of the ideal by the artist, is the creation out of nothing, in time.

(*e*) *Psychology:* In man's soul are three parts; (α) the external senses; (β) empirical understanding, and the appetitive faculty; (γ) memory, will, and reason. There are, then, three kinds of cognition; (α) sensible; (β) rational; (γ) supra-rational; only the latter reaches the whole truth, and, with true knowledge, all images, instructions, dogmas, cease; for the ground of the soul is a Divine image, free from all activities, the organ of mystic contemplation, which sees pure being, the "Godhead," unconscious of self: this alone is immortal.

(*f*) *Ethics*, is the end of all wisdom, that man, by direct intuition, may arrive at absolute rest in union with the Infinite, the "Godhead." This is the deification of man as the Son of God, made one with the eternal Son; for God became man that man might become God; this, however, is not annihilation. Yet E. is not antinomian; the stillness of reason, in this life, is not inconsistent with use of the faculties which belong to the earthly nature.

The conditions of this oneness with God are,

(α) Freedom from sin, entire, perfect; then only the will is perfectly free, it wills only what God wills, the good. Moral laws are for the imperfect; the perfect is free from them, being above them; he is not virtuous, he is virtue's self;

(β) Withdrawal from all outward things into the soul; moral acts are only a step towards this; better is holy rest; (Quietism.)

(γ) Death to self and all its powers, passions, affections, will, reason, that God may speak, act in man: man must cease to act for a reward; he is "deceased," and so,

(δ) Unification with God is accomplished; man is not only the adopted son of God, he is one with the eternal Son. This is the (necessitated) emanent begetting of the (immanent) eternal Son of God.

(2.) *John Tauler*, popular preacher at Strasburg and Cologne, (d. 1361, A. D.), did much to bring before the people the mysticism of Eckhart. Natural light of reason gives no true knowledge, it must be renounced for the mystic light of grace.

(3.) Author of the "*German Theology*," (14th or 15th

cent.) ; self-love is the root of all sin ; GOD's love, of all good ; self, *ego*, must be wholly renounced, so man is deified. (Note influence on Luther and the German Reformation.)

The "brothers of the Common Life" gave practical form to German Mysticism. (See also "*De Imitatione Christi.*")

Among philos. less purely mystic, but with marked tendencies thitherward may be placed,

(1.) *Gerson*, (*a*) (1363-1429, A. D.) was chancellor of the Univ. of Paris ; took an active part at the Council of Constance ; was banished by the Duke of Burgundy for denouncing the murder of the Duke of Orleans, and found a refuge in Bavaria ; subsequently entered the cloister at Lyons, and taught little children. G. was a man of universal learning ; but though he attempted a reconciliation of realism and "terminism" (nominalism), his distrust of hnman powers found utterance in his "Mystic Theology, speculative and practical," "*De Illuminatione Cordis*," etc.

(*b*) True science is that of the religious sentiment, the immediate intuition of GOD by the soul ; this makes even the fool a true philos. (Cousin, Hist. Gen. Phil. c. v.)

(2.) *Petrarch*, (1304-1374, A. D.) who, towards the close of his life, abandoned profane studies for the contemplative phil. and wrote "*De Contemptu Mundi*," "*de Vita Solitaria*," etc.

(3.) *Raymond* of Sébonde, professor of medicine at Toulouse, (d. 1432, A. D.), who wrote *Theologia naturalis*. (See Montaigne, Essais, ii. 12.)

The book of nature proves to us what the book of Revelation gives on authority. Through knowledge of nature man may arrive at knowledge of himself, and through that, of God. This is better than physics, logic, or metaphysics; in the first we learn (*a*) being, (*b*) life, (*c*) the sensitive; in the second, thought; and then the first cause, sc. God. Grateful love must lead to union with the loved.

(See also the life of S. Theresa (1525-1582) written by herself.)

CHAPTER IX.

PHILOSOPHY OF THE RENAISSANCE.

1. INTRODUCTION. 2. PLATONISTS, CABALISTS, MYSTICS. 3. PERIPATETICS. 4. INDEPENDENT PHILOSOPHY AND SKEPTICISM

[*References*:—See, beside those already named, and special ref. below, Ritter, Stöckl, Lecky (Hist. Ration.), Blakey, Cousin (especially Frag. Philos. vol. iii ;), Erasmus, Enc. Moriæ and Epistles ; Epist. Obsc. Vir.; Lubke's Hist. Sculpt. v. ii. ; Hallam's Hist. Lit. Europe.]

1. INTRODUCTION.

(A.) *Character:* (1.) Phil. took a position of *independence* with respect to Christian dogma ; highest truths were to be determined by reason alone, not even an appeal for verification to Christian Rev. recognized. Ancient systems were reconstructed without any reference to the teaching of the church, or it was maintained that philos. truth might be false according to faith, and conversely.

(2.) The underlying *unity* which, generally, marked scholasticism in all its schools was now lost ; as, in society, the unity through Pope and Emperor was abandoned. The only remaining unity was one of antagonism to scholasticism, (on both sides a war of bitter words), a retention of some of its forms of thought, a general attempt to ignore all that had passed since the downfall of Anc. phil., and a tendency to a certain method (psychological) as well as to certain subjects, *e. g.* human faculties, the means or limits of knowledge, and physical and mathematical inquiries, at first associated with cosmological and theosophic speculations (Cabalistic), and often with magic.

(3.) The sixteenth century was a period of *transition* of *confusion*, without settled method or principle; there was no predominating school, no originality, but a vague following of every ancient school. Greek thinkers were now read in the original, and men, no longer scholastics, were Platonists, Peripatetics, etc., but rather as scholars, classicists, than with any comprehensive or productive grasp of the principles which they professed.

(4.) Without great names, there was a *widening* of the sphere of phil.; it was popularized, but the influence of classicism made the culture of mere form as extreme as the neglect of it among the later schoolmen; but philos. at the same time exerted, particularly through the "humanists," a more manifest influence on general literature, science, and social life.

(B.) *Causes.* Beside (1.) inherent causes in the state of scholasticism; and (2.) the religious movement which, from the German Mystics, took form as the "Reformation," and which, in attacking the church and religion of the Mid. Ages, also attacked (though not invariably) its phil., and, at least, developed a demand for change, or scientific progress, with distrust of all existing principles, may be noted as special causes,

(3.) The *renaissance* of classical art and literature, beginning with the second half of the 14th cent. Here was found deep thought in a beauty of form to which, in such subjects, the age was a stranger ; theory spoke to heart and imagination, and was not covered up in harsh and repulsive forms.

The Ren. began in Italy. Petrarch and Boccacio, in the first half of the fourteenth cent., had done much to extend a taste for the classics, especially for the Greek. But the fall of Constantinople (1453 A.D.) was a most productive agent in spreading through Italy its teachers. Greek MSS. were diligently collected and translated.

(Note Politianus, Bembo, Erasmus, Ficino, the Picos, etc.) Especially the Medici in Florence, through their Platonic Academy, spread abroad the enthusiasm for Greek art, poetry, and phil.

(4.) The invention of *printing*, together with the increase of wealth in the free cities, widened immensely the interest in philos., and brought it sensibly into general literary culture and political life.

2. Platonists and Cabalists.

The contention between Greek teachers for the supremacy of Plato or Aristotle, soon created two rival parties which divided the advocates of the new learning in western Europe. The followers of the former were Neo-Platonists, and sought in the Cabala, a Divine Rev. for their philos. ; Plato had learned of Moses. (On Platonism in Literature, see Fleming's Dict., "Idea" ; *e. g.*, Calderon, El Purg. de S. Patr. ii.)

(A.) *Marsilius Ficinus*, (1433–1499, A.D.) a Florentine, taught at the Platonic Academy in Florence; translated Plato and Plotinus, and (partly) Porphyry, Jamblichus, and Proclus ; wrote, also, "*Theol. Platonica*," etc.

The sensible species cannot beget the intelligible spec.

whereby the subject of knowledge is united with the object: this spiritual form is innate in the soul, and sensible experience only awakens the soul to consciousness of it. The object of knowledge, the true essence of the thing, is the Div. idea, which by the soul is seen, immediately, in GOD: "*signatum est super nos lumen vultus Tui.*" As the eye in seeing by light, so the soul sees not the species, nor GOD in Himself, but the object through the idea, and GOD in His relation to the finite.

(B.) *John Pico de Mirandola,* (1463–1494, A.D.) devoted himself to Platonic studies at Florence, and, through the Hebrew, to the Cabala; for Pythagoras and Plato had derived their principles from the inner meaning of Hebraic Ss. At the age of twenty-four, he devoted his property to founding a Platonic Acad. at Rome, which was suppressed by the Pope: (note the 900 theses to be maintained against all opponents.) There are three worlds, the counterparts of one another, (1) the super-celestial, (2) the heavenly, (3) the sub-lunar; man is a union of the three. With him is associated his nephew, John Francis Pico de M.

(C.) *John Reuchlin,* (1455–1522, A.D.) b. at Pforzheim, devoted himself at Paris to the new learning and Hebrew; studied law; was envoy of the electoral princes to Florence and Rome; there introduced to the Cabala and Neo-Platonism, he transferred them to his native land, writing "*de Arte Cabalistica,*" etc.

The Cabala as doctrine, contains, through Div. Rev., all truths; as art, it deals with the mystic meaning of letters, words, and S. Ss.; but the Cabalist himself must, through purification and contemplation, receive Div. inspiration, in order to know super-sensual truth. Distinguish

(1) *ratio*, for scientific knowledge of the sensible; (2) *mens*, the eye of faith, which by Div. light sees, immediately, the super-sensual world. Syllogistic theology only leads to a maze of errors.

(D.) *Cornelius Agrippa*,(1487–1525, A.D.) at Paris devoted to law and medicine, a humanist, taking the practical side of the Cabalistic Pythag. and Neo-Plat. phil. of his day, seeks, in his "*occulta philosophia*," the hidden power of nature, through geomancy, hydromancy, pyromancy, chiromancy, necromancy, etc., etc.: at length, a skeptic, he wrote "*de Vanitate et Incertudine Scientiarum.*"

(E.) In the Lutheranism of Germany appeared a mystic element, strenuously opposed by dogmatic Lutherans, but finding utterance in Weigel and

Jacob Boehme, (1575–1624, A.D.), (1) *b.* at Goerlitz, an illiterate shoemaker, began to have visions early in life, in which was "such a wondrous inward clearness of vision, that it seemed he could look, unhindered, into the deepest and last principles of all things." His numerous works are the popular gospel of German mysticism; from nature, the Bible, the ideas of earlier German mystics, he developes a new and complete "Cabala," in most fantastic forms, confounding ideal and sensual, spiritual and physical, ethical and natural. God is, in Himself, the purely undetermined, from which proceed, in Self-Rev., the contradictories (1) darkness, eternal nature, the first principle; (2) light, His spirit. From the harsh "fire-principle," the Father, emanates the Light-Principle, the Son, (the second principle). The world is a third being produced from these two (*gnostic emanation*). This is ethical also: from the one, God=nothing, in development proceed good and evil, a cosmical necessity in things.

In man, also, the image of GOD, the microcosm, is a three fold soul, the fire-soul from the first principle, the light-soul, the Divine image, and the animal-soul (for earthly knowledge). Three principles then strive for the mastery in man.

(Note the rise of the Rosicrucians, on a mystic basis.)

(3.) PERIPATETICS.

Averroism had maintained itself in Padua in the latter half of the middle ages, at first in the extreme form, *sc.*, the oneness of the intellect in all men, but subsequently made more orthodox, by many, *sc.*, the unity of primary principles in all men. The introduction of the Greek text gave a fresh stimulus to this sect of Peripatetics, but also produced another, the *Alexandrists*,(Alex. Aphrodis.) teaching a deistic naturalism. The individual reason is inseparable from the phantasma and sensation, and disappears with the bodily organs ; but what is true in phil. may be false in faith. Most conspicuous was

(A.) *Petrus Pomponatius*, who in 1516, A.D., wrote "*de Immortalitate Animæ*." (1) Vegetative-sensive functions are as valid proof of the materiality of the soul, as intellectual, of its spirituality; (2) it is the entelechy of a body, therefore it is corporeal ; it depends on sensuous images ; in and for itself, therefore, it is material, mortal, though in certain relations it possesses a similarity with the immaterial and immortal. Virtue and vice need no reward or punishment but in themselves.

In like manner Aristotle and his Alex, commentators are used against miracles, and the freedom of the will; what happens on earth is due to stellar influence. (Note opposition to astrology among the Platonists.) Prominent among Averroists may be named

(B.) *Andreas Cæsalpinus*, (1509–1603, A.D.), physician to Clem. VIII., and the first writer of a systematic botany. He discards the comment. on Arist. GOD is the soul of the universe, the one intellect of stars and men, individualized only in bodies and for a limited time.

Through Melancthon Peripateticism was established in the Protestant Universities.

(4.) INDEPENDENT PHILOSOPHY AND SKEPTICISM.

Entire independence of ancient systems is not to be looked for in the 16th cent.; but attempts may be noted taking different directions with different classes of thinkers who agree only in rejecting the old, but without any common principles of reconstruction. First may be named

(A.) The *Humanists*, Philologists, most bitter opponents of Scholasticism, especially in dialectics, which they strove to make chiefly an aid to rhetorical elegance: hence their special devotion to Cicero and Quinctilian. In addition to Von Hutten, to Erasmus, and his friend Vives, of special note is

Peter Ramus, (1) (1515–1572, A. D.), b. in Picardy studied at Univ. of Paris, was Prof. in the Coll. of France, against scholasticism (“*quæcunque ab Aristotele dicta essent commentitia esse*”), sought to give phil. elegance of form, to reform dialectics, physics, metaphysics; his works were suppressed by his adversaries, and he was forbidden to teach; finally he was murdered by personal enemies on S. Bart.'s day, 1572, A. D.

(2) There is a natural logic of which the dialectic art must give scientific account; it consists in (*a*) invention, finding the principles by which to solve the question; (*b*) judgment, attaining from this the proof. For (*a*) R. gives commonplaces, from which arguments may be attained; for (*b*) he shows how to apply them in judging rightly; (*α*) by syllogizing, (*β*) by arranging, *collocating* as a whole, by definition and division.

The "Ramists" formed a party in Eng., Germ., and France. Milton translated his dialectics.

(B.) The *Naturalists.* (1) *Telesio,* (1508–1588, A. D.) a Neapolitan, (b. at Cosenza,) educated at Rome, Milan and Padua, founded at Naples the first Acad. for the nat. sciences; in his "*de Naturâ rerum,*" he sought to establish the nat. sciences on a new foundation.

His method is to "follow sense and nature, which is always at one with itself, always produces the same result in the same manner."

Knowledge is of *entia realia non abstracta,* by means of sense-perception (empirical), from which are concepts and deductions; for the animal soul is conscious of change in itself produced from without, and thus has (*immediate*) perception of the object which causes it. Perception of like and unlike changes gives the universal concept. On memory of past perceptions is based deduction (*commemoratio*), which is imperfect knowledge when compared with immediate perception.

The three principles in nature are (*a*) warmth, the expansive; (*b*) cold, the contractive; (*c*) matter, the passive recipient of these: in heaven (*a*) is active, in earth, (*b*); all things have sensation of these two principles, and hence a universal sympathy and harmony.

The bodily nature is an animal soul whose seat is in the brain, and thence through the nerves it expands itself over the whole body.

Man has an immortal soul, also, of intellect and free-will, created by GOD, "*forma superaddita*," which, through the animal soul, is connected with the sensuous world. (Note Telesio's relations to Bacon.)

(2) *Campanella*, (1568–1639, A. D.) b. in Calabria, a Dominican, devoted to nat. sciences, 27 years imprisoned for conspiring against the (Span.) government, spent his last years at Paris.

Besides physics, C. sought to reform also metaphysics. All finite beings are a complex of being and non-being; in the former are three principles, (*a*) power, (*b*) knowledge, (*c*) love; in the latter, (*a*) impotence, (*b*) ignorance, (*c*) hate.

GOD is absolute being, in whom, not distinct, are (*a*) power, (*b*) wisdom, (*c*) goodness. Deity produces ideas, angels, men, the world, mingling non-being with His being. The proof of His existence, anticipating the Cartesian, is from the concept of the Infinite, which we did not, could not, produce.

(3) *Paracelsus*, (1493–1541, A. D.) physician, naturalist, undertook to reform the medical system of Galen, as well as the nat. sciences, by Cabalistic ideas. All created things issue from one prime matter, the *limbus*, the egg, from which is developed, through the brooding world-spirit, the universe. Each thing has its own vital spirit, unconscious, instinctive. Man, the microcosm, with a threefold nature, earthly, sidereal, divine, has a threefold light, natural, rational, divine, (faith). In his steps follows closely

(4) *Joh. Baptist Helmont*, (1577–1644, A. D.) who, in

his numerous works, developes still more fully and applies to medicine, the mystic Cabalism.

(5) *Giordano Bruno*, (*a*) (1548–1600, A. D.) b. at Nola (Neapolitan), entered the Dom. order, abandoning which, he went to Genoa, Venice, Geneva, France, Eng., Germany; at length, returning to Venice and Rome (1593, A. D.), was brought before the Inq., condemned as an Atheist, burned at the stake. He had devoted himself to physics, math., astron., and found the Copernican system irreconcileable with Catholic dogmas.

(*b*) B. developes scientifically a materialistic pantheism; opposing dualism, he finds one matter, infinite, eternal, developing from itself a plurality of beings by the plurality of forms whose potentiality is in it: form is the "*actus substantialis*," which, as an inherent energy, actualizes matter; this, then, is efficient as well as formal cause of all things, the intelligent soul of the world. Matter and form are, in essence, one, differentiated as the active and passive whose independent existence is unthinkable.

Through all changes of the plurality of different forms this essence remains unchanged. It is GOD. He is *natura naturans*; plurality developed from this unity is *natura naturata*, a universe necessitated, unlimited in extent or duration. The elements of all things are indestructible, unchangeable monads, at once psychical and material.

Our knowledge is perception of similitudes and relations, a seeking for the hidden unity of the first principle above indicated.

(6) *Vanini*, (1585–1619, A. D.) a Neapolitan, educated at Padua, setting out from Alexandristic views, developed a naturalism of his own, in "*de Admirandis Naturæ, reginæ deæque mortalium, Arcanis*." There is no intelligence

in matter ; the world is moved by its own inherent powers. Virtue and vice depend on climate, temperature, food, etc. The sole end of man is sensual pleasure. He seems to have put in practice his own principles. (On Bruno and Vanini, consult Cousin, especially Fragm. Philos. M. Age.)

Connecting this period with the next, we may note

(7) *Gassendi,* (1592–1655, A. D.) taught at Dijon and Paris, devoted to math. and physics, the correspondent of Hobbes, Des Cartes, Galileo, wrote various works on the Epicurean system, which he followed though with some independence. (See Lange, Gesch. d. Hist. Materialismus.)

Atoms and vacuum are neither infinite nor eternal; order and design prove an originating, superintending cause. The irrational soul is formed of atoms, but not so the rational.

For this life the Epicurean ethics are alone valid.

(C.) *The Jurists.* (1) *Nicolo Machiavelli,* (1469–1527, A. D.) b. at Florence, wrote Hist. of Florence, "*Il Principe,*" etc., notorious for its moral principle, that means employed for the independence and power of the state are to be morally estimated solely by the end proposed.

Platonic ideals of the state appear among the "Utopists ;" most noteworthy of whom is

(2) *Sir Thomas More,* (1480–1535, A. D.) who wrote, before the troubled later period of his life, "*De optimo Reipublicæ statu, deq. Nov. Insula Utopia,*" which was discovered by "Raphael," a companion of Americus Vespucius.

Property among the Utopians is administered by the community, which is purely agricultural ; hence, no need of a commercial class. The government is republican, the prince being chosen for life by the protophylarchs. All children are educated (compulsory) by the State.

Religion is free, except that none are to deny the immortality of the soul and Div. Providence.

Hugo Grotius, (1583–1645, A. D.); b. at Delft, driven from Holland, took refuge first in France, then in Sweden; wrote "*De Jure Belli et Pacis.*"

He distinguishes *jus divinum* (Revealed) and *jus humanum:* the latter is (*a*) *jus naturale,* (*b*) *jus civile.* Reason and language predetermine man to society, and whatever is necessary to its existence belongs to *jus nat.* Society rests on natural consent, *i. e.,* contract; its right to punish is only for *custodia societatis,* not for retribution, but to deter from crime: community of goods is the law of nature; division is by compact. The State has *dominium eminens* over the property of its citizens.

From *jus nat.* arises also the law of nations.

Puffendorf (1632–1694, A. D.) follows essentially the same principles.

In opposition to the "Divine right of kings," immediate and absolute authority from GOD, as maintained by many of the Reformers against the Papacy, some Catholic Divines, *e. g.* Bellarmine and Suarez, reproduced the political phil. of the Schoolmen, that authority was immediately in the people, mediately in the prince, though, by *jus nat.,* he should rule, being selected by the people's choice.

(D.) *The Skeptics*, the invariable product of conflicting systems, and overthrow of established principles, find utterance in

(1) *Michael de Montaigne,* (1533–1592, A. D.), b. in Perigord; popularized skepticism in his brilliant essays: especially noteworthy is ii. 12 (see also i. 19; ii. 1, and Pascal's Pensées). Since sensuous experience is the

source of all knowledge, what warrant have we that our notions correspond with the object? If reason tries to judge, where is the criterion of its correctness? Philosophers vary endlessly, even in practical morals. "Ignorance and incuriousness (*que sçais-je*) are two charming pillows for a sound head."

(2) *Pierre Charron* (1541–1603, A. D.), friend of M., in his "*De la sagesse*," maintains, in similar manner, that man is born to search for truth: its possession is with God only.

(3) *Fr. Sanchez*, (1562–1631, A. D.). Prof. of Med. and Phil. at Toulouse, reduces skepticism to scientific form. Beings are possibly infinite in number: how can we know them all? or, if limited, yet we can know only part of the whole, which uncomprehended, no part is truly known: some are too great, some too little. In sensation and consciousness we perceive only states of ourselves, — nothing, not even the soul, in itself. Imperfect beings are incapable of true, *i. e.*, perfect knowledge.

CHAPTER X.

DEVELOPEMENT OF ENGLISH EMPIRICISM.

1. PHILOSOPHICAL CHARACTER OF THE SEVENTEENTH CENTURY. 2. BACON. 3. HOBBES. 4. LOCKE.

[*References* :—Mansel's Met.; Whewell's works ; Mackintosh.]

1. PHILOSOPHICAL CHARACTER OF THE SEVENTEENTH CENTURY.

(A.) We notice at this period marked attempts at entire reconstruction of phil., with absolute freedom from authority, not only that of the scholastic, but of the ancient systems, as well as of the theosophic conceptions of the previous age. Very few, until and including Kant, read or knew much of the ancients, — neither Descartes, Spinoza, Malebranche, Hobbes nor Locke. (See De Quincey, Phil. Writers, i. 116 ; note also Bacon, passim, "*aut inveniam viam, aut faciam.*")

(B.) To theol. and eccles. authority are left supernatural truths ; but, in the natural, reason tries to pursue its own course without reference to these. There are few priest-philos., and the religious orders lose their pre-eminence ; in place of these are, first, the Universities, then the Academies in the middle of the 17th Cent.; *e. g.*, R. S. Lond., 1645 ; Acad. Paris, 1665 ; Berlin, through Leibnitz, 1700.

Bacon is a lawyer and statesman; Descartes, a soldier, etc., both men of the world, and elegant in literary style. Hence, also, the rise of a "deistical" school of nat. theology.

(C.) Whatever variation in results, a similarity in method may be observed, an inquiry into human faculties, (Psychology, Goclenius), into the origin, truth and certainty of human knowledge,—an *analysis* of the facts of nature and consciousness.

(D.) The art of printing, the discovery of gunpowder, of the mariner's compass, modifying civilized life lead to a popularizing of phil., and to the fruitful discoveries of nat. science: these give an impulse to their methods in phil., *sc.*, to

Empiricism, the method of experiment and observation, and combination of facts so obtained. Assuming the validity of such facts, and neglecting analysis of the primary principles involved in the investigation, knowledge is limited to the objects of experience. Its tendency is to (*a*) sensualism, (*b*) materialism, (*c*) positivism, or (*d*) skepticism.

(E.) The developement of math. is closely connected with *Rationalism*, which bases itself on the deductions from universal principles given by pure reason.

(F.) Independent national life gives a marked character to the progress of national thought, and compels a recognition of national schools in a manner previously unknown; although these, of course, act and react upon one another.

2. BACON.

[*References*:—Whately's Ed. of the Essays; Macaulay; Campbell's Lives; Whewell's Hist. Ind. Sc.; Sir Wm. Hamilton's Discussions; Mansel's Aldrich.]

(A) Bacon's *life*, so prominent in political history, need not be recounted here; Francis Bacon, b. in London (1561, A. D.); although the "Essays Moral, Econ. and Polit." appeared in 1597, and the "Advancement of Learning in 1605, it should be noted that his chief contributions to Phil. were made after his busy practical life was ending in his disgrace in 1621; "*De Aug. Scient.*" appearing in 1623; "*Nov. Org.*" in 1620; the "*Historia Nat.*," or "*Sylva Sylvarum*," after his death (d. 1626).

(B) *Principle.* He recognizes the ideal as existing in the Div. mind, but man is to attain it by gradual induction from particulars. He opposes scholasticism, which, beginning with principles given in pure reason or by rev., had proved unfruitful in discovery; yet he assumes a moderate realism, that though in nature exist only individuals, yet true knowledge is of their forms: (Aph. Nov. Org. l. ii.)

He attaches himself to Democritus, (De Aug. iii. 4; Phil. Essay on D.), though he declares that all received opinions and notions must be laid aside, for Phil. has neither produced useful result, nor shown capability of advancing; "*auctoritas pro veritate, non veritas pro auctoritate:*" (see Nov. Org. i. Aph. lxxxi.) a new and safe way must be opened, resting, not on authority, but on "*experimenta lucifera:*" (Aph. lxxxiv.) Hence the title, "*Instauratio Magna.*"

(C.) *Divisions:* B. first reviews the whole field of the sciences which are contained in (1) Hist., resting on memory ; (2) Poesy, on imagination ; (3) Phil., on the understanding ; it is (*a*) *Phil. prima*, the concepts and principles common to all sciences, which he makes no attempt to determine, assuming some, *e. g.* "*Ex nihilo nihil fieri, necque quicquam in nihilo redigi :*" (*b*) all sciences, either (1) divinely revealed, Theology, or (2) Philosophy, ("*altera oritur a sensu.*" De Aug. iii. 1.) Phil. has three objects (α) God, (β) nature, (γ) man.

(β) strikes our intellect by direct ray ; (We must diligently listen to nature's own voice, mingling nothing from ours with hers) :

(α) by refracted rays only, and Phil. can answer objections to Rev. merely, not give any affirmative decision (De Aug. iii. 2, ix. 1) : the subject is referred to Theol.

(γ) Man's intellectual nature also is not cognizable. ("*Sin ipsa in se vertatur, etc.*" De Aug. i.)

"Philosophy," *sc.* of nature, is (*a*) speculative ; (α) physics, for laws of nature and efficient causes ; (β) metaphysics, for forms and final causes :

(*b*) Operative ; (α) mechanics ; (β) nat. magic.

(D.) *Method and Theory of Knowledge.* This is B.'s almost exclusive work. (See Nov. Org. l.ii.) The object of Phil. being to attain power over nature, through "*interrogatio naturæ,*" we must (1) strip Phil. of its Theosophic character. *A priori* reasoning in physics from final causes is absolutely false and misleading.

(2) The *syllogism* is applicable to human laws and Divine Rev., not to discovery ; it may answer for probable conclusions in ethics ; but lower principles in physics cannot be so deduced from higher, for the very terms may be badly abstracted from things. (De Aug. v. 2.)

(3) The mind must be rid of its *idols*, for though all

all knowledge originates with sense perception, yet the senses need to be guided, to be guarded from error by judicious procedure. (Aph. Nov. Org. i.)

(*a*) *Idola tribus*, deceiving phantoms originating in our common nature, *e. g.*, arguing in physics from final causes, imagining parallel cases, following will and feelings, neglecting less sensible for grosser phenom., etc.;

(*b*) *Id. specus*, in individual idiosyncracies, innate, from education, custom, prejudice, etc.;

(*c*) *Id. fori*, in the common use of words; definitions must be continually tested by example;

(*d*) *Id. theatri*, in dogmas of Philos. schools, in mingling Theol. with Phil.; (*e. g.*, Genesis and book of Job; Nov. Org. i. Aph. lxv.. lxxxix.)

(4.) True "*interpretatio naturæ*," then is by

(*a*) Establishing facts through observation and experiment;

(*b*) Arranging them, and thus basing Phil. on Nat. Hist. (See Inst. Mag. Pt. iii.; "*Sylva Sylvarum*.") For positive *instantiæ*, we must look at the most opposite matter: we must consider privative inst. in similar matter; distinguish solitary, analogous, monstrous, crucial, inst., etc. (Nov. Org. l. ii.); thus definitions may be obtained: (the bee, not the spider).

(*c*) By induction proceeding, step by step, to higher and higher laws; not by mere "*ind. per enumerat. simpl.*," but by exclusions, etc.; nor by "*anticipat. mentis*," leaping from a few instances to the highest generalizations (Nov. Org. i. Aph. 19, 104), a most fruitful parent of error.

(*d*) "*Descendendo ad opera*, since *axiomata* may point out new experiments.

(E.) *Psychology* and *ethics*. B. is not a philos. in the

widest sense of the term ; his empirical method may, he maintains, be applied to all sciences ; to ethics, politics, etc. ; but see his tables of Nat. Hist., Inst. Mag., p. iii. Psychology can have little place in his system, for little can be known except of the irrational soul, which is corporeal, (motion, sense, found in all bodies ; but distinguish sense from perception.) In his essays he is a moralist without a doctrine ; the "light of nature," indeed, gives forth a feeble ray, but even that needs Rev. to make it clear enough to be a rule. The rational soul is referred to Theol. (Pref. Inst. Mag.)

In brief, B. marks out a path for empiricism, but does not himself follow it. The 6th part of his Inst. Mag. would have been a Phil. founded on legitimate interpretation of nature, but he did not expect to reach it.

3. Hobbes.

[References:—Whewell, Hist. Eth. ; Cousin, Phil. 18th Cent.; Hallam, Lit. Europe.]

(A.) *Life.* *Thomas Hobbes*, of Malmesbury, (1588–1679, A.D.) studied at Oxf., then in France, etc., a friend of Gassendi, pursued Math. and Nat. Sc., the disciple and secretary of Lord Bacon ; in the civil war, siding with the king, he took refuge in Paris, (1640) and became tutor of Chas. II. ; returned to Eng. in 1653 ; thereafter occupied himself with literary labor. Works "Elements of Phil." in three parts, appearing in reverse order, (1) "*De Corpore*," (1655–6) (*a*) Logic ; (*b*) *Phil. Prima ;* (*c*) Motion ; (*d*) Mechanics, etc. (2) "*De Homine*," "Human Nature," (1650) ; (3) "*De Cive*," (1642) ; "Leviathan," (1650) ; (*repeats de Hom. and de Civ.*, but adds "a Christian Commonwealth, etc."; (4) "*De Corpore Politico*," (1650) ; various discussions on "Liberty and Necessity," in answer to Bishop Bramhall and others, (1656) etc.

H. is remarkably clear, simple, and vigorous in style, and develops his system with strict logical consistency. (Comte claims him as the father of "Pos. Phil.")

(B.) *Principle,* a rigid materialism; the subject of Phil. is every body which can be generated or have any properties; (Corp. i. 1, 8); spirit is a corporeal substance (having extension) of such subtility as not to act on the senses. (*De Hom.* xi. 4, 5; cf. divisions of Science, Lev. 1, 9.)

H. is, of course, a nominalist; but individuals are known only in their (phenomenal) relations to the sentient. There are two kinds of learning; the "mathematical" from reason, *sc.* of magnitudes, numbers, motions; and the "dogmatic," from passion. (*De Hom.* xiii.). Anc. Phil. is "a phantasm full of fraud and filth."

Phil. is the knowledge of causes from phenom. (effects), and of phenom. from causes (note def. of causes); its end is practical benefit through foresight of effects.

(C.) *Theory of knowledge.* Absolute knowledge is impossible; it is limited to (1) phenom., (2) the chain of sequences. (Lev. i. 7.)

Motion, the cause of sensation, communicated to the sentient, by reaction produces the phantasm, the aggregate of sensible qualities, which exist only in the sentient: continued, decaying sensation is named imagination; with the added element of time, *i. e.* sequence of phenom., it is memory, "*sentire se sensisse,*" (*De Corp.* iv. 25; 1, 2, 7.) Images in memory follow the order of their origin, ("assoc. of ideas"), (Lev. i. 3).

Cognition is the power of retaining images. To these

phantasms are applied (1) analysis, (2) synthesis, (advance upon Bacon.)

Words are arbitrary marks and signs, to register past sensations ("thoughts"), and to convey them to others. (Lev. i. 4.) They stand for (1) matter or body; (2) accidents or qualities (motions, objective and subjective); (3) phantasms; (4) names. (*De Corp.* i. 5, 2.)

Common names denote any one of a multitude; abstract, the supposed cause of the concrete, of our concepts.

Logic. In propositions two names are copulated, which stand for the same thing; syllogistic reasoning is the joining of three names, for adding or subtracting; (*ratioc. = computatio*); *i. e.* it is reckoning by means of word-signs. (*De Corp.* i. 1, 2; Lev. v.) Discursive reason connects consecutive concepts as they were first connected in sense.

Truth and error are in propositions; the latter arises in passing from one image to another, or in joining a name of one class with a name from another.

(D.) *Divisions.* (1) *Phil Prima,* with H., is definitions of fundamental concepts.

(2) Science (phil.) is (*a*) *natural,* of consequences from the accidents of nat. bodies, either accidents common, *sc.* quantity and motion, determinate (Geometry, etc.); or indeterminate (*Phil. 1ma*); or qualities of bodies (Physics) ethereal or terrestrial (ethics, logic, etc.);

(*b*) *Civil,* of bodies politic, the commonwealth. (Lev. i. 9; *De Corp.* i. 1, 9.)

(E.) *Philosophia Prima.* H. adopts scholastic forms from the nominalists, though unmeasured in condemnation of scholast. and "metaphysics." He is weak in met. and psych., devoting himself chiefly to political ethics, yet his whole system is based on logical deductions from primary definitions.

The nature and attributes of *God* are referred to theol.; only his existence can be otherwise known. (Lev. i. 12; *De Hom.* xi. 2, 3); but note, in his ans. to B'p Bramhall, "GOD is infinite spirit corporeal," *sc.* having extension (universally diffused, moving ether?), and that man's relations to GOD are based on His power.

Cause is "the sum of all accidents in agent and patient which concur to the *producing* (note) of the effect, so that if they exist the effect existeth;" not, if any one be absent: cause = active power. (*De Corp.* i. 6, 10.)

The cause of universal things is known by nature, viz. *motion*, (*De Corp.* i. 6, 5); efficient, is in the agent; material, in the patient (ii. 9); where is no effect, there is no cause: we may imagine a part of the chain, and then the first is called cause only; the next, cause and effect.

Space is the phantasm of a thing existing without the mind; time a phant. of before and after in motion of a body.

All *change* is motion produced by a body contiguous (no void) and itself moved. (ii. 9, 9.)

Contingent accidents are those which do not depend on the immediate antecedents of the other accidents which are under consideration, but they are equally necessitated: contingents are so named when we do not know their causes.

(F.) *Psychology* (vid. supr.) There must be a corporeal organ to retain motion: this distinguishes sentient from non-sentient bodies. (*De Corp.* iv. 25, 1.)

It need only be added here, that appetites and aversions, in H., are vital motions of the heart, as modified by motions from without, reaching it through the brain. (iv. 25, 12.)

(G.) *Ethics* are a strictly logical developement of his def., his object being chiefly political ethics.

(1) *Individual.* To comprehend H., we must first consider his theory of

Liberty and Necessity. "Will is appetite;" exterior motions reaching the "vital motion" help or hinder it. (*De Hom.* vii.) This we name desire or fear, the motives of all our actions. Either actions follow immediately the first appetence, as when we act suddenly; or, to first desire succeeds thought of resulting ill, a fear which impedes action. To this may succeed a new appetence, etc. This is "deliberation:" the last desire or fear (the same in brutes as in men) is called will. (*De Hom.* vii. 1; xii. 1; *De Corp.* iv. 25, 13; Lev. i. 6.)

Every act of will is caused by antecedents. (Lev. ii. 21.)

Liberty is the power of doing what we will,—freedom from external restraints.

Thus necessity determines each man's moral views, and each calls good what is agreeable to him, and evil what displeases him (*De Hom.* vii.), either immediately or through prudence, by expectation of future benefit, or fear of future ill.

Hence, *ethics of selfishness; e. g.*, "no man giveth but with intent of good to himself, because gift is voluntary, and the object of the voluntary is a man's good." (Lev. i. 15.)

Repentance is from knowledge that the action misses its end (*sc.* of appetite, enjoyment). (*De Hom.* ix. 7.)

Honor is the acknowledgment of power, whether in the invisible (God=ether in motion?) or in man.

Praise and *blame* declare a thing good or evil for me or some one else, etc., etc.

Sin is transgression of a law, civil or natural; sc. "to do to others," etc.; (note, no account of personal sins, *e. g.*, of lust; *Corp. Pol.* ii. 9, 3.)

(2) *Civil.* The *state* is an artificial body, (see title-page of Lev.) "*Corp. Polit.*"; The multitude united as one man by a common power for common peace, defence, and benefit.

The *natural state of man* is one of equal rights to all things; equal right to the end gives equal right to the means: then it is necessary that the strongest obtain, and thus perpetual war. (*Corp. Polit.*, i. 2 seq.) In the natural state is no right or wrong, just or unjust, (Lev. i. 13), no *meum* and *tuum*: what each one can get, that is his as long as he can keep it.

Society originates in (*a*) conquest, (*b*) compact. Thus peace is secured by the law of right reason (prudence) that it is expedient to give up something (i. 14). The cause of the commonwealth, then, is man's foresight of what is needful to his preservation.

Jus (right) is, in nature, the freedom from external restraints to action: this is totally surrendered in society to (*a*) one man (monarchy, which is best); (*b*) to a few (aristocracy); (*c*) to the community (democracy). This surrender unites all powers, all rights, all wills. This sovereignty is absolute, unlimited. (Lev. ii. 17.) Assured power confers the right to reign. (Lev. i. 14.) Tyranny, etc., the "same forms misliked." (Lev. ii. 19.)

In this compact minorities have no rights, no redress; subjects have none towards a sovereign; for there can be no injury: resistance puts one in the state of nature.

Property originates in the sovereign power assigning to each; it does not exclude dominion of the sovereign.

Religion is fear of invisible powers recognized by the state; and private conscience may not oppose public, or the law. (*Corp. Polit.* ii. 6, 11, 12.) Good is what the state sanctions, as far as law extends. (Lev. ii. 26.)

Punishment rests on power, removing the noxious, and deterring from future wrongs. God may punish by right of His omnipotence, for the same reason.

Between nations is no *jus*, no moral obligation. Hobbes should be thoroughly studied with reference to the subsequent progress of materialism.

IV. Locke.

[*References*:—Leibnitz, Nouv. Ess.; Cousin; Morell's Hist. Mod. Phil.; Hallam; Reid's Inquiry etc., cc. i. vii; Brown's Lectures, xxvii; Whewell's Lectures on Moral Phil.; Mackintosh.]

(A.) Life, *b.* in Somersetshire; (1632); ed. at Oxf. and Fellow there. He devoted himself to medicine and the natural sciences: he followed the fortunes of the Earl of Shaftesbury, and was tutor to his son: in France (1675–1679,) was then recalled by the Earl: went into exile with him to Holland, returning in 1688; devoted himself to literary labors: d. 1704.

His works are, "Letters on Toleration," (1685); his "Essay on the Human Understanding," written in his exile, pub. in 1689; Two discourses of Civil Government (1689); on Education, (1693); "Reasonableness of Christianity," (1695), etc., etc.

His clear common sense, his manly honesty, his vivacious style, and even his somewhat unscientific modes of thought and expression were calculated to give him the wide-spread and powerful influence which he exerted. Empiricism with him seemed to have reached its full developement; his many followers in the 18th cent. added little, except in applying his method and principles to special investigations.

(B.) *Method.* L. proposes to analyze the faculties of the human understanding and their limits, and so determine the grounds and extent of human knowledge (psychological, empirical); but instead of an induction from our cognitions as given in consciousness, he begins by investigating their origin, (Cousin).

(C.) *Theory of Knowledge.* An *idea* is defined as "anything with which our minds are immediately occupied when we think;" (concept, or image?) Ess. i. 18).

(1.) There are no *innate ideas;* the mind originally a *tabula rasa;* no innate theoretical principles; children and the uneducated know nothing of them: fundamental principles contain the most abstract ideas, which are least known. Still less are practical principles innate, which differ so widely among mankind; not even the being and nature of God, about which men in the same nation vary so widely. (Ess. B. i.)

(2.) All ideas are from *experience;* (*a*) sensation; (*b*) reflection; (*a*) for knowledge of the sensuous qualities of external objects; (*b*) for knowledge of our inward states and activities; *e. g.*, feeling, thinking, willing, etc.

Thus, the idea of space is derived from sight and touch; of time, from succession of ideas; the infinite, is a purely negative idea, or the indefinite.

On "reflection," note that L. limits the word in his def., "the notice which the mind takes of its own operations and the manner of them," (consciousness). But extend the word to defining, judging reasoning, etc., and his proposition is nugatory. Refl., as he uses the word, is vague, fluctuating, and requires analysis ; the French sensualists, more consistent, discard it from its place as one source of knowledge.

(3.) *Genesis of ideas ; (a)* the *simple*, by sensation and perception, in which the soul is passive ; (α) ideas through one sense, as of colors, heat, smoothness ; (β) of sensuous qualities through more than one sense, as extension, from motion ; (γ) given in "reflection," as thinking, willing ; (δ) given in sense *and* reflection pleasure, pain, power, existence, unity, ; (Ess. ii. 7).

Distinguish (α) *primary* qualities, given objectively, in bodies, extension, solidity, figure, motion, number, form ; (β) secondary qualities, in the sentient, signs of changes in things, as color, sound, etc. (L. does not inquire how corporeal qualities are converted into ideas of the mind.)

These are the original ideas of all our knowledge, and as such, undefinable ; the soul is their passive recipient.

(b) *Complex ideas ;* after sensation and perception, (consciousness of sens.) (α) memory ; (β) discernment. (Distinguishing, separating,) (γ) comparison ; (δ) composition ; (ε) abstraction, a power peculiar to man. Ideas of single objects are separated from accidents, from space and time ; thus arises a universal concept whose name is extended to all objects resembling the concept, (conceptualism). (Ess. ii. 9–11.) These are acts of the understanding, (the soul active). Comp. ideas are defined by analysis to the simple ideas. (Note, L. cannot explain unity ; *e. g.*, man remains a complex idea.)

They are ideas of (α) substance an unknown something, substrate to qualities ; (β) modes ; (γ) relations, as cause and effect, time and space relations, moral relations, etc.

(4.) *Modes*, compound ideas of qualities existing in something, considered at length (ii. 13 seq.), are—

(*a*.) *Simple modes*, whose elements are homogeneous; *e. g.*

Space, body, extension, of co-existent parts;

Time, duration, eternity, (indefinite repetition of measured duration,) of successive parts (ideas) not separable.

Number, finite and infinite, (a negative idea, indefinite addition of number applied to the determinate);

The *good*, that which increases pleasure or diminishes pain;

Power, from change of ideas, the idea of the passive, receiving change; from choice and determination, the idea of the active, making change;

Liberty, (*vid. infr.* psych. and ethics.)

(*b*.) *Mixed modes*, the mind actively combining unlike elements into "notions," to which names are arbitrarily applied, as in bodies, (passive powers); in spirit, (active powers, thinking, motivity); in God, from enlarging to infinity modes which we experience in ourselves. (Note, L. cannot, empirically, separate his "mixed modes" from substances); words (Ess. iii.) represent not substances, but the idea of collected qualities.

(5.) *Relations* arise from comparing two ideas, and hence come new "ideas," and terms, (husband, whiter, old, great); thus the rel. of *cause* and *effect* from marking the change or becoming which follows the application of one thing to another (antecedent and consequent); as heat and wax.

Identity and *diversity*, come from comparing the idea of a thing in one time and place, with the idea of the same in another; id. and div. are relative. Distinguish personal identity given in consciousness though the thinking substance may change. (Ess. ii. 27).

Other relations are proportional, natural, instituted, moral; (to a law,) (*vid. infr.* ethics).

(6.) *Knowledge* is the perception of agreement or disagreement of ideas, under the notions of (*a*) identity or diversity, (*b*) relation, (*c*) co-existence, (*d*) real existence. (iv. 1). (*a*) is perceived at once in the individual;

(*c*) is of "ideas" in the same subject;

(*d*) when the idea or complex of ideas represents reality out of the mind.

Degrees of knowledge (iv. 3) are (*a*) intuitive, instantaneous perception that two ideas agree or disagree; (*b*) demonstrative, two ideas brought together by some intermediate, (admitting of doubt); (*c*) of particular, finite beings, by sens. and perc. Judgment is contrary to reason, when it implies contradiction, or is of ideas not clearly conceived; it is true, if we think ideas to be related as they actually are. The mind cognizes by the intervention of ideas; knowledge is real, if the idea (simple) conform to the thing which produces it. Complex ideas are of the mind's own making and therefore subjectively real, as in mathematics; ideas of substance are from such qualities as are naturally united, (iv. 4, 5), (*essentia realis*, unknown; *ess. notionalis*, the ground of genera and species). Knowledge then can be true, without being real. Knowledge also of the supersensual must be impossible. according to L.'s principle, but herein L. holds back, and merely limits that knowledge.

God is proved from the world, His works (cosmological); but the idea is negative.

(D.) *Psychology :* The soul is, probably, an immaterial substance, but this cannot be proved (IV. 3.6; see letter to Bp. of Worcester); God may give a material substance the power to think, and what we call spirit may be a mode of body.

The primary ideas of mind are (*a*) perceptivity, (*b*) motivity.

Will must be distinguished from desire, since they often oppose one another: actions, either thinking or moving, are free, when a man has power to think or act, or not to do so; there is no liberty where there is no thought and will, but there may be thought and will without liberty.

The question is not whether the will is free, which is nonsense, but whether the man is. A man is not free to will, because the thing presented determines his will.

The will is nothing but a power of the mind to direct the operative faculties to motion or rest, the motive being satisfaction or dissatisfaction. Uneasiness determines the will, and not the greater good; but the will (the man) can suspend decision for clearer judgment. (II. 21.)

(E.) *Ethics.* (1) *Individual. Happiness* is the utmost pleasure, and we call good what produces it, and evil what produces pain. Men do not place it, indeed, in the same things; the wrong judgment may prefer the present to the absent; but men are responsible for their judgment.

Moral good or evil is conformity to a law or violation of it, whereby good or evil, *i. e.*, pleasure or pain, is drawn on us by the law-maker's will (II. 28): law is

(*a.*) Divine, which measures sins;

(*b.*) Civil, which measures crimes;

(*c.*) Law of opinion, which measures vices. Moral rectitude is *relative*, to one or all of these. One word is often used for the positive act and the moral idea, which misleads: *e. g.*, stealing. (L. fails to show the obligation of obedience.)

(2.) *Political.* L. may be called the father of mod. Pol. In his two treatises on Government, he (*a*) opposes the Patriarchal theory; (*b*) inquires into the *origin,* extent and end of civil Gov.

The *state of nature* is (*a*) perfect freedom of action and property; land originally common; labor gives property in it;

(*b*) perfect equality;

(*c*) every man executive of the law of nature; (not a state of war.)

Civil Society originates when men voluntarily resign their natural rights to the community, the majority ruling, ("Contrat Social").

Its end is the preservation of property.

Government is dissolved when the executive, legislative, etc., act contrary to their trust. Tyranny is the exercise of power beyond right.

All religious opinions should be tolerated, so far as they are not dangerous to the commonwealth.

Locke's influence in Eng. during the 18th century is almost supreme, and many apply his empiricism to special investigations in ethics, etc. (See Gibbon's Autob. "Since phil. has exploded all innate ideas and natural propensities.") Three separate developments however must receive attention: (1.) Idealism of Berkeley; (2.) Sensual ism in France; (3.) Skepticism of Hume, etc., (vid. inf.)

CHAPTER XI.

DEVELOPMENT OF RATIONALISM.

1. DESCARTES. 2. CARTESIAN SCHOOL. 3. SPINOZA. 4. LEIBNITZ. 5. IDEALISM IN ENGLAND IN THE 17TH AND 18TH CENTURIES.

[*References*:—Morell's Hist. Mod. Phil.; Cousin; see also special ref. infr.]

1. DESCARTES.

(A.) *Réné Descartes*, (1596–1650, A. D.) b. in Touraine, ed. by the Jesuits of La Flèche, for a time a soldier, travelled extensively, (Eng., Denmark, Germ., It.); dissatisfied with traditional phil. resolved to investigate its principles anew; retired to a village in Holland (1629); devoted himself to physics, math., medicine, optics, etc., in addition to met.; invited by Queen Christina to Sweden, shortly after died there.

Works : Discours sur la Méthode (1637), (for guiding the reason in search of truth) with Dioptrics and Meteorology; *Meditationes de Prim. Phil.* (1641); *Principia Phil.*, (1644); *Les Passions de l'Ame*, (1650), (physiological psychology), etc.

D. may be called one of the founders of mod. science; treating the laws of the universe as a mechanical problem, and verifying his solutions by experiment, applying algebra to geometrical problems, (Anal. Geom.) etc.

His clear, simple style ranks him among the first (French) prose writers of his day.

(B.) *Method.* While the Eng. school, devoting itself to the phenom. of external nature, was developing sensualism, D., analyzing the internal phenom. given in consciousness, was founding mod. *idealism.*

Aristotle's method had proved unfruitful in the knowledge of things, for dialectics only teach us how to set forth what we know already. Like Bacon, he would find a new way ; for a true logic will lead to discovery ; (Ep. ad Voet.) Math. already point out the way ; consider (1) the Method ; (2) Metaphysics, which contain the principles of cognition concerning GOD and the soul from which we can deduce, (3) physics, the principles of nature. The method, then, is (1) To begin with universal *doubt*, even holding for false what seems doubtful, *e. g.* sensuous impressions, but doubt as means only to a certainty not yet possessed ; setting aside all prejudice or hasty judgment, to receive nothing as true when obscurity or indistinctness in *idea* (vid. infr.), leaves reason to doubt or possibility of refusal ; (Princ. Phil. i. 1–6) ; for practice, meanwhile, to follow the probable, the commonly received.

(2) To *divide* each difficult problem into as many parts as possible, (analytical) ;

(3) To proceed from the simplest to the complex ; (geometry has proceeded thus with fruitful result) ;

(4) To count up and review and see that nothing is omitted.

In special investigations proceed from causes, from innate principles, to effects, by deduction, verifying in experiments, thus distinguishing the actual from the possible.

(C.) *Theory of Knowledge.* Knowing (*percipere*) is (1.) *sentire*, (2.) *imaginare*, (3.) *intelligere.*

The objects of knowledge are (1) things, material or spiritual;

(2) Affections or modes, (*a*) of matter, as duration, order, number, (" clearly and distinctly conceived ") ; (*b*) of spirit, knowing and willing ; (*c*) from union of the two, senses and passions ;

(3) Eternal verities, existing in the mind only, common notions, axioms innate, as that all properties are in a substance. (Note: No attempt to determine these primary principles.)

All these as thought in the mind are called *ideas;* consequently, there are three classes ; (1) those which we create (images) ; (2) those which we acquire from external objects ; (3) those which are born with us (innate ideas). *Innate* ideas, at first regarded by D. as entities impressed by God on the soul, (*res cogitatæ quatenus objective sunt in intellectu*), are, afterward, viewed as developed from the soul itself in which they exist potentially ; sense-perception is the *occasion* of their actuality, they are not abstracted from what is thus given. They conform to objective realities because so disposed by God.

In judgment, the subjective knowledge (innate ideas) is turned to the objective reality, and this is an operation of the will, which assents in affirmation or negation.

Error lies in abusing this freedom of the will, and judging before the mind has clear and distinct ideas.

The *criterion* of knowledge is the clearness and distinctness of the idea, (i. 43) ; such we have of created thinking substance, *i.e.*, soul, of matter, of God, though the last inadequate, (i. 54) ; we may not be able to create images, for these are only of the sensible ; but in sense is nothing certain except what intellect supplies. (Denies "*nihil in int. quod non prius in sensu.*") In sensations and passions is the greatest difficulty as respects clearness and distinctness; they are referred to the things which produce them, an error in judgment ; they are clear and distinct, *as* sensations, etc. ; if they are considered to be things, then no clear perception what they are.

Supernatural truths are to be received by faith, not being discovered by reason, though not contradictory to it.

(D.) *Principle*, is dogmatic, without criticism of the faculty of cognition and its limits, a pure rationalism ; phil. is perfect knowledge of all which man can know through clear and self-evident first principles ; the knowledge of other things being deduced from these ; this is man's highest good. (Ep. ad. Voet.).

(1.) To doubt is to think ; "*cogito, ergo sum ;*" (no syllogism, but the pure apperception of a mode in a subject.) (cf. Kant. Crit. P. Reason, ii. 2–4.)

(2.) Thought is action in *ego ;* this gives "clear and distinct notion" of *substance*, which is therefore a primary notion, self-evident, certain. (i. 11.)

(3.) But *ego*, *mens*, is known as distinct from body, unextended, etc. I could think away body, but not *ego ;* a clear, certain knowledge of the spirituality of the soul.

(4.) Existence of mind, not thinking, is absolutely inconceiveable ; the essence of mind is clearly and distinctly known as simple, immaterial, thinking substance ; this is the *first step* in knowledge.

(5.) Among ideas which are known in consciousness, is that of infinite, perfect being, the idea of omniscience, omnipotence, goodness, etc., an idea not originated by *ego,* for it is above the imperfect, limited soul, neither to be unmade nor modified by it: it is clear and distinct, therefore objectively real.

The idea of this perfect being involves infinite fulness of reality, consequently the (limited) *ego* cannot produce it, for the effect cannot exceed the cause, nor contain what the cause does not (*formaliter or eminenter;* principle of causality.)

The idea of perfect being embraces all perfections, among which is objective existence (i. 14: vid. S. Anselm, and distinguish here psychological and ontological arguments). On this is based the possibility of Revelation (i. 25).

We may not comprehend these perfections, we understand (*intellig.*) them as filling thought, clear, not obscured by limitations. (See further development in Fénélon, "*De l'Existence de Dieu,*" and Bossuet, "*De la Connaissance de Dieu et de Soi-même.*")

(6.) *Ego* does not exist of itself, but from the cause which produces this idea; it is not sufficient explanation to derive existence from parents, for *regressus in infinitum* is inadmissible, for continued existence is not caused by the *ego*.

God's existence is the *second step* in knowledge.

(7.) The senses in themselves give no certain knowledge of an outer world; every hypothesis leaves room for doubt. But in the idea of GOD is absolute veracity; on this we base certainty derived from sense-perception; error, if it exist, is in our (voluntary) judgments.

On the same ground is based trust in clear and distinct ideas.

Note: vicious logical circle; the truth of GOD's existence rests on clearness of the idea; and objective truth of ideas on the veracity of GOD; (Gassendi).

(E.) *Metaphysics.* (1.) *Substance*, "a thing which so exists that it needs no other thing for its existence," strictly taken, applies to GOD only; but, equivocally, to created substances, which exist by the ordinary concurrence (*concursus*) of GOD. (i. 51, cf. Spinozism.)

(2.) *Infinite*, as applied to *God*, is positive as well as negative; and we must distinguish the indefinite in created things, *e. g.* extension and divisibility in bodies, from the proper infinite which can only be predicated of the Creator.

GOD is also pure spirit, for the idea of matter or extension involves divisibility, which is an imperfection. As such, He is intelligence and will, which constitute the idea of spirit; but these are not modes of His being. With a single operation, he knows, wills and works all.

(3.) *Attribute* belongs to substance; in and through it we know each substance; it constitutes the essence of the thing, it is essential to the concept of the thing, and to all ideas belonging to it (i. 53.) *e. g.* of matter, extension; of spirit, thought.

All other properties are *modes*, modifications of substance, and admit of change; they pre-suppose the attribute; *e. g.* figure supposes extension, but extension does not pre-suppose figure.

Qualities are only actual, present, not permanent.

Note: The attribute of body being extension, space and body are not really distinct but only different in concept; space being the same extension whatever body occupy it.

(F.) *Physics.* Like Bacon, D. excludes all inquiry into final causes; he relegates them to ethics.

Denying vacuum and atoms, (cf. def. of body, ii. 16, seq.) he reduces all physical changes to motion, change (relative) of place. All phenom., consequently, are reducible to geometric and mathematical principles (ii. 64; iii. 4), and nature is viewed as a mechanism moved by God.

Even the brutes are living automata; in them there is no animal soul as their substantial form. They, like machines do some things better than we can, with our finite intelligence.

The quantity of motion (*mv*) imparted by God to a limited portion of matter is unchangeable; finite will can only modifiy its direction (ii. 36). Since there is no vacuum, motion is rotary, and vortices account for the bodies of the universe.

(G.) *Anthropology.* (1.) In thought, the attribute of soul, distinguish knowing and willing. Vegetative and sensitive powers belong to the body. The latter is a living automaton in which the soul inhabits (pineal gland).

(2.) *Sensation.* The vital spirits, produced from the blood through rarefaction by animal heat in the heart, ascend to the brain, and thence are diffused through the nerves. The qualities (secondary) of bodies, except figure, motion, etc., are various dispositions affecting our nerves.

When an object impresses a sense, the vital spirits convey the impression to the brain, and the mind takes note of the effect on the organ: this is sensation.

Imagination and memory are accounted for by internal motions of the animal spirits; so, also, all animal functions and bodily motions.

(3.) *Passions.* The mind may affect the heart through the nerves, and, by reflex action, a passion be produced in the brain, a perception of an internal state.

(4.) The *soul* passively receives sensations conveyed to the brain (perception), but is active in will, imag., thought, and so may act upon the body.

How this mutual action is accomplished, D. cannot explain: the concept of "occasional causes" is the nearest approach to explanation: the concurrence (*assistentia*) of GOD. (Br. Quarterly, Jan. 1874.)

(5.) Distinguish *will* from desire (iv. 190); the former is known in consciousness as free; we can voluntarily affirm, (assent,) or we can abstain from believing (doubt).

Our will is not determined by anything except as intellect shows it to be good or the reverse; and this is freedom, for there is no constraining cause outside of the mind which assents to the good and chooses it. (Med. 4.) (intellectual determinism.)

2. CARTESIAN SCHOOL.

Both the needs of the age and the analytical power of Descartes gave him a wide spread and permanent influence; the psychological method in phil. became the predominating one, while a foundation was laid for pure idealism.

The Dominican and Franciscan orders, which in the 13th and 14th cent. had taken the lead in phil., had lost their intellectual position, but while many Jesuits were active in opposition to Cartesianism on theological grounds, the Jansenists warmly supported it for similar reasons, while philos. questions agitated society itself (to a remarkable degree.) The universities were divided; that of Paris, in 1671, by royal decree, forbade the teaching of the new phil. Notwithstanding, it made great progress in France and the Netherlands, advocated, to a greater or less degree, by Arnauld, Pascal, etc., especially by

(A) *Geulincx*, of Antwerp, (1625–1669, A. D.), taught

at Leyden, wrote on Logic, Metaphysics, Ethics, and a Commentary on Descartes.

Direct action of soul on body or body on soul is impossible. The essence of soul is in thought only, consequently it is not capable of any other activity, such as producing motion in body: the same reasoning applies to body.

Bodily affections indeed may afford occasion for sensations, and *vice versa,* but the efficient and immediate cause of this harmony is GOD only ("occasionalism").

Hence a fuller development of the Cartesian principle which pointed to a *passivity* of nature in respect of GOD as the one efficient cause of all spiritual and physical operations. Secondary causes, so called, are but *occasional,* the only efficient cause is GOD. What we call laws of nature are this law of occasional causes which GOD follows. (Tendency to Spinozism.)

(B.) *Malebranche,* (1.) (1638–1715, A. D.) b. at Paris, ed. at the Sorbonne, priest of the Oratory: wrote *De la Récherche de la Vérité;*" "*Traité de Morale;*" "*De l'Amour de Dieu,*" etc. His style is luminous and attractive.

(2.) We know the *ego* in consciousness, all beside through "ideas." Empirically we obtain only relations of objects to our own bodies: ideas cannot originate with ourselves; we see them immediately in GOD. (cf. Reid ii. 8.) He has in Himself all ideas, and the material world rests, for our knowledge of it, on revelation from Him. (cf. Berkeley.) He is always immediately present to our spirits, the universal reason, the light of all spirits: (tendency to mysticism: See Pref. to "*Récherche,* etc.")

But it is not GOD's essence which is seen, except in the limited relation which it has to limited things; and a condition, also, is our own voluntary attention. Sensuous experience is the occasional cause of awakening this attention.

Thus also we discover the relations of ideas to one another, and arrive at truths.

M. develops "occasionalism" in the same manner as Geulincx. (vid. sup.) The will is only the working of GOD in us; each natural attempt to attain the good is caused by GOD only.

But to particular goods the will is undetermined; the intelligence judges between them which is the higher good, and to this the will is determined, but may withhold assent, and in this consists its freedom.

Evil in us is, consequently, limited to not doing what we can and should do.

M. has a special value in tracing the causes of error, *e.g.*, illusions of the imagination.

Finally, abandoning Cartesianism, he finds a refuge in Christian dogma alone.

3. SPINOZA.

[Ref. Cousin, Fragm. Philos. v. iii: Bayle; Goethe, Dichtung und Wahrheit; Ueberweg's Notes on his Fundamental Propositions; M. Arnold, in MacMillan's Mag., vol. ix.]

Descartes' definition of substance and his theory of continued creation contained a germ of pantheism which found its full development in Spinoza. He should be thoroughly studied as a key to modern idealism, and even to some recent philosophical speculations from "scientific" ground.

(A.) *Life. Baruch Despinoza,* (1632-1677, A. D.) b. in Amsterdam, of a family of Portuguese Jews who found a refuge from persecution in Holland, was thoroughly ed. in

Hebrew literature, devoting himself for many years to the Bible and the Talmud. He then forsook the synagogue and theology for physics and metaphysics, adopting Cartesianism ; was excommunicated by the Jews (1660) ; (changed his name to Benedictus de Espinoza) ; he lived in seclusion, though he received some flattering offers ; without family, he supported himself by making spectacle lenses. His life is represented as simple, of gracious manners, and unreprovable integrity.

Works. "Principles of Desc. geometrically arranged," (1663,) with appended "*Cogitata Metaph.*" In this S. for the most part, closely follows Desc.

(2.) "*Tractatus Theologico-Politicus ;*" which excited wide-spread attention and discussion: for his principles however, we must consider chiefly his

(3.) Posthumous Works, "Ethics," which is chiefly metaphysics and psychology ; "*Tract. Politicus ;*" "*De Emendatione Intellectus*" (fragm.) etc.

(B.) *Method.* S. adopts a geometrical method to develope his principles, (unattractive in form and injurious in results,) attempting to deduce, in strict logical order, a system from definitions and axioms. (Note ; assumption of a reality answering to thing defined ; but the criterion of reality, as with Desc., clearness and distinctness of the idea.)

Knowledge is of three kinds :

(1.) *Opinio*, *imaginatio*, confused, inadequate ideas from the words of others, or through the senses.

(2.) *Notiones communes,* clear and adequate ideas through *ratio.*

(3.) Intuitive knowledge, proceeding from the adequate idea of some one of GOD's attributes to adequate cognitions of the essence of things.

Falsity consists in inadequate, mutilated or confused ideas (2d class), otherwise ideas are true.

The fundamental idea is substance = Being = GOD. His method then is *à priori*, beginning with the idea of GOD, deducing in logical order all resulting principles. The empirical is, as far as possible, avoided.

(C.) *Principle* is a rigid monism; the mind, spirit, force, is identical with the material, the idea with the *ideatum*, there being but one substance, one Being, mentally comprehended in its essence = attributes, *sc.* extension and thought, infinite, eternal; it is known in varied modes. Substance and cause are identified. Our chief attention must be given to

(D.) *Metaphysics.* (1.) *Substance* is that which exists *in se*, and is conceived *per se;* it is "*causa sui*," *i. e.*, its essence involves existence; it is infinite; *i. e.*, it cannot be limited by another nature of the same kind, for there can be but one substance of the same nature or attribute; it is one, indivisible; necessary, eternal, it is GOD (Eth. i. Def., and Prop. 1-10.)

(2.) *Attribute*, is that which the mind perceives to constitute the essence of substance. Substance may have many infinite attributes (i. 11). Neither body nor soul are substances, but they are (i. 14.),

(3.) *Modes*, affections of the attributes of GOD.

(4.) *God* is being, absolutely infinite substance consisting in infinite attributes, "*constans infinitis attr.*," each of which expresses His eternal and infinite essence.

(5.) No substance can be created by another (Eth. i. 6); therefore *extension* is one of the attributes of GOD (i. 15); infinite, eternal. Substance cannot be *finite*, for then, by def., it would be limited by another of the same nature, which is impossible.

(6.) *Thought*, also, is an attribute of God; He is *res cogitans*, *res extensa*.

(7.) God is *free*, *i. e.* he exists from necessity of nature alone, and is determined to act by Himself alone. He acts by necessity of nature (freedom from external restraints); all things are determined by Him (i. 29).

(8.) *Nature*, substance and cause are, by S., identified; (*vid.* 9, *inf.*) Thought and will in God are one; He is *natura naturans*; *natura naturata* is all which follows from His nature and attributes, modes, or affections (i. 24), at once the result of his decree, his thought, the necessity of His nature (i. 29). Things could not be produced otherwise than as they are (i. 33); they are infinite in number; they are called contingent, only with reference to our own ignorance.

(9.) *Cause.* God is cause of all, but *causa immanens*, not *causa transiens*; He is the substance of all that which follows from his eternal and infinite essence, (essence = that which being given the thing is necessarily assumed, and the contrary,) *i. e.*, particular things are the determinate affections of His attributes.

The reason why He acts and why He exists, is one and the same; as there is no final cause of existence, so none of His acts (i. 17). God needs nothing (i. 36).

Finite things, which have determined existence, are determined in operation as well as existence, by other finite and determined causes, and so *ad inf.*, (pre-existent modes of Div. attributes.)

No attempt is here made to give S.'s strict logical sequence from def. and ax.; or to trace his paralogisms; but we must not overlook the fatal *petitio princ.* in the def. of substance.

(E.) *Psychology*, with S. is identical with physics, for man is a part of "*nat. naturata*."

(1.) *Bodies* are the modes in which the Div. essence is expressed in determined ways, according to the attribute of extension. They are distinguished by the idea of motion in varying degrees, and this, in one body, is determined by another body, and so *ad inf.*

(2.) *Ideas* are those modes in which the Div. essence is expressed according to the attribute of thought. The only object of our mind is body; and to each determined body answers its idea, which is "adequate" when it has all the properties of a true idea; reality and perfection are the same thing; and the more perfections the body has, the more in its idea. (Note: Distinguish idea from *image*.) The order and connexion of ideas answer to the order and connexion of bodies, and conversely.

Man's essence is constituted by determined modes of GOD's attributes; and body and soul are consequently one *individuum*, being, so to speak, a part of GOD. As the body is part of *nat. naturata*, in which is GOD's attribute of extension manifested, so is the soul, with its affections, will, desire, love, a part of *nat. naturata*, as the manifestation of GOD's attribute of thought, (i. 31.) To attribute affections to GOD, *natura naturans*, (i. 17, 31) is anthropomorphic error.

The two functions of the soul are knowing and willing.

(1) Knowing, (*a.*) its own body of which it is the idea, in sensation having the idea of the body and all its parts,

(*b.*) It perceives also the "*affections*," which arise from the action of other bodies on its own, and so also the affections, and, through them, the nature of other bodies; (sense-perception.)

(*c.*) The ideas of past affections can be represented (imagination) ; and if the body have been affected in two modes at once, when the mind imagines one, it will immediately recall the other, a "concatenation" of the affections of the body, of those ideas which involve the nature of things ; the same thing is true of affections of the mind. (iii. 14.)

(*d.*) Through these perceptions, arises in the intellect the idea of the thing in itself ; the confused, inadequate idea has become the adequate, perfect idea.

(2) *Willing*, only relatively differs from knowing (ii. 49) ; will and intellect are collective names for acts of willing and ideas, which are one and the same. Both these as determined modes are necessarily determined to existence and operation by other modes *ad inf.*, and consequently freedom of choice does not exist, (ii. 48.) Error arises from man's being conscious of effort, but not of its cause.

(F.) *Ethics.* (1.) *Affections* (*affectus*) are transient states of the body as part of *natura naturata*, through which its activity is increased or diminished, aided or hindered, and ideas of these. When man is the adequate cause of such an affection it is *actio ;* when this is not the case, *passio.* The primary affections are desire, joy, and sadness. The passions proper are inadequate and confused ideas, in which man finds himself suffering ; attaining to the adequate, the mind becomes active, passion ceases ; a state never perfectly reached.

(2.) The chief effort of man is to preserve his being, and he calls that *good* which contributes to self-preservation and self-perfection, and *evil* the contrary : they are modes of thought, they are relative (iii. 39), for everything in nature is, in its degree, perfect.

(3.) The moral in man is this strife and opposition. *Virtue* is the power to accomplish the object ; it is action according to the laws of one's own nature ; but nothing is as useful to man as his fellow men, on whom he so much depends ; a rational life, a life according to nature's laws, includes justice, fidelity and honesty.

(4.) But true *knowledge*, is the life, the activity, the perfection of spirit; this consists therefore in having adequate ideas, and highest is the adequate cognition of the eternal and infinite essence of GOD. (ii. 47.) Herein is the highest good, the chief virtue of man, the perfection of his intellect, his beatitude ; (iv. app. c. iv.) : joy, love of GOD is the result of this cognition.

(5.) *Moral evil, sin ;* man cannot sin against the will, the knowledge of GOD, for this is the same as the necessary laws of *nat. naturata*, which cannot be violated. All human affections, love, hate, envy, etc., are properties of nature (i. 31), inconvenient sometimes, but necessary, having determined causes ; for nature, of which man is a particle, regards many things besides his convenience (Tract. Pol. i. 4 ; ii. 8). Whatever we do, we do of necessity, being thereto determined ; but the consequences of the deed may be privative of some perfection.

Repentance is sadness with the concomitant idea of some deed which we believe we have done freely; this sadness is due to education, etc. (Eth. iii. Def. 27.)

(6.) *Immortality* is not personal ; it is in the Div. idea.

(7.) *Politics.* Each man exists and acts *jure naturæ*, necessarily, and, by the same right, judges what is good and evil for him, useful, etc.

This natural right = natural power = power of GOD (Tr.

Pol. ii. 4); *i.e.*, the right of individuals extends by nature as far as their power does; it is not determined by reason, but by desire.

If harmonious, according to reason, to the law of nature, men would be most useful to one another; but affections necessitated overpower virtue = power, and men oppose one another; they must therefore give up natural rights for common security; thus society or one man (better the former) receives the right of judging what is good and evil, of making laws, which it enforces, not by reason but by threat, of punishing, etc. This compact, based on utility and reason, or any other is void when the utility ceases. (Tr. Theol.-Pol. xvi. 16, seq.)

In the natural state is no sin; sin is (outward) disobedience to the laws of the state, and by it punishable; the contrary is merit.

In the same state also is no property, therefore no justice and injustice, (Eth. iv. 37.) Men therefore for security, though by nature enemies, agree to have collectively what each would have separately, of two evils choosing the less; of two goods, the better.

Imperium is in the community: the power transferred is absolute, (Tr. Th.-Pol. xvi. 27,) and the citizen must submit to unjust decrees; the power of the state is limited only by that which belongs to him as man, which no compact can destroy, *e.g.* thought, speech, free interpretation in religion.

In the externals of religion, the state is sole judge.

Of special interest in connection with recent "scientific" discussion is S'.s. theory of

(8) *Miracles*. (Tr. Th.-Pol. i. 6.) When men do not understand the cause of an operation, they call it God's

work ; they think His Providence is not concerned in what they can explain by nature's laws, and that natural causes are suspended when He acts ; and so they imagine two powers, (*a*) of God, (*b*) of nature ; the heathen view of inconstant, unstable gods.

But nothing happens contrary to the immutable laws of nature, and in this we can know the existence and Prov. of GOD, not in miracles, which, as determined works, do not show infinite power ; if there were works surpassing our understanding, we could conclude nothing from them ; "against nature" and "above nature" do not differ.

All which GOD wills or knows, involves eternal necessity and truth ; the universal laws of nature are His decrees, following necessarily from His nature as "*nat. naturans.*"

A miracle, then, is a work of whose laws we are at present ignorant.

4. LEIBNITZ.

(A.) *Life. Gottfried Wilhelm Von Leibnitz*, b. 1646, at Leipzic, studied there and at Jena, law, history, politics—learning an eclectic peripateticism. In 1670, he was in the service of the court of Mayence, producing some of his earlier works at the age of 24 and 25. As counsellor of his Prince, we next find him at Paris, for three years studying math., phil., theology ; (he met Malebranche.) In 1673, he was in Eng., meeting the R.S., then in Holland, conferring with Spinoza. In 1684, he published his Diff. Calc. (cf. Sir Isaac Newton.) In 1688, he was received with great distinction at Rome. In 1690, he entered the service of the Elector of Hanover ; about this time we find him corresponding with Bossuet and others upon a reunion of Catholics and Protestants, seeking also to unite the

Lutherans and Calvinists. He founded the Acad. of Berlin (1700), and was consulted by Peter the Great upon his plans for the civilization of Russia. In 1712, we find him imperial counsellor at Vienna. He died at Hanover in 1716.

L. was a man of universal intelligence, of extraordinary penetration, of unbounded learning, devoting himself with energy and wide-reaching liberality, to the most varied topics; a metaphysician, mathematician, geologist, jurisprudent.

Works. Never systematizing his own views for publication, he wrote voluminously as special points presented themselves. Most noteworthy for phil. are, among others, "*Nouveaux Essais sur l'Entendement Humain,*" (1704, against Locke), "*Théodicée,*" (1710); "*Princ. Phil.,*"(1714, *Monadology, etc.,*) for Prince Eugene of Savoy.

(B.) *Method and Theory of Knowledge.* L. seeks to avoid the extreme idealism of Spinoza and Malebranche, but still more the empiricism of Locke. (Nouv. Ess.) Like Desc., he seeks a math. method of demonstration from necessary metaphysical truth, whose certainty is not proved in experience, but in the soul itself. (Rationalism.) In general, he is *eclectic;* the majority of sects are right in what they affirm; error, for the most part, is in negation.

Ideas are clear or obscure, distinct or confused, adequate or inadequate, sensuous or intellectual. The senses give indistinct representations of what takes place, not what necessarily is, or ought to be, neither causes nor reasons. Adequate ideas are from *à priori* concepts of the reason. Truths, accordingly, are contingent or necessary, empirical or rational.

All intellectual ideas and principles, being marked by universality and necessity, are *innate;* we therefore assent to them as soon as they are presented to us. The empirical proposition "*nihil in intellectu, quod non prius in sensu,*" needs, at least, the addition, "*nisi intellectus ipse.*" Not that the soul is conscious of these innate ideas and principles, but the soul *virtually* possesses them, as a condition of thought itself, conscious or unconscious. As perception, which is of the essence of the soul, becomes apperception by occasion of sensuous experience, so is this latter also the occasional cause which brings into consciousness the corresponding innate idea, and the virtual becomes actual.

Impressions in sense also become empirical ideas in the same way; for the soul "has no window" through which sensible objects can enter it.

The fundamental *principles* are (1) identity and contradiction, for necessary matter; (2) sufficient reason for contingent matter.

In finding a *criterion,* L. tries to avoid the imperfections of that of Descartes, *sc.* "clearness and distinctness." Adequate knowledge implies possibility of complete analysis of every thing that makes up the clear and distinct conception; the ideas must involve no contradiction, and the proposition must be warranted by exact observation, and strict logical demonstration. (Cf. Kant's Critique, P.R.; "L. intellectuallized Phenomena.")

L. does not attempt to discriminate and separate the subjective element in thought, nor does he distinguish well logical possibility from reality.

(C.) *Monadology.* Unable to recognize matter as purely passive, and nature as lifeless mechanism, L. reinstates a dynamical theory. If matter's essence be extension it is infinitely divisible, but this is inconceivable; bodies are an aggregate of monads. These are not atoms, but simple elements, without extension, imperishable from without, unchangeable, whose essence is force. Monads are analogous to the human soul; their powers are (1) "perception" for representations of all in each individual; (2) "appetite" or tendency to new perceptions.

Their perpetual changes are due solely to internal energy; but each strives (*appetitus*) to represent the universe; and each is a microcosm, but in different manner from every other. (Note the "law of continuity," "everything in nature goes by steps.") Substances which differ can have no mutual influence; but in creation a relation has been established between ideas in the monads and their motions, the

Pre-established harmony. God has made each monad, in its activity and internal changes, to answer to every other. (cf. the Clock-maker.)

But this is in widely different degrees; (1) in some monads, wholly obscure (inorganic bodies); (2) in others, with sense-perception; (3) in others, (human souls) with clear and distinct apperception.

Inorganic bodies are aggregates of (1), known empirically as phenomena only (*materia prima*). *Extension,* then, instead of being the essence of matter, is purely phenomenal, and caused by the aggregate unity of monads. Matter is "*phenom. bene fundatum.*" *Space* is purely ideal, the order of co-existing phenomena. *Time* is the order of succession in them.

Organic bodies are constituted by a central monad of the second class, the substantial form, around which are gathered monads of a lower order. This central monad, a soul, (plant or animal) is the principle of unity.

(D.) *Psychology.* L. considers human nat. in the light of his monadology. The human soul is in the highest grade of monads, possessing intelligence and will, the central monad of the human body. The ideal world in it expresses the actual world, and, confusedly, the perfect ideas which are in GOD, the *Monas Monadum.*

The mutual influence of soul and body, also, can only be explained by the "*pre-est. harm.*"

All monads, including human souls, were created at once; but soul-monads, through GOD's power, pass from unconsciousness ("naked monads") to consciousness. In death, monads of organic bodies lapse into the first grade, from which they came; not so man's soul-monad; it is *immortal.*

Freedom of the will, is not "freedom of indifference," which is irrational. It is analogous to the Divine: it chooses the higher good, by moral necessity, and this does not annihilate the will's freedom.

(E.) *Theodicea and Ethics.* GOD is the monad of monads, the necessarily existing essence, the sole, unlimited cause of all, producing by His will the best, the most perfect world (optimism); other worlds, in Divine Intellect, are metaphysically possible, but morally impossible, because GOD's perfection, a law unto Him, is the ground of determination in Him to the best world.

L. combines the mechanical theory of nat. with the teleological; the principles of physics and mechanics depend on Supreme intelligence and forethought; and all efficient causes with their results in the kingdom of nature, the world-machine, answer to the final causes and their results in the world of spirits, where God is ruler, rewarding the good, and punishing the evil.

Morality is grounded in the object of man's being, eternal happiness in God, and ever-increasing felicity ; on this is founded the obligation of virtue and righteousness.

Evil must be distinguished as (1) metaphysical, the necessary limitations of finite beings ;

(2) physical, the defects and pains incident to this life ;

(3) moral, the violation of the Divine law.

(1) is the root of (2) and (3) ; God's will is not the efficient cause of evil ; for it is grounded in (1), which results from the very nature of the best possible world ; and power of choice, from which results (3), is the very foundation of morality.

(F.) *Leibnitz' School.* L., as might be expected, had numerous followers, and, whether among friends or opponents, he exerted an immense influence on German thought, which, at least until the middle of the 18th Cent., took an idealistic direction. Chief in importance is

Christian von Wolff, b. at Breslau, (1679, A.D.) ; prof. at Halle and Marburg ; d. 1754. Without originality, he yet gave to the thoughts of his master what they lacked, a clear, logical and consistent system. He modified only minor points, *e. g.* more clearly distinguishing material and spiritual monads ; the former do not possess perception.

He distinguishes more clearly than his predecessors the various subjects of philosophical investigation.

Phil. is, (1) speculative ; (2) practical :

(1) is (*a*) logic ; (*b*) metaphysics :

(*b*) is (α) ontology ; (β) rational psychology ; (γ) cosmology ; (δ) natural theology :

(2) is (*a*) ethics ; (*b*) international law ; (*c*) politics : Empirical psychology precedes all parts of phil.

The Leibnitz-Wolff School gradually lost its credit through its own pedantry, and the prevailing empiricism of Locke.

5. English Idealism in the Seventeenth and Eighteenth Centuries.

[Ref., Dr. Porter's App. to Ueberweg's Hist. Phil. ; Burnet's "Hist. of His Own Time ;" Tulloch's "Rational Theol.," etc.]

Here for convenient study we may consider a succession of thinkers who opposed more or less successfully the prevailing empiricism of Eng. thought, with a more or less decided tendency to find the ground of truth in the innate principles of the soul itself, a modern Platonic school.

(A.) *Edward Herbert, Lord Cherbury*, (1581–1648, A.D.) espoused the Parliamentary cause in the civil war; wrote "*De Veritate*," "*De Religione Laici*," etc. Innate cognitions are directly given in intuitive reason ; the mind is not a "*tabula rasa*," but a closed book.

H. lays the foundation for the Eng. "deistical school" in a religion of reason, resting on original immediate knowledge in all men. (See Dr. Porter's App. to Ueberweg, vol. ii.)

(B.) *Ralph Cudworth*, (1617-1688, A.D.,) Professor of Hebrew at the Univ. of Cambridge, where he spent his life. Besides his "Treatise on Eternal and immutable Morality" and on Free-will, against the Fatalism of Hobbes, his "Intellectual System of the Universe," worthy of special note, is a work of vast erudition, directed against atheistic cosmology. He claims final causes for physics; to explain motion in matter, he maintains the necessity of assuming a "plastic nature," the medium whereby God is the cause of individual things: thereby all things, even the evil, are made to contribute to the good, the end of the universal whole.

C., with Henry More (vid. infr.) and others, founded a school of Platonism at Cambridge, which, however, was devoid of permanent influence.

(C.) *Samuel Clarke, D.D.* (1675–1729, A.D.) wrote on the "Being and Attributes of God," "The Obligations of Nat. Religion, etc." His attempt at *à priori* demonstration in the first treatise received general attention and caused wide-spread controversy. Immutable, absolute Being must eternally exist, one, self-existent, omnipresent. C. supplements his demonstration by *à post.* args. concerning the attributes of God. These, not mere decree or utility, are the foundation of moral obligation. Activity of the soul is, as such, spontaneous, necessarily free.

(D.) *Joseph Butler*, (1692-1752, A. D.) preacher at the Rolls chapel, bishop of Durham, (1750), pub. (1726) his fifteen sermons, preached at the Rolls chapel, and in 1730, an essay on the Nature of Virtue. (App. to the Analogy.) Although unsystematic, practical rather than speculative, and carefully avoiding scientific terminology, he yet asserts the existence of a Moral Faculty whose judgments are independent of the consequences of actions, ruling the affections and passions and directing them to definite moral ends; *e. g.* settled Resentment is naturally directed to the administration of justice against vice and wickedness. (See Whewell's Lect.)

(E.) *George Berkeley*, though he set out from the empiricism of Locke to develop its conclusions against materialism, (phenomenalism, idealism,) yet reached a stand-point which assimilates him in many respects to the rationalistic or the Platonic School. (See Prefaces, in Frazer's Ed.; Reid; Br. Quarterly, Jan. 1874.)

(A.) *Life.* b. 1684, in Ireland; distinguished for math. attainments; fellow at Trin. Coll., Dublin: his early Philos. works at the age of 25, among the most remarkable contributions ever produced at so early an age: associate of Pope, Swift, etc. In 1728 renounced prospects of promotion for a mission in Am. Failing, returned and was made Bishop of Cloyne, (1734); d. at Oxf. 1753. *Works.* "New theory of Vision," (1709) in which appears already his reduction of Locke's theory of ideas to phenomenalism: "Principles of Hum. Knowledge," (1710) on a basis of nominalism and sceptical acosmism; founding positively a duality, subjective, of *ego* and ideas; objectively, of sensations and Deity: (cf. changes in 2d ed. 1734); "Dialogues between Hylas and Philonous;" (1713) defending B.'s theory of matter; "De Motu" (1721); "Alciphron, or the Minute Philosopher," (1732), seven dialogues written in R. I., in defence of Christian ethics and theism; "Siris," (1744) Platonic Ontology. B.'s style clear, vivacious, glowing with warmth and fancy, together with the precision of his reasoning, and his relations to more recent positivism, makes him one of the most attractive and important of Eng. Metaphysicians.

(B.) *Method*; always empirical, and originally following Locke almost implicitly, nominalist and skeptical, he yet proceeds at length from psychological ground to pure ontology, as demanded by reason, which alone can give true science. (Siris, § 264; Theory of Vis. Vind. § 11.)

(C.) *Principle.* (1.) *Negative.* Material substance is a mere empty abstraction; its qualities are sensible, *i. e.* in the mind (Princ. §§ 16 seq.). Its *esse=percipi.*

(2.) *Positive.* A dualism of spirit and ideas; (in his earlier works the latter examined; in his later more fully the concepts of reason.) the subject-object in the *ego* given in consciousness. Infinite spirit the cause of ideas.

(D.) *Ideology.* "Ideas"=sensations or sensible images, are,

(1.) Ideas imprinted through special senses; there is no *communis sensus;* (Th. of Vis. § 127;) accompanying ideas are indicated by one name; (Princ. § 1);

(2.) Ideas perceived in the passions of the mind;

(3.) Ideas formed by memory and imagination, compounding, dividing, or representing (1) and (2), suggesting those which previously existed. (Th. Vis. Vind. § 9.) Ideas become general only when a particular one stands for others of the same sort. (Introd. Princ. § 15.) They can exist only in a mind which perceives them.

Primary and secondary qualities are equally ideas; *e. g.*, extension, motion (relative).

Ideas can be only like ideas, and could give no notion of objects, if such existed.

Physics is only concerned with phenomena (§ 102). What we call *causes* in nature are only the invariable connexions of phenom., the rules and method of motion. (*De Motu*; Siris, § 261 seq.; cf. Martineau, Cont. Rev., Jan. Feb., 1876.)

The senses indeed are to be trusted, but their only product is ideas.

What we call *nature* is the series of sensations in our minds.

(E.) *Metaphysical Principles.* (1.) Substance = spirit; something perceives the ideas, *sc.* spirit, *ego;* it is one, simple; (*a*) perceiving, it is the understanding; (*b*) producing ideas, etc., it is the will. Of it we have no "idea," for the passive cannot represent that which acts, but we have in consciousness the notion of an agent, perceiving, knowing, willing, etc. (Hylas and Phil. iii. p. 328.)

(2.) *Cause;* reason derives the concept from our consciousness of the active power of the will in producing effects; (ideas, etc.; Princ. § 28; Siris, §§ 155, 160.)

(3.) *God.* In ideas excited through sense, the mind is passive recipient; therefore some other will or spirit produces them, hence arg. *à post.* to the Being of God; their connexion shows foresight, His Providence; their order, etc., shows wisdom, power and goodness. The material world is a sensible language in which He speaks to our spirit. (Princ., § 146, seq.) All things exist "in God," as eternal ideas, seen by pure reason through phenomena. (Siris §§ 231–368.) Thus B. arrives empirically at transcendental realism. There are, revealed in the Logos, self-existent, necessary, uncreated principles.

(4.) *Force,* residing in bodies, is a mathematical hypothesis (§ 234); senses tell us only of motion, but power or force is a metaphysical concept of reason derived from consciousness of volition.

Time is succession of ideas.

Space is the sensation of unresisted motion of our body. (Princ. §§ 97, 116.)

Extension, also, is an abstract idea, and as such, non-existent; we can divide to the limit of our perception; but ideas are not infinitely divisible. (Princ. § 123.)

(5.) We infer the existence of other spirits from phenomena, referring ideas produced in us to other agents, supposed to be like ourselves. (Princ. § 145.)

(F.) *Ethics.* In "Alciphron," dialogues in the Platonic manner, B. opposes the selfish theory of Mandeville and the sentimentalism of Shaftesbury. (vid. infr.) Belief in immortality, deity, a future life, is not of custom or education, but grounded in human nature. The rule and measure of good is its tendency to promote the general interests of mankind.

Freedom of will is an activity of the soul known in consciousness. (Alc. VII. § 19, seq.)

CHAPTER XII.

SKEPTICISM AND MYSTICISM IN THE SEVENTEENTH AND EIGHTEENTH CENTURIES.

1. CONTINENTAL SKEPTICS. 2. ENGLISH SKEPTICS BEFORE HUME. 3. HUME. 4. MYSTICISM.

1. CONTINENTAL SKEPTICS.

Philos. Skepticism, a despair of human reason, may take two unlike forms ; (1) a negation of all dogmas, as in the New Academy; (2) a reception by faith of dogmas wholly undiscernible by reason; (note mystical tendency in 2). To the second class of skeptics belong *Huet,* (1630–1721, A. D.) Bishop of Avranches, and

(A.) *Blaise Pascal,* (1) b. 1623, at Clermont, early distinguished for his attainments in math. and physics, an earnest adherent of the Jansenists, ("*Lettres Provinciales,*") ; d. 1662.

(2.) P., in part, follows Descartes, (*e. g.* Pensées, ii. 15, ed. 1867) ; but reason can give no certainty, although in our nature lie an irresistible searching after truth, and a tendency towards certain principles. "We cannot escape from both these sects (sc. Pyrrhonists and Dogmatists), nor subsist in either."

"Les grandes âmes qui, ayant parcouru tout ce que les hommes peuvent savoir, trouvent qu'ils ne savent rien, et se rencontrent en cette même ignorance d'où ils étaient partis." (IV. 15, 17, 18.)

The knowledge of truth comes from another source, revelation, received by faith, an immediate illumination from God, which has its seat in the heart; one must love, in order to know. (cc. xi, xii.)

(B.) *Pierre Bayle*, (1.) (1648–1706, A. D.) b. in Foix, a Protestant, then a Catholic, then Protestant again; to avoid persecution under Louis XIV. took refuge in Holland at Rotterdam, and wrote his *Dictionnaire Historique et Critique.*

(2.) Of immense erudition, enlivened by satirical wit and elegance of style, B. is skeptical in spirit, rather than with a system. He contents himself with exposing the weaknesses, imperfections and inconsistencies of all dogmatic systems. Reason is clear sighted enough to detect errors, but not to arrive at truth. In the same spirit, he points out the apparent antagonisms between phil. and Christian dogmas.

(C.) *Voltaire*, (1.) (1694–1778, A. D.) b. in Paris, a pupil of the Jesuits, a friend of Lord Bolingbroke, in London (1726–9,) followed the R. S. in physical researches with the phil. of Hobbes as a basis; in England changed his name from Arouet by an anagram; from poetry turned his attention to philos. questions, but without earnestness or depth. He returned to France, introducing there the physics of Newton and the empiricism of Locke. (See Morley; *Soirées de S. Petersburg*, vol. 1, p. 186; Blackwood's Mag., Mar., 1872.)

(2.) His only guide to truth seems to be good sense under the inspiration of Locke; he turns the polished shafts of his brilliant wit, and sarcastic ridicule equally against the ideas of Plato, the Cartesian demonstration of the existence of GOD, and Leibnitz's theory of matter, and his optimism (*Candide*). He ridicules equally virtue and vice, Aristotle and Rousseau: "Most men are wolves and foxes, with a few sheep among them."

V. is, *au fond,* sensualist; all knowledge is through the senses. Yet he believes that the existence of a creator is, *à post.,* demonstrable. "If God did not exist, it would be necessary to invent Him," for the support of a moral order: future rewards and punishments, however, are doubtful.

2. English Skeptics.

[Ref. Mackintosh, Eth. Phil. in 17th and 18th Cent.; Hallam's Lit.; Morell's Hist. Mod. Phil.; Whewell's Lect. Moral Phil.]

We have already seen the skeptical element in Berkeley's earlier phil., and have now to glance at a succession of emp. thinkers in a narrow sphere of thought, with their opponents, terminating in the greater genius and more searching analysis of Hume.

(A.) *Joseph Glanville,* (1636–1680, A.D.) (1.) F. R. S., Court-preacher to Chas. II., wrote "*Scepsis Scientifica, confessed Ignorance the way to Science, etc.;*" "*Sadducismus Triumphatus*" (posthumous), etc.

(2.) He opposed all dogmatism. Causes are the alphabet of science; but since experience gives only phenomena, we can only resort to hypotheses: "*Post illud, ergo propter illud.*"

(B.) *Henry Dodwell,* (1641–1711, A. D.), of Trin. Coll. Dublin, Prof. Hist. Oxf., gave a new impulse to discussion upon the immortality of the soul. It is naturally mortal, but made immortal in Christians by the gift of God (cf. "body, soul and spirit." N. T.)

(C.) *Antony Collins*, (1676–1729, A. D.) of Cambridge Univ., a friend of Locke, wrote "Reason in Theology," "Free Thinking," "Liberty and Necessity," etc.

Liberty is "a power in man to do as he wills and pleases," but he is determined by reason and senses; "*moral* necessity;" an exhaustive arg. for "Philos. Nec." Collins is one of a group of writers who endeavored to establish the relations of Rev. to phil. by denying all supernatural truths, accepting the empiricism of Locke, but denying the limitations by which he had surrounded it. Other writers ("deistical") are *Toland*, (1669–1722, A. D.) "Christianity not Mysterious," and *Tindal*, (1657–1733, A. D.) "Christianity as old as the Creation," (cf. Bishop Butler's Anal.) etc.

(D.) *Bernard de Mandeville*, (1670–1733, A. D.) b. at Dort, Holland, resided in Eng.; pub. (1714) "Fable of the Bees, or Private Vices Public Benefits."

Setting out from Locke's denial of innate practical principles, and from the "utilitarian" theory of morals, he shows that there is no essential distinction between vice and virtue, and that the former may be beneficial to society. All natural impulses are legitimate, and restraints upon them by priests and magistrates are a usurpation. (cf. Berkeley's Alciphron.)

(E.) *David Hartley*, (1.) (1704–1757, A. D.) ed. at Cambridge, a physician, produced in 1749 his "Observations on Man," etc. (See Coleridge, Biog. Lit. cc. v.–vii.)

(2.) He is the founder of the "Associational Psychology." Following Locke, he offers a physiological sensualism which abandons any attempt to bridge the gulf between mind and matter, by reducing phenom. of the former to terms of the latter. Sensation is explained as vibrations in the nervous system: they leave vestiges, ideas of sensations: repeated, they create a disposition to certain vibratiuncules. Simple vibrations may combine into the complex.

Association of ideas = "any combination of thought or feeling which is capable of becoming habitual by repetition." As the vibratory movement acquires a tendency to repeat itself, so one may tend to produce another naturally associated with it. Three things are associated, sensations, (include emotions,) ideas, muscular movements; any one of associated sensations, A, B, C, may recall the ideas, a, b, c. Volition is explained as muscular action excited by an idea.

Passions, affections, are caused by assoc. of pleasure or pain with ideas. All reasoning is to be explained by assoc. of ideas; it is the ground of assent.

Note, also, the "law of transference," with its ethical applications. (Obs. on man, iv. 4–6.)

It may be so old and habitual as to seem innate instinct. H. disclaims the materialist consequences of his principle.

(cf. Bain etc.)

(F.) *Joseph Priestley*, (1733–1804, A. D.) of wide reputation in physics and chemistry, and for his liberal politics. He wrote (1777) "Disquisitions relating to Matter and Spirit;" "Materialism and Philosophical Necessity," etc. He adheres to Locke against Hume's skepticism, while controverting also Reid's appeal to intuitive beliefs. He expands Hartley's principles into materialism, philos. necessity, Utilitarian ethics. Thought = sensation. (cf. Condillac). Yet he tries to reconcile his views with "natural religion," recognizing a Divine spirit, and looking for a future state in the resurrection of the body.

(G.) *Erasmus Darwin,* (1731–1802, A. D.) ed. at Univ. of Cambridge and Edinb., physician, botanist, poet; wrote "Zoonomania," (1794) attempting a still further systematizing of Hartley's Psychology, leaving out the theological element of Priestley.

At this point might be considered the ethics of Paley; but, deferring their consideration for a subsequent chapter, before examining the most complete skeptical development of empiricism, we may glance briefly at some leading

Opponents. (A.) *Richard Cumberland,* (1632–1719, A. D.) fellow of Magdalen Coll., Camb., Bishop of Peterborough, wrote "*Disquisitio de Legibus Naturæ,*" (1672) in which, against Hobbes, he seeks to establish inductively the existence of a universal ethical rule founded on human nature, the law of universal benevolence; the proof of it is, it tends to the highest happiness of all. This is evidence of a Divine purpose, of the law of a Supreme Lawgiver. Moral rules are discernible by right reason, the capacity to discern first principles as well as practical laws by which to attain the ethical end. He lays a foundation for utilitarianism, though we see an element of rationalism in his phil.

(B.) *Anthony Ashley Cooper, Earl of Shaftesbury,* (1671–1713, A. D.), author of the "Characteristics of Men, etc." (1711), wrote also "Inquiry concerning Virtue and Merit," (1699.) He takes essentially the same ground, seeking to avoid injurious practical inferences from Locke's empiricism. Virtue consists in harmony of our social and selfish propensities, so that each individual may regard the good of the community.

Nature and reason give rise to some moral conceptions, a "moral sense." Morality does not require a religious basis.

In general, of these opponents of skepticism it may be said that unable to rest ethics on immutable *à priori* principles, yet unwilling to accept the epicurean morals of expediency, or extreme utilitarianism, they offered a "morality of consequences." (Whewell, c. vii.)

3. HUME.

[Ref. T. H. Green's Introd.; Reid; Sir W. Hamilton's Disc.; McCosh, Scottish Philos.]

Hume marks a most important stage in the Hist. of Mod. Phil., especially of empiricism. By his bold, clear, logical development of Locke, and his searching and universally destructive analysis, he impelled other minds to renewed and deeper search for truth (cf. Kant). Empirical principles, vanishing in feeling, "perception," were reconstituted as generalized experience transmitted from the past.

(A.) *Life. David Hume*, (1711–1776, A. D.) b. at Edin.; abandoned law for phil. and belles lettres; in France (1734–7). His Treatise on Hum. Nat. in 1739 received but little attention. In 1747 he was Sec. to the Embassy at Vienna and Turin. His position as librarian at Edin. in 1752 gave him facilities which he employed in producing his Hist. Eng. (1754–1762); was Sec. to Emb. at Versailles (1763), and Under-Sec. of State (1767). (Note his quarrel with Rousseau). He died at Edin.

Works: (1) "Treatise on Human Nature;" v. 1, of the Understanding; v. 2, of the Passions; v. 3, of Morals (1739–40).

(2) "Inquiry concerning the Hum. Understanding and Principles of Morals" (1748): (chiefly abridged from (1).

(3) "Essays, Moral, Political and Literary": (1742).

(4) "Dissertation on the Passions;" (principles of morals): (1751).

(5) "Nat. Hist. of Religion" (1755); "Dialogues on Nat. Rel." (Posth.)

Hume is distinguished for depth, consistency, and correct and elegant style.

(B.) *Method.* H. aims at strict empiricism, accepting without question or proof Locke's theory of ideas; but, with greater logical consistency, (cf. Treat. on Hum. Nat. "being an attempt to introduce the experimental method of reasoning, etc.,") he aims to investigate thus the extent and force of human understanding, the nature of ideas, and of reasoning.

(C.) *Principle.* "After the most accurate and exact of my reasonings, I can give no reason why I should assent to it; and feel nothing but a strong *propensity* to consider objects strongly in that view, under which they appear to me." (Hum. Nat., i. iv. 7). Experience is a principle for the past; habit creates expectation concerning the future. (Note "propensity to feign.")

All knowledge is reduced ultimately to subjective transitory impressions; it exists = it is felt. (Sensualism.)

(D.) *Theory of knowledge* is based on Locke's ideology. "*Perceptions*" are (1) impressions produced in feeling (= thinking);

(2) "Ideas" reproduced by memory and imagination from precedent impressions: these may produce (*a*) secondary impressions, desire, or aversion, (reflection); (*b*)

secondary ideas of these, in mem. and imag. *Thinking* is a less lively feeling. Mem. and imag. differ only in liveliness ; the latter less lively and may admit a different order of impressions.

The *understanding* (= reason) judges of

(1) The relations of ideas, (Geom. Alg., etc.): but science never attains precision or certainty (i. ii. 4.) ;

(2) The relations of objects, of facts (*sc.* feelings).

" Reason is and ought to be the slave of passions, to serve and obey them," (ii. iii. 3), merely combining, separating, etc.

Perceptions are *associated,* by natural "propensity," according to three relations ; (1) resemblance ; (2) contiguity ; (3) cause and effect : (i. iii. 1).

Philosophical relations are also (4) identity, (5) proportion, (6) degrees, (7) contrariety. (H. does not show that "impressions" give relation of impressions, or a synthesis of them : he falls back on "propensity to feign." He re-introduces unity under the name of "relations.")

Belief is the vivacity of an idea, a quality conveyed to it from the vivacity of a present impression ; (*e. g.* belief in the continued existence of unfelt phenom.) (i. iv. 2).

A *general* term raises the idea of a particular thing, "along with a custom," *i. e.* associated ideas of resemblance, (extreme nominalism).

(E.) *Speculative Metaphysics.* (1) Principle of *Causality,* is not known *à priori,* nor *à post.* (i. iii. 3). A cause is an object precedent and contiguous when all resembling objects hold the same relation ; or when the idea of the one determines the mind to the idea of the other. This determination is in the sensitive nature ; custom induces a propensity of passing from the idea of a past impression recalled in the presence of a similar impression, to the associated image, which we name *effect*, (i. iii. xiv).

From this habit arises expectation of similar relation in the future ; of necessary connection we have no idea, because we have no "impression" ; the expectation rests on a natural "propensity" ; but anything may produce anything, since *cause* is only conjunction of perceptions, (i. iii. 3 ; i. iv. 5). "Laws of Nature" are assured habits of expectation.

(2) *Identity, i. e.* continued existence, is a fiction of the imag. ; we discover similarity of impressions, and "uneasiness" leads us to suppose existence of perceptions when not perceived. (i. iv. 2).

(3) *Substance* is a collection of ideas, capable of being indefinitely enlarged ; our knowledge is, of course, purely subjective.

Its "primary qualities" are as much feelings as its secondary. (i. iv. 2).

(4) *Time* and *space*, are impressions of the manner in which impressions appear in the mind.

(5) The idea of *God*, then, disappears as an outward reality ; ideas of human wisdom, goodness, etc., are magnified in imag. We cannot go from the finite to the infinite ; all ideas are anthropomorphic.

(6) *Mind or soul* is but "a heap or collection of different perc. united together by certain relations, and supposed, though falsely, to be endowed with a perfect simplicity and identity." (i. iv. 2). We have neither idea nor impression of self, of soul.

The materiality or immateriality of it is an unmeaning question. Spiritual substance = Spinozism. (i. iv. 5).

(7) Senses do not reveal an *outer world ;* nor does

reason, which simply discusses relations of perceptions. The belief rests on the "propensity to feign" continued existence when perc. have a certain degree of coherence and constancy in repetition. *Extension* is feeling, and motion is perceived change in bodies.

But yet a natural instinct and the liveliness of the impressions make us act as if the outer world were real.

(F.) *Practical Philosophy.*

(1.) *Passions*, are impressions of reflection, produced by ideas which cause pleasure or pain, (include emotions and desires.)

Will is included in these, the internal impression we feel when we give rise to new motions of body, or perc. of mind, (ii. iii. 1), in order to attain a good (pleasure), or avoid an evil (pain).

"Direct passions" (violent impressions) are desire, joy, hope, with their opposites. Yet beside passions founded on pain and pleasure, are some, (revenge, benevolence etc.,) which rest on a natural impulse. (H. breaks down in explaining pride, involving *self.*)

(2.) *Freedom of will.* Necessity in material things is a determination of the mind to pass from one perc. to its usual attendant; actions of matter have no other necessity, and this is equally true of mind (uniformity = necessity); man's mind is conditioned as nature is. Will is not guided by reason; that is the "slave of passions."

(3.) A *moral sense* is a feeling of pleasure in what is pleasurable or useful in the general. Sympathy is an original instinct (ii. ii. 7), whereby the same test of pleasure or pain is extended to others, so that moral approbation is extended also to what is agreeable or useful to them.

(4.) *Justice*, like other obligations, civil and moral, arises from interest and sympathy; it is an "artificial virtue" produced by the general sense of common interest, which creates society.

(5.) *Beauty* is either the sensuously pleasurable, or grounded in the useful, the anticipation of the former, (ii. i. 8.)

Leaving Hume, we might pass to that continental "illuminism," with which he is so closely allied, and thence to the attempt to re-establish phil. on an empirical basis; but this would lead us into our own century, and as mysticism often has its roots in the same soil with skepticism, we will first retrace our steps.

On the reaction to spiritualism, cf. Cousin; LeMaistre, Soirées de S. Pet. p. 293 seq.; Wordsworth's Exc. ii. "They the wisest, etc."

4. Mysticism in the Seventeenth and Eighteenth Centuries.

As sensualism developed into skepticism, so Platonism produced a mysticism, most frequently the "mysticism of sentiment." (See Cousin, the True, the Beautiful and the Good: Lect. v.)

(A.) *Henry More.* (1614–1687, A.D.) Fellow of Christ's Coll. Camb., with Cudworth and others, the "Latitudinarians." (Tulloch's Rational Theol.) He began his philos. course by opposing Hobbes and defending Descartes from skepticism; he took refuge in Platonism terminating in (Neo-Pl.) mysticism, from Ficinus, etc., and wrote "Immortality of the Soul," "*Defensio Cabalæ triplicis*," etc. All knowledge is from direct and divine intuition. Phil. is a Divine Rev., whence Pythag., Plato and the Cabala obtained it.

(B.) *Fénelon,* (1651–1715, A. D.) tutor of the Duke of B. (1689), then Archbishop of Cambrai, defended Mad. Guyon against Bossuet; his opinions at last condemned by the Pope, to which decision he instantly and unhesitatingly submitted; he wrote "*De l'Existence de Dieu,*" and "*Les Maximes des Saints.*" Contemplation is preferable to thought and action, love to virtuous piety: (quietism.)

(C.) *Poiret,* (1646–1719, A.D.) a Prot. min., d. in Holland; wrote many myst. works, opposing all spec. phil.

(D.) *Emanuel Swedenborg,* (1688–1772, A. D.) b. in Stockholm, lived many years in London and died there: at first devoting himself to physical sciences, from 1745 he turned his attention to the spiritual world. A portion of his voluminous works, ("Prodromus," "Econ. of the An. Kingdom," etc.) have a philos. bearing. (Note also "Arcana Cœlestia," etc.) He taught a doctrine of series, of degrees: the material world is a key to the spiritual, culminating in God, whose type is the sun; heat and light = Love and Wisdom.

Man has a threefold nature; (1) spirit; (2) soul = spiritual body; (3) material body. Mind is, (1) the spiritual principle communicating directly with God and the celestial hierarchy; (2) the rational, intellectual princ.; (3) the sensuous, for the material world.

(E.) *St. Martin,* (1713–1804, A. D.) b. in France, trans. Boehme, opposed, ineffectually, the sensualism of Condillac, etc.; in himself and in God of whom he is a type, he discovers all truth.

CHAPTER XIII.

FRENCH SENSUALISTIC SCHOOL OF THE EIGHTEENTH CENTURY.

1. EMPIRICAL POLITICAL PHILOSOPHY. 2. CONDILLAC. 3. MATERIALISM.

[Ref.—Lange, Gesch. d. Materialismus ; Cousin, Phil. Sens. 18me Siécle ; Morell.]

1. EMPIRICAL POLITICAL PHILOSOPHY.

Under this title may be considered a class of writers, inspired by the empiricism of Locke, and distinguished for "liberal" opinions in politics and religion, although differing more or less widely from the sensualism defended by Condillac.

(A.) *Montesquieu,* Baron de M., (1689–1755, A. D.) in his "*Lettres Persannes,*" (1721) opposed absolutist principles in church and state ; and in "*l'Esprit des Lois,*" marked out a constitutional form of government, separating the legislative, executive and judicial functions, the aristocracy and the democracy, for mutual limitations and safeguards ; yet this form, though resting on nature, may not always be expedient.

(B.) *Jean Jacques Rousseau,* (1712–1778, A. D.) (1) b. at Geneva, met with distinguished literary success at Paris ; retired to Geneva ; returning to Paris, produced *Emile,* and *Contrat Social.* (Note, in Émile, the "*profession de foi du Vicaire Savoyard,*" against the sensualism of Helvetius).

R., for a time in Eng., quarrelled with his friend Hume. He presents his own life and character in the most repulsive light.

(2) R. defends spiritualism against the prevailing materialism of France. Matter cannot move itself; its changes show will; its laws, intelligence, *sc.* GOD.

Will and reason in man evince that he has a soul. A moral instinct, conscience, is innate; it is our natural guide, and its guidance leads to happiness. Morals and rel. rest on needs of the heart. (Nat. rel.) R.'s chief philos. relation is to

Politics. (*a*) The state of nature is not, as Hobbes describes it, a state of war; it is one of savage isolation and freedom, guided by natural instincts. A sense of needs leads to voluntary association, the social compact, the state.

(*b*) Natural rights, unlimited freedom, are given up. "*Volonté générale*" aims at the good of the community. An unlimited sovereignty is thus transferred to the State, enunciated in laws, which regulate moral right.

For an executive, the people must appoint their officer, their servant (cf. Hobbes); this is no new compact; the *sovereign people* may appoint one to execute laws in their name, may limit or take away his power. If he assume powers not given to him, *e.g.* making laws, he is a despot; *ipso facto*, he loses his authority. A republic is best, as least liable to this danger.

The people retain the law-making power.

2. CONDILLAC.

(A.) *Etienne Bonnet de Condillac*, (1715–1780, A.D.) b. at Grenoble, Abbé, friend of the Encyclopædists at Paris, produced his "*Essai sur l'Origine des Connaissances Humaines*," (1746); "*Traité des Systêmes*," (1749); "*Traité des Sensations*," (1754); ' "*Tr. d. Animaux*," "*Logique*," etc.

C. was the ablest French metaphysician of his century. At first following Locke with comparatively few deviations, we must look to his Tr. d. Sens. for his perfected system. (See Cousin, Phil. Sens. de 18me. Siécle.)

(A.) *Method.* Locke's empirical theory is developed, systematized, rendered consistent, not by observation, but by rigid analysis. C. proposes to go back to the origin of our ideas, and so to fix the extent and limits of our knowledge (Pref. to *Essai sur l'Or.*); professing to follow strictly observation and experience, regarding phenom. in every point of view, analyzing and comparing, his object leads him to imagine a process of development.

(B.) *Theory of Knowledge.* To show that all knowledge is "transformed sensation," he imagines a marble statue, organized as man, receiving the sense of smell.

The order of knowledge is :

(1) Sensible impression, *sensation;* perception = consciousness of sens.; (Ess. sur l'Or. ii. i. 3); (he confounds the active and the passive).

(2) *Attention*, is continued active sensation, vivid consciousness excluding all perc. but one; (note passivity).

(3) *Memory*, is feeling when the sens. impression is ended. *Ideas* thus originate, (images); they are feelings as viewed objectively; sensations are the same viewed subjectively; sensible ideas represent the present; intellectual, the past feeling.

(4) *Consciousness* of the *ego* arises from memory of changed feeling.

(5) *Comparison,* originates in two sensations, or, a past and a present idea, "attention to two ideas" ; (Tr. d. Sens. ii. 10). Memory (passive) may recall a succession of ideas ; imagination is a lively retracing of them (ii. 15) ; hence *judgment.*

(6) *Reflection* is carrying our attention from one object (collection of qualities = sensations) to another, considering them separately ; attention passing from the present to the remembered.

(7) *Abstraction* is attention fixed on one quality of an object.

(8) *Reasoning* is a double judgment. Imagination, reflective, may combine images. Pleasure accompanying sensible impressions suffices to call out this chain of "transformed sensations." (Pref. Tr. Sens.) Understanding is a collective name for the above processes ; reason = orderly conducting of these steps to knowledge. Judgments are identical propositions ; and true science is based on a succession of these (algebraic, Tr. d. Syst.) ; it is well-constructed language ; by use of the latter grow up judgment, reasoning, etc., its (arbitrary) signs assisting mem., imag., etc.

Hearing, taste, etc., are added to the statue ; through touch, idea of body and space. (ii. 4).

(C.) *Speculative Metaphysics.* (1) *Substance* is the unknown ground of qualities (sensations) ; of it we have no idea (Tr. d. Syst. ii. x. 1).

(2) *Self* and *Body* are collections of qualities present or remembered. (Tr. d. Sens. vi. 3).

(3) The *infinite* = indefinite ; eternity = indef. duration, *sc.* succession of ideas ; immensity = indef. space.

C. does not follow out his one princ. to its consequences; he believes a first cause because effects cannot be in an inf. series. He recognizes (inconsequently) God, immortality of the soul (indivisible subject of perc.), free will, virtue; knowing nothing of substance he may rather be called phenomenalist than materialist.

(D.) *Practical Philosophy.* (1) C. lays a foundation for ethics in tracing the origin of ideas, without expressly discussing morals. As all intelligence is transf. sens., so all principles of action originate from pleasure or pain, (thus based on the passive), which produces

Desire; a passion is a dominant desire; all forms of pass., love, hate, etc., are forms of self-love, desire of pleasure, aversion from pain. (Tr. d. Sens. i. iii. 1).

The *Good,* primarily, is what pleases smell and taste; the *beautiful,* sight, hearing, and touch.

Secondarily, the good is a sensible action conformed to a (sensible) law.

Will = desire, when the thing desired is in our power. (Tr. d. Sens. i. iii. 8).

Thus unity of principle is attained, for attention and desire = feeling. (Tr. d. Sens. vii.)

(2.) In *a State of Nature,* not absolutely savage, but simply agricultural, property originates in division; and a contract, expressed or implied, arises which binds each to contribute to the common good.

3. Materialism.

Condillac laid down the principles of sensualism, but was restrained by religious feeling or other causes from their ultimate consequences, and an absolute consistency. Materialism, however, joined to the ethics and politics of the Revolution, seemed, for a time, to absorb all phil. in France.

(A.) *Helvetius, Claude Adrien,* (1715–1771, A. D.) b. at Paris, produced in 1758 "*L'Esprit.*" It was condemned by the Sorbonne and the Parliament; whereupon he made formal retractation. "*De L'Homme,*" (pub. 1772), was a more extreme statement of the same views. (cf. Rousseau; *ubi supra*, and see Cousin; Phil. Sens. 18me S.)

(1.) The mind has two passive powers; (*a*) to receive impressions from exterior objects, physical sensibility; (*b*) to preserve those impressions, memory = continued, weakened sensation. Every capacity reduces to these; "*je juge = je sens.*"

(2.) Men, in this regard, are by nature equal; differences are due to education, etc.; man's superiority over the brutes is due to his physical organization; his mind also is the result of it: men, *e. g.*, without flexible fingers would have no arts, no civilization, would be wild beasts.

(3.) Passions are the cause of all human activity; liberty is free exercise of man's limbs, etc.

(4.) Pleasures, physical in origin, are what all men seek according to their various passions. ("Ethics of interest," egoism.) To actions useful to a man he gives the name of virtue; to those injurious, vice; so also society. The vicious are to be pitied; for, through ignorance, they do not understand their own true interests, and society should, by educating, enlighten them.

The compassionate and the inhuman both seek their own pleasure. "'Tis a man who has told everybody's secret."

(5.) The state can appeal only to the enlightened self-interest of the people.

(6.) He revives the calculus of probabilities of Carneades; it is applicable to all subjects, to the existence of the body, the spirituality of the soul.

(B.) *Diderot, Denis* (1713–1784, A. D.), with D'Alembert, editor of the *Encyclopédie des Sciences*, etc., (1753–1782, A. D.), to which contributed Voltaire, Rousseau, d'Holbach, Turgot, etc., wrote "*Pensées sur l'Interp. de la Nature*," etc., (1754.)

Atoms have sensations, which become conscious in animal organisms; from sensation thought is awakened. D., eventually rejecting rev. truth, finds GOD, (pantheistically) in natural truth, beauty, and goodness.

(C.) *D'Alembert, Jean* (1717–1783, A. D.), author of the admirable preface to the Enc., skeptical in phil., can form no idea of matter or mind, although the union of parts in organized beings seems to be the work of intelligence.

(D.) *D'Holbach, Baron Paul Heinr.*, (1723–1789, A.D.) b. at Heidelsheim, friend of Diderot, d. at Paris, produced in 1770 his "*Système de la Nature*," a complete gospel of materialism, its most systematic statement.

(1.) All that exists is matter, endless, necessary; its essence is motion, endless, necessary.

Nature is the result of its motion, producing different combinations. The activities of things are likewise the (necessitated) motions of their atoms.

(2.) Fears and ignorance on one side, and abstractions of theologians and metaphysicians on the other, have personified these energies as World-soul, Spirit, GOD.

(3.) Man is an organism material and sensible; soul is body considered relatively to its sensitive activities and functions. Soul, *in concreto* = brain ; otherwise, a metaphysical abstraction.

(4.) All nature strives for self-preservation : this in man is self-love, love of what aids, hatred of what injures. This is the determining principle of all action.

(5.) The good = useful; the evil = hurtful. Virtue is the art of making one's self happy, by advancing the happiness of others, and of governing the passions. Civil law by threats and punishments restrains them, or prevents their injuring.

(E.) *Condorcet, Marie Jean Ant.*, (1743–1794, A. D.) marquis, mathematician, friend of D'Alembert ; proscribed by the Convention, he poisoned himself.

In his "*Tableau Historique des Progrès de l'Esprit Humain*," as an epicurean sensualist, he maintains the perfectibility of mankind. Progress is through education and physical improvement.

(F.) *St. Lambert, Chas. Fr.*, (1716–1803, A. D.) in his "*Catéchisme Universel*" (1797) developed, in practical ethics, the princ. of Helvet. with general applause. (Note the Acad.)

Man is an organized and sensitive body ; from pleasure and pain his knowledge and actions ; but his happiness is bound up with the happiness of all. Vices are injurious passions ; virtues, useful ones. Belief in God is dismissed as an arbitrary superstition, not concerned in "*Principes des Mœurs*."

CHAPTER XIV.

SCOTCH PHILOSOPHY.

1. Period of Development. 2. Reid. 3. Period of Criticism.

[References:—McCosh, Scottish Phil.; Porter, App. Ueberweg; Cousin; Hamilton's Notes on Reid; Morell's Hist. Phil. 19th Cent.; Mackintosh.]

1. Period of Development.

(A.) *Introduction.* Here we may find, with few exceptions, a general unity of method, and even of matter. An inductive method, from facts observed in consciousness, with observation of the acts and words of others, of universal language, a method applied especially to psychol. and ethics, may entitle this school to be called the "phil. of consciousness," or, of "the common sense." (Sir Wm. Hamilton's App. to Reid. A). It may incline toward the empiricism of Locke, rarely accepting it unqualifiedly, or be influenced by the criticism of Kant; it may not be thorough and profound; yet principles are obtained which are not mere products of observation and experience, but are, partially at least, supplied by the mind itself; (Hutcheson, "senses"; Stewart, "laws of thought"; Brown, "Original intuitions"; Hamilton, from Kant, "*à priori* forms.")

(B.) *Francis Hutcheson,* (1) (1694–1746, A. D.) b. in n. of Irel., of a Scotch family, ed. at Univ. of Glasgow, min. in Irel., prof. of Mor. Phil. at Glasgow (1729), wrote "*Inquiry into the Original of our Ideas of Beauty*" (1725); on the "*Nat. and Cond. of Passions and Affections—The Moral Sense*" (1728); "*Moral Phil.,*" (posth.) (1754.)

(2.) H. finds in man certain cognitive powers, '*menti congenita intelligendi vis;*" and internal "*senses,*" "determinations of the mind independent of will, and of the pleasurable or painful."

Senses are (1) bodily; (2) of beauty, which is (objectively) a compound ratio of uniformity and variety; (3) of sympathy;

(4.) Moral Sense, which has for its object actions which tend to give happiness, (eudæmonism).

Moral goodness is an "idea of a quality in actions which procures approbation and love towards the actor" independent of utility; moral evil, the idea of the opposite, (cf. "honor and shame, etc.")

The civil power rests on an implied contract, etc.

(C.) *Henry Home, Lord Kames,* (1696–1782, A. D.), lawyer and judge, wrote, in 1751, "*Essays on Principles of Morality*"; in 1762, "*Elements of Criticism.*"

Man has a "moral feeling" by which he judges of his various motives, self-love, benevolence, utility, etc.

He has intuitions of truth.

Like Hume, Kames argues for phil. nec.; will is determined by desire; but motives do not destroy responsibility.

Beauty is intrinsic and relative.

(D.) *Adam Smith,* (1723–1790, A. D.) (1) b. in Scotl., ed. at Univ. of Glasgow, a pupil of Hutcheson's; at Oxf.

seven years ; Prof. at Glasg. ; in France (1764–6) ; spent his last years in Edinb.; author of "*Theory of Moral Sentiments*," (1759) ; "*Wealth of Nations*," (1776.) Style, fluent, discursive. (See Stewart's Life.)

(2.) S. develops the "*Ethics of Sympathy*"*;* the objects of moral perc. are, primarily, other men's actions ; if one feel himself affected in the same manner as another is, he approves that other ; secondly, "we suppose ourselves the spectators of our own behavior."

With sense of "propriety," is sense of merit, arising from sympathy with the agent and the recipient of benefits, considering also the tendency of the action to promote happiness.

Hence, the rules of morality originate in society.

2. Reid.

(A.) *Life. Thomas Reid,* b. 1710, near Aberdeen, ed. there, min. of the Kirk, Prof. of Phil. at Aberd. (1752), at Glasgow, (1763), d. 1796. (See Stewart's Life.)

Works : "*Inquiry into the Human Mind on the Principles of Common Sense*," (1764) (chiefly analysis of sensations, against Hume, and Locke's Theory of Ideas.) "*Intellectual and Active Powers of Man*" (1785–8), etc. Rarely profound, or critical, often superficial, Reid's shrewd common sense gave him great power in detecting prevailing errors based on partial inductions.

(B.) *Method,* is induction from facts given in consciousness (its veracity assumed), confirmed by observation of men, their universal language, their common acts. "The whole of phil. consists in discovering the connection between natural signs and the things signified, and reducing them to general laws." (Inq. v. 3.)

R. does not attempt a "*prima phil.;*" neglecting metaphysics, the laws of the human mind and its faculties are to be established from unquestionable facts, from data admitting no question, requiring no criterion.

(C.) *Principle.* Intuitions, self-evident truths, are the basis of higher knowledge; our senses testify to what is, not to what must be. (Int. P. ii. 19, 20.)

The testimony of sense, memory, etc., must be received without questioning their veracity.

Some propositions may be distinctly apprehended, and reason see no necessity of believing; others must be assented to by "common sense." These have no apodeictic proof, but admit *red. ad abs.;* they have the consent of all men. If rejecting an opinion lead to a thousand absurdities, that opinion is a first principle. (Int. P. vi. 4.) (*vid inf.*)

All knowledge obtained by "reason" (*ratiocinatio*) rests on these.

(D.) *Theory of Knowledge.* (1) There are no "*ideas*" (Locke) intermedia between the mind and external objects;

(2) No process of reasoning in conceiving them.

(3) Sensation "suggests" the notion of present existence, by a law of the mind which compels assent.

(4) Memory suggests past existence in the same manner.

(5) Sensation and thought thus testify to the existence of self; change, to a cause; power, to will; touch, to extension, etc., etc.

Mind and body are not known in their essences, but in their powers and operations.

Powers of the mind are (1) intellectual, (2) active; or, (1) natural; (*a*) active = faculties, (*b*) passive = capacities requisite to acquire habits; (2) acquired = habits.

(E.) *Intellectual powers.* (1) Powers by *external senses.* R. distinguishes (*a*) *sensation,* which is only in the sentient mind; our sens. are not images of bodies; they are "signs" of an outer world. (Inq. vi. 21);

(*b*) *Perception;* it has an object which may exist, whether perceived or not. Distinguish (α) original perc., given by "the constitution of our mind;" (β) acquired from custom, of which original perc. are only signs; (γ) perc. gained by inference.

Both primary and secondary qualities belong to external things, and sens. suggests both. (Inq. v. 6; vi. 20.)

Observe that in attention the mind is active.

(2) *Memory,* giving belief of past realities.

(3) *Conception,* apprehension of individuals, or of the meaning of general terms.

R. does not distinguish conc. clearly from imagination; the latter is limited to "pictures of the visible." (Int. P. iv. 1.) Consciousness tells us the difference between perc., imag. and remembrance, therefore they are not one.

(4) Analyzing and *combining;* common terms are

(*a*) attributes, by abstraction;

(*b*) general, for collections of attributes, by generalization (Int. P. v. 3), (conceptualism). Distinguish extension and comprehension in terms. (Int. P. v. 2.) Realities are complex. Simple and distinct notions are gained by abstraction; the most distinct complex ones, by combining these; and others again are necessary for reasoning or language. Brutes have them not. (Int. P. v. 5.)

Space is an empirical notion given in perc. of bodies, not by sens.

Time is given similarly, in memory. (Int. P. iii. 3.)

Eternity is time unlimited; immensity, space undefined.

Notion of *power* is derived from consciousness (relative, a quality,) from our voluntary activity. (Act. P. i. 5.)

(5) *Judgment.* Here distinguish (*a*) *contingent* truths depending upon some effect of will and power, and capable of change; they rest upon some other mental operation, as sense, memory, etc.;

R. gives twelve examples of these; (Int P. vi. 1, 5) *e. g.* existence of what is given in consciousness and of self; the validity of our faculties; power over actions and determinations of will, etc.;

(*b.*) *Necessary* truths, in "pure judgment;" these are (*α*) grammatical; (*β*) logical; (*γ*) mathematical; (*δ*) æsthetical; (*ε*) ethical; (*Z*) metaphysical; (i) substance; (ii) causality, (against Hume); (iii) design, final cause. All these first principles rest upon "common sense."

(6) *Reasoning.*

(7) *Taste,* power of relishing the agreeable, while discerning (judgment) the excellent, is applied to (*a*) novelty; (*b*) grandeur, that degree of excellence which awakens admiration; (*c*) beauty, the agreeable with judgment of perfection or excellence. (Int. P. viii. 4.)

(8) *Moral Sense.* There are intuitive princ. of morals, self-evident, from which, by reasoning, contingent, practical truths are derived.

(9) *Consciousness is* knowledge of the operations of our own minds. R. makes it a special "power," distinguishing it, *e. g.* from remembrance. (Int. P. i. 1, 2.)

Reid considers "social principles" in the original constitution of the mind, for language, (1) truth-telling; (2) belief of others' words;

For nature, the "inductive principle," expectation of the continuance of past experiences.

(F.) *Active powers.* (1) We have no idea of power apart from volition; active power is an "attribute of a being by which he can do certain things if he will." (Act. P. i. 5.)

(2.) *Will,* has reference to our own actions, and to what is believed to be in our power; desire may not so refer, and may oppose will; therefore they are different in kind. Voluntary operations are (*a*) attention, (*b*) deliberation, (*c*) purpose, resolution.

(3.) *Principles of action* are (*a*) *mechanical,* involuntary, (α) instincts; (β) habits;

(*b*) *animal,* voluntary, but without judgment;

(α) *appetites,* periodical, not moral, neither social nor selfish;

(β) *desires,* constant, unlimited, (i) of power; (ii) of esteem; (iii) of knowledge;

(γ) *affections,* having persons for their objects, are (i) benevolent, agreeable feelings, and desire of others' good: *e. g.*, of parents and children, gratitude, compassion, esteem (?), friendship, sexual love, public spirit, social affection;

(ii) Malevolent, emulation and resentment.

Passions may be defined, as vehement desires and affections, sensibly modifying the body, controlling the will and biassing the judgment. (Act. P. iii. ii. 6.)

(*c*) *rational,* determining the ends we pursue;

(α) What is *good for us* upon the whole (enlightened interest);

(β) *duty,* moral obligation, a relation of the agent to the act, determined by "moral sense."

There are self-evident principles on which moral reasoning is grounded, on which particular duties rest. (Act. P. iii. iii. 6.) These are the ground of moral approbation and disapprobation.

(G.) *Ethics.* (1) *Liberty* of a moral agent is "power over determinations of the will," with conc. and judgm. of what is willed as useful or good. On this is based the power to do well or ill, and without this no praise or blame, no accountability.

The *proof* of moral liberty is the consc. that we are efficient causes in our deliberate and voluntary acts; (*a*) natural conviction (consider (α) conscious power, (β) deliberation, (γ) promises, (δ) blame); (*b*) accountability, choosing means (design.)

Rational beings, indeed, are and ought to be *influenced* by motives, but these are not causes, they do not act, (iv. 4).

The law of necessity supposes an inert, inactive being, which, like matter, is only acted upon. To say that because rational beings act from motives, they have not liberty, is to confound the rational with the irrational, (the brute.)

On this is based moral government of those who have power to obey or disobey; criminality supposes not only voluntary action, but moral liberty.

(2.) *Moral principles;* some are intuitive (no complete analysis), *e. g.*, omission may be culpable, obligation to inquire our duty, and to do it, to "do to others, etc."

Justice is a natural virtue, etc. (against Hume, v. 5-7.) Noticeable throughout all Reid's works is his *polemical* attitude.

With Reid may be mentioned,

James Beattie, (1735–1802, A. D.), author of "*The Minstrel*," Prof. at Ab. (1760), who wrote "*Nature and Immutability of Truth*" (against Hume); superficial and popular, not widely differing from Reid.

Geo. Campbell, (1709–1796, A. D.), min. of the Kirk; (1746); Prof. at Ab. (1771), author of "*Dissertation on Miracles*" (against Hume); "*Phil. of Rhetoric*," (1776) recognizing as sources of knowledge, consciousness, intuition, common sense; distinguishing necessary from contingent truths, like Reid.

Adam Ferguson, (1723–1810, A. D.) ed. at St. Andrew's, Prof. at Ed., wrote "*Ess. on Hist. of Civil Soc.*," (1761); "*Moral and Pol. Science*," (1792.)

3. Period of Criticism.

(A.) *Dugald Stewart*, (1) (1753–1828, A.D.), b. at Edin., ed. at the Univ. there, spent a year at Glasgow under Reid; Prof. of Moral Phil. at Edin., (1785), of Moral and Political Science, (1792). His technical skill, elegance of style, and scholarly tastes form a marked contrast with the unpolished simplicity of Reid. He illustrated the doctrines of his master with a wide range of attractive and interesting facts, and exerted a marked influence on many of the most prominent men of the age.

Among his distinguished pupils were Brougham, Palmerston, Russell, Jeffrey, W. Scott, Sydney Smith, Brown, Chalmers, Alison, etc.

Among his voluminous works are, "Elements of the Phil. of the Human Mind," (v. 1, 1792; v. 2, 1814; v. 3, 1827); "Moral Phil.," (1793); "Philos. Essays," (1810); "Act. and Moral Powers," (1828) etc.

(2.) *Method.* Disregarding ontology, "a most idle and absurd speculation," he proposes to "rise slowly from particular facts" given in consciousness, proceeding by strict Baconian induction "to general laws." (El. Phil. i.) Cautious and critical, always turning from metaphysics to the concrete, modern psychologists offer us no more attractive or valuable guide.

(3.) *Theory of knowledge.* The mind for discovery of truth employs various faculties whose authority is indisputable, guided in their exercise by "fundamental laws of belief," "constituent elements of human reason" ("common sense" of Reid); these are (*a*) Math. axioms; (*b*) Laws of belief in consc., mem., and reasoning; these are, in consc., of (*α*) the ego, our existence, an (indirect) "suggestion;" (*β*) of personal identity, similarly given in memory; (*γ*) of the material world, and the uniformity of nature (El. ii. 1.) These being merely laws, no inference from them is possible.

Like Reid and Campbell, S. criticizes the Aristotelian logic; the syllogism is nugatory (cf. Whately); he attempts, (not very successfully), a logic of inference. (El. ii. 3.)

Notions of mind and matter are "relative" merely; we know these only in sensible qualities, which give "irresistible" conviction of self, mind, body.

(4.) *Intellectual Powers.* Classification is based on Reid's, improved.

(*a*) *consciousness*, made a separate faculty, by which we are cognizant of our other mental operations, "suggesting," *à post.*, self; personal identity is an acquired conviction;

(*b*) *perception;*

(*c*) *attention*, made "an act of the mind," the active exertion of the will apparently overlooked;

(*d*) *conception* = "simple apprehension," *i. e.* of absent objects of perception, the representative faculty;

(*e*) *abstraction*. S. places himself with the nominalists; conceptualism is not intelligible; names are originally individual, applied to many on the ground of resemblance, so expressing qualities common to a genus;

(*f*) *association of ideas,—i. e.* of thoughts of all kinds; this, and the resulting power of habit, are discussed at length with admirable illustrations in taste, morals, etc.;

(*g*) *Memory* is spontaneous, recollection voluntary;

(*h*) *Imagination*, (far in advance of Reid,) is the "power of modifying conceptions, combining, etc." (El. i. 3; i. vii. 1); it is a complex of conception, abstraction, judgment, taste and fancy (presenting different materials);

(*i*) *Judgment*.

On the whole div. we must remark an unscientific grouping of powers, laws, exertion of will, etc.; the divisions are plainly not co-ordinate. But varied illustrations, good sense, and scholarly taste, render him none the less interesting and instructive.

(5.) *Active Powers*. Still following Reid, though rejecting the "mechanical," (*a*) appetites; (*b*) desires, (add to Reid's des. of society and of superiority, R.'s "malev. aff.," emulation); (*c*) affections; (*d*) self-love; (*e*) moral faculty. Will is relegated to an App., and not thoroughly examined; duty, obligation implies free-will.

(6.) *Ethics*. S. follows Reid, though with wider research: he makes no attempt to inquire what is "the good," why it is good: but, (*a*) negatively, it is not given in judgments based on utility, nor on positive law; (*b*) there is in the mind a moral faculty which gives, (α) perception of an action as right or wrong, (a quality of action);

(β) accompanying emotion of pleasure or pain;

(γ) perception of merit or demerit.

Duties are carefully examined;

(*a*) To God. His existence is not given intuitively but by two "first principles," *à post.;*

(α) everything which begins to exist has a cause;

(β) combination of means to an end implies intelligence. On this foundation he builds a Nat. Theol., the existence and attributes of God and a future life, with resulting duties. (Moral Phil. ii. 2.)

(*b*) To fellow-creatures; benevolence, justice, veracity;

(*c*) To ourselves.

(7.) *Æsthetics* are considered at length, but, as ethics, in subjective view; the pleasurable leads to our confounding sensuous beauty with pleasures intellectual, in assoc. of ideas, utility, fitness, relations, design, etc. In these he can find no unity. (Phil. Ess. ii. 1.) The term beauty, primarily applicable to the agreeable in objects of sight (color, form, motion,) is transferred to sounds, etc.

Taste is partly nat. sensibility, partly acquired intellectual power, derived by induction from the agreeable.

The pleasure is due to (*a*) organical adaptation of the human frame to the external world; (*b*) associations from experience, (α) common to mankind; (β) custom and fashion, "arbitrary beauties," classical, local, personal.

But S. gives many interesting and valuable observations.

(B) *Dr. Thomas Brown,* (1) (1778–1820, A. D.) studied law and med. at Edin., associate Prof. with Stewart, (1810); his chief works are "Inquiry into the relation of

Cause and Effect," (1818); "Phil. of the Human Mind," (1820); marked by diffuse and ornate style and acute analysis.

(2.) He departs widely from Reid, giving far more value to assoc. and relation.

The mind has original intuitions, "irresistible beliefs" of identity and causation.

Of mind we know nothing but states or feelings which form our momentary consciousness; consc.=the series of states of mind, of feelings; although they give the belief of pers. identity, etc. (Hamilton's Cosmothetic or Hypothetical realism).

These states or feelings are, (*a*) external affections (sensations); "a muscular sense" and touch give belief in an external world.

(*b*) internal affections, are (*α*) intellectual states; (*β*) emotions.

Intellectual states are explained by—

(i) simple suggestions,=associations of resemblance, contrast and contiguity; these will account for conception, mem., imag., habit;

(ii) "relative suggestions," of relations between two objects, which will account for generalization, classification, judgment, reasoning, (from particulars to particulars; cf. Mill's Logic Ind.)

Relations are (*a*) of co-existence; position, resemblance or difference, degree, proportion, comprehension, (whole and parts); (*b*) of succession, causal priority.

Causation. Disregarding the knowledge of power given in conscious volition, B.'s tendency to physical inquiry leads him to resolve the notion of cause into invariable succession (Hume), but he refers it to intuitive belief. (Hamilton, Met. xxxix.)

Volition is permanent and prevailing desire after deliberation.

The *Moral Faculty* is a class of emotions of approbation and disapprob., into whose cause or ground he does not inquire. (cf. Hamilton's Disc.)

(C.) *Sir James Mackintosh,* (1765–1832, A. D.) b. near Inverness, ed. at Aberdeen, in the midst of his active political and literary life, found time for philos. thought. In ethics he follows Brown and Hartley; conscience is explained as a class of feelings guided by assoc., having authority from the element of voluntary dispositions and desires; the common quality in their objects causing approbation, is beneficial tendency.

(D.) *Sir William Hamilton,* (1) (1791–1856, A. D.) b. at Glasgow, ed. at Univ. there and at Baliol Coll., Oxf.; soon distinguished for varied and profound learning; in 1811, advocate at Edin.; Prof. of Univ. Hist. there, (1821); later, Prof. of Logic and Met. (1836). In 1852 were collected his "Discussions;" in 1856, appeared his ed. of Reid, with notes and extended App.; his Lect. on Met. (chiefly cognition, little on the Feelings, "conation" nearly a blank) and on Logic were pub. (1858) by Mansel and Veitch. (see Mill's "Exam. of Sir Wm. H.'s Phil.")

His vast learning, and deep and logical analysis of previous views, his scientific method in division and def., suggest Aristotle (note his study of A.) and S. Thom. Aq., though his works give us but a fragment of a completed system. Based on Reid, his phil. shows a marked influence from Kant, (but cf. H.'s Reid; Note A, § vi. 86).

(2.) *Principle.* Phil. is "the science of mind"= psych. Met. The primary data of consc. are to be [illegible] they are (a) incomprehensible.

(" that it is," not "why it is;") (*b*) simple, (*c*) necessary and universal; (*d*) certain. He calls himself a "natural realist," or, "natural dualist." (See his div. of phil.)

(3.) *Theory of knowledge. Divisions of Phil.* are (*a*) Phil. of Facts, (empirical Psych.), (α) cognitions, (β) feelings, (γ) conative powers, (will and desire);

(*b*) Phil. of Laws, (rational Psych.), (α) logic (of cognitions); (β) æsthetics, (of feelings); (γ) Moral Phil., Political Phil.;

(*c*) Phil. of Results, Ontology.

Mind is a common name for states of knowing, seeing, feeling, etc., which the thinking subject recognizes: (consc. no "faculty;" there may be latent mental modifications): an unknown substance is an inference. So also matter. Knowledge, then, is "relative."

Relativity of knowledge. (*a*) Existence is not cognizable *in se* (ding an sich), but in special modes;

(*b*) these modes are known only to our own faculties;

(*c*) and under modifications determined by the mind itself (sense or intelligence). (Met. viii.)

Theory of the Conditioned. The Absolute and the Infinite are a negation of the thinkable; (read letter to Calderwood, App. to Met.) "Positive thought lies in the limitation or conditioning of one or other of two opposite extremes, neither of which as unconditioned can be realized to the mind as possible; and yet, of which, as contradictions, one or the other must, by the fundamental laws of thought, be recognized as necessary;" (Reid, note A § 1. n.) *e. g.*, space finite and inf., time, etc. To think = to condition, (to think as limited or related.)

The sphere of our beliefs, however, is more extensive than the sphere of our knowledge.

The *non-ego* is not only conceived, but directly perceived as external, but only as existing in relation to self.

(4) *Cognitive Powers:* (*a*) *Presentative,* (α) external, *sc.* perception of *non-ego* under the form of space;

(β) internal, *sc.* self-consciousness, of spirit under the forms of time and self. This power is intuitive, immediate, (natural realism.) Distinguish sens. which belongs to the feelings, subjective; as perc. to knowledge, objective; they are co-existent, but their energies in inverse ratio.

Perception is of what is present to the subject; of distant objects it is not immediate.

Primary qualities of matter are attributes of body as body, and may be deduced *à priori* from the notion of substance (*a*) as occupying space (extension); (α) divisibility, (β) size, (γ) figure, (δ) incompressibility; (*b*) as contained in space; (α) mobility, (β) situation.

Secundo-primary qualities are given by induction, *à post., sc.* attraction, repulsion, inertia (accidents).

Secondary are known as subjective affections, color, etc.

(*b*) *Conservative,* memory, acting out of consciousness.

(*c*) *Reproductive,* (α) suggestion, (involuntary); (β) reminiscence (voluntary): (α) is thought suggesting thought under the laws of assoc., "simultaneity" and affinity. The one law of "redintegration" will explain all the phenom. "Those thoughts suggest each other which were parts of one "entire act of cognition." (Met. xxxi. xxxii.)

(*d*) *Representative,* imagination; distinguish concepts from images; (Begriffe, anschauungen.) Imag. (popularly) adds to this comparison, etc. (H. makes little of creative imagination.)

(*e*) *Elaborative,* the faculty of relations, comparison,=

conception or simple apprehension, judgment, reasoning, (Met. xxxiv. See also Logic.)

In (*a*) is contained the *ego* and *non-ego*, a primary, native notion of existence, awakened in the first act of experience; here is duality; then follows plurality of phenom. with resemblance and difference; next, as conditions of thought, substance and causality; by act of will abstraction is made of common properties; then follow general notions, under which plurality is recognized as unity; so far as objects resemble, they are, relatively, the same.

Distinguish extension and comprehension of general terms.

(*e*) is, next, the discursive faculty in its two processes of deduction and induction from judgments.

(*f*) *Regulative*, reason, common sense, cognizing laws by which the mind is governed in its operations. ("Phil. of the conditioned," in H.'s opinion, his most important contribution to phil.)

He adds to laws of identity, contradiction, and excluded middle, the law of reason and consequent (logical, L. vi.), the principle of the *conditioned.* This is applied as (*α*) princ. of cause and effect; (*β*) of subst. and phenom.

Causality. "All that is now seen to exist has previously an existence under a prior form;" effect previously existed in its causes, it is "the sum of all the partial concurring causes." The mind is unable to think commencing existence. That there is a cause is a judgment from "impotence of the mind;" causation = mutation. (Met. xxxix.) Similar are the notions of God and free will, nec. beliefs beyond the sphere of knowledge. (App. to Met., and Mill's Ex.) Moral liberty is inconceivable, because we can only conceive the determined, the relative, ("phil. of the cond.")

(5.) *Logic*, (*vid. sup. e.*) is an *à priori* science; the laws of thought as thought, (cf. Thomson's Laws of Thought). Distinguish immediate inferences without a middle term. H. attempts an extension of the sphere of the science by "quantification of the predicate." He fails to analyze the laws of induction, only recognizing purely logical ind.

(6.) *Feelings*, (*a*) pleasurable, accompanying the unrestrained energy of any mental power, *e. g.* sensation; (*b*) painful, from excessive or restrained energy. "Pleasures of the imag." are accounted for in the same way; order and symmetry facilitate the acts of reproduction and represent.: hence variety with unity is called beautiful, as giving free play to mental energy (Met. xlv.), the understanding judging the whole to have unity.

Of Hamilton's school may be mentioned:

(E.) *Henry Longueville Mansel*, (1820–1871, A.D.) fellow of St. John's Coll., Oxf., Prof. of Eccles. Hist., Dean of S. Paul's, author of "*Prol. Logica*," "Limits of Rel. thought," (Bampton Lect. 1858), "Metaphysics," (1860), etc., who adopts the "phil. of the conditioned," although he maintains an immediate knowledge of the *ego*, and rejects Hamilton's explanations of causality. (cf. Calderwood, "Phil. of the Inf.," McCosh, "Intuitions, etc." See notes to "Limits, etc." against German "phil. of the Absolute.")

(F.) *James Frederick Ferrier*, (1808–1864, A.D.) b. in Edin., ed. Edin. and Oxf., Prof. of Hist. Edin., of Moral Phil., St. Andrew's; pub. "Institutes of Metaphysics" (1854,) in bold re-action from the psychological school.

Few Eng. met. have so clear and lively style, remarkable equally for vigor and precision.

Absolute existence is the synthesis of obj. + subj., the *ego* + the *non-ego* = *substance*. Matter *per se* cannot be known at all; nor can the ego. The particular (*e. g.* sens. exp.) is only known with the general, and conversely; and every cognition, and therefore every concept, must contain these two elements.

CHAPTER XV.

GERMAN CRITICAL AND IDEAL PHILOSOPHY.

1. KANT. 2. FICHTE. 3, SCHELLING. 4. HEGEL. 5. OPPONENTS OF PURE IDEALISM.

1. KANT.

Kant's influence has been so great, second only, if second, to Aristotle's, that references must include the great majority of subsequent writers on spec. phil. or its hist. But see, as most accessible, Cousin, Ueberweg, Morell, McCosh's thorough criticism in "Intuitions etc.," and, as illustrating K.'s influence on Eng. thought, Carlyle, Misc. Ess. v. I; De Quincey, Biog. Ess., Ch. Qly Rev., Oct., 1875.

(A) *Life. Immanuel Kant*, of Scotch descent, b. at Königsberg (1724), ed. and taught there; Prof. of phil. at the Univ. there (1770–1797). He took a lively interest in the political questions of the day; a liberalist. His "Religion within the limits of Pure Reason" (1794) incurred a prohibition from King Wm. II. At the King's death he published "Strife of the Faculties;" his uneventful, retired life gradually became the centre of an ever widening circle of disciples, but he declined all invitations to leave his philosophical seclusion at K. He died in 1704.

Of chief import among his *works* are:

(1) "Critique of Pure Reason" (1781);

(2) "Critique of Practical Reason" (1787);

(3) "Critique of the Judgment" (1790).

(B) *Object and Method.* Empiricism had terminated in the skepticism of Hume, or in a materialism which was equally the negation of phil. Rationalism had produced pantheism, or empty hypotheses. It was necessary to inaugurate a "criticism" of the human faculties, in order to ascertain if phil. were possible, and, if so, what its limits were. K.'s process is equally independent of the historical development of phil., and of christian Rev.

It is certain that all knowledge *begins* with experience; but whence is that knowledge derived? It is necessary to analyze cognitions, to determine critically the functions and the limits of human faculties, and so to secure right use of the "organon" for. phil. (Pref. 1st and 2nd eds. Crit. P. R.)

(C) *Principle,* a dualism of realism and idealism, "transcendental idealism."

(1) Empirical intuitions, valid in their sphere, supply *all* the materials of knowledge, (contingent, variable); the forms of thought are supplied by the mind itself; their criteria are universality and necessity.

(2) "Things in themselves," though as such they are unknown, affect an internal sensibility, and then are known, but only as conformed to the laws of our own mind.

Reason impels us to think the *unconditioned* (transcendent), but it cannot be thought without contradiction.

Synthetic judgm., *à pr.,* furnish a ground of certitude, as in Logic and Math.

Before proceeding to the Crit. of the Mental faculties, a word may be needed of Kant's

(D) *Terminology*. (1) *Cognitions* are (*a*) intuitions, (*b*) conceptions.

(*a*) are singular, individ., immed., of phenom. ;

(*b*) are free from all emp. elements (concepts, notions), from understanding alone.

(2) *Ideas* are nec. concepts of reason for which no real object is found in the sphere of the senses.

(3) *A priori* knowledge is that which is independent of all experience (cf. Arist.) ; *à post.* has its source in exp.

(4) *Analytic* propositions or judgments are amplifications of the identical, giving, *e. g.*, one or more elements of the subject in the pred.

In *Synthetic* prop. and judgm. the pred. adds to the subj.

(5) *Transcendental* knowledge is the knowing how cognitions are applied *à pr.;* (transcendental in *passing over* from intuitions to concepts. K. fails to harmonize these,) *transcendent* is that which is beyond all possible experience, though reason may find it necessary to be assumed, (unconditioned, absolute).

(6) Before *criticism,* it is necessary to observe that in the mind are three faculties ;

(*a*) *Sensibility,* a passive receptivity ; the mind is affected by phenom., possesses intuitions ;

(*b*) *Understanding*, (Verstand) an active spontaneity, judging of phenom., of experience ; the faculty of conception by means of intuition ;

(*c*) *Reason,* (Vernunft) which gives unity to the variety of concepts, reduces particulars to the general, and deduces the part. from the general, (ratiocination). Understanding gives rules ; reason gives principles.

(E) *Judgments* are (1) *à priori,* from the mind itself, universal, necessary ;

(2) *A posteriori*, from experience, particular, contingent. They are also

(1) *Analytic*, explicatory; (*e. g.*, the whole = the sum of all its parts); resting on the principles of identity and contradiction;

(2) *Synthetic*, augmentative, adding to the concept of the subject. These are

(*a*) *A post.*, from experience, (*e. g.*, gold is ductile);

(*b*) *A priori*, univ. and nec., found in math. and physics; (*e. g.*, a line is the shortest distance between two points).

Some are, (*a*) *pure*, absolutely independent of experience;

(*b*) *relatively* pure, concepts deduced indirectly from exp.

How are synth. judgments *à pr.* possible? Ans.; the matter is given in exp., a synthesis of perceptions, not things in themselves, but phenom. existing in consciousness; the pure form comes from the mind. This is the condition of all experience, which the *ego*, the "transc. synthesis of apperception," supplies. Abstract the thinking subject, and all phenom., all qualities, all relations of objects disappear.

(F) *Transcendental Æsthetic.* The essential forms of sensibility, separating what the understanding thinks, isolating sensib., then separating sensation, are,

(1). *Space*, for external sensib., the co-existence of intuitions; hence the possibility of geometric judgments;

(2) *Time*, for internal sensib., succession in phenom. These are the formal conditions *à pr.* of all phenom. Transc. objects are related neither to space nor time. Magnitude, extension, duration, are thus in the subject, the mind; they are limitations of our knowledge of things.

(G) *Understanding.* Its essential function is judgment.

reducing the plurality of intuitions to the unity of the concept, in the unity of apperception. Judgments are rendered possible by the *categories*, pure, *à pr.*, concepts of the understanding, not applicable to things in themselves, but to phenom. in our consciousness ; for understanding is limited to the finite and conditioned. In the categ. is nothing known, for thoughts without percepts are void of meaning, (cognition = intuit.+concept). Abstracting all contents of judgments we find twelve forms of judgments under four heads :

(1.) Quantity.	(2.) Quality.	(3.) Relation.	(4.) Modality.
(*a*) universal.	(*a*) affirmative.	(*a*) categorical.	(*a*) problematical.
(*b*) particular.	(*b*) negative.	(*b*) hypothetical.	(*b*) assertory.
(*c*) singular.	(*c*) infinite.	(*c*) disjunctive.	(*c*) apodeictic.

In the same manner, taking the synthesis of representations which the imag. provides, the understanding gives unity to this pure synthesis, by the concept, the third requisite for the cognition of an object. Pure concepts, applicable to objects, *à pr.*, are the *Twelve Categories.*

(1.) Quantity.	(2) Quality.	(3) Relation.	(4) Modality.
(*a*) unity.	(*a*) reality.	(*a*) inherence, substance.	(*a*) possibility ana imp.
(*b*) plurality.	(*b*) negation.	(*b*) causality.	(*b*) existence, non-ex.
(*c*) totality.	(*c*) limitation.	(*c*) reciprocity.	(*c*) necessity, contingence.

(cf. Hamilton's Disc.)

In order to apply pure concepts of the understanding to empirical intuitions a "*schema*" is needed ; the transc. determination of time serves this purpose. The schema is a product of the imag., but distinct from an image.

The schema of (1) quant. is number; of (2) qual., in reality, time filled; in negation, vacuum in time; in limitation, transition in time; of (3) relation, in substance, permanence in time; in causality, succession; in reciprocity, co-existence; of (4) modality, in possibility, existence at *any* time; in reality, existence in determined time; in necessity, existence at all times.

The *Principle* of judgments, (1) analytical, is contradiction;

(2) Synthetical, of pure understanding,

(*a*) axioms of intuition, "all intuitions are extensive quantities;"

(*b*) anticipations of perception, "in all phenom. the real has intensity," *i. e.*, degree;

(*c*) analogies of exp.; "it is possible only through the representation of a necessary connection of perceptions;" (α) permanence of substance;

(β) all change according to law of cause and effect;

(γ) all substances in space at the same time exist in reciprocity.

(*d*) postulates of empirical thought;

(α) that which agrees with formal conditions of exp. is possible;

(β) that which coheres with the material conditions is real;

(γ) that whose coherence is determined according to univ. conditions of exp. is necessary.

(H) *Reason.* (1). We must dist. phenom. from *noumenon*, negatively, the latter means a thing so far as it is not an obj. of our sens. int. (ding-an-sich); but intellectual int. of noumena is a faculty not possessed by man. But reason, the principle of *à pr.* knowledge, strives to rise to the noum., the unconditioned; and by a "transc. illusion" we convert its regulative princ. into objective realities, as if they were constitutive. ("Transc. dialectic.")

The proper function of reason is only to give unity to our conceptions, to regulate the understanding; beyond that it is powerless. For this purpose it uses the three forms of syllogism (logical reason, faculty of mediate judgment), categorical, hypothetical, disjunctive. By these it attains—

(2) *Ideas*, necessary concepts of reason for which no real object is found in the sphere of sense:

(*a*) by the categ. syll., as resting on the categ. (3. *a.*) of absolute subj., soul, the psychological idea; (*b*) by the hyp. syll. (categ. 3. *b.*), absolute connection of parts in a whole, the world, the cosmological idea; (*c*) by the disj. syll. (categ. 3. *c*) absolute union of all realities or perfections, GOD, the theological idea.

These ideas have no objective validity, being produced by reason according to its own laws; as noumena they serve as regulative princ. We have indeed no right to assert their non-existence (objective); on the contrary they give conceivable suppositions, possibilities of objective reality which practical reason renders nec. By dialectical (sophistical) inferences, they are converted into constitutive princ. Let us examine more closely;

(*a*) *Ego*, which is conceived only as subject, is thus made objective; *sc.*, "I am a thinking substance, simple, immortal, etc.," which is a synthetic judgment, and an illusion; proofs which are pure paralogisms, the intuitions of experience in consc., under the forms of time and space, having been, by the understanding, under the forms of its categories, embraced in the unity of the concept, are, by illusion of the reason, regarded as transcendent objects of cognition. Hence rational psychology, whether in the form of spiritualism or materialism, involves contradictions —is impossible.

(*b*) In the intuitions of *nature*, the same process, the same illusion. In attempting to regard the world as real in a transc. sense, arise four *antinomies* :

(*α*) The world has a beginning in time, a limit in space : Antithesis ; The world is infinite in time and space :

(*β*) Every composite substance consists of simple parts : Antith. ; There is not in the world any simple substance :

(*γ*) A free causality is necessary to account for phenom. : Antith. ; Everything in the world happens according to nat.'s laws :

(*δ*) Absolutely necessary being is either a part or a cause of the world : Antith. ; Abs. nec. being does not exist.

The proofs of each of these are unanswerable, but each regards the transcendent, and becomes meaningless when we regard intuitions of exp. as the limit of cognition.

(*c*) *Ens realissimum*, the ideal of pure reason, is made an object, hypostatized, personified.

(*α*)The *ontological* arg. for GOD's existence is a paralogism : in the prop. " GOD is," we substitute a synth. for an anal. judgm. (cf. Anselm and refut.)

(*β*) The *cosmological* arg. of nat. theol., from contingent to nec. being, when analyzed proves to be the ontological with additional paralogisms ; *e. g.*, the contingent must have a cause.

(*γ*) The "physico-theol. arg." has authority, deserves respect, but is not scientific. If the Supreme Being is a link in an empirical chain, then a member of it ; if not, how to bridge the abyss ? At most, this arg. might lead to an architect, of limited power, not to a creator, of absolute power. These three ideas of reason, then, are *regulative ;* our thought is conditioned, we are compelled to think as if (*a*) a simple substance, the ground of personal. id., exists;

(*b*) the world must be considered as a totality;

(*c*) we must view the content of all concepts as if a perfect, etc. Being made and orders the Universe.

But the language of a firmly rooted faith is permissible in the presence of reason, even where knowledge has been renounced.

(I) *Critique of the Practical Reason.* Here also proceed as with spec. reason, and distinguish the material, empirical, *à post.*, from the formal, rational, *à priori.* Nature and freedom, inclination and duty, are opposites. The former is directed to emp. ends, to personal happiness; it opposes morality; the matter of desire is indeed the concrete object of the will, but

(1) *Moral law* is distinguished by its universality; principles by virtue of their form, are universal; and consciousness attests the "autonomy" of the will, as free to be determined by the power of univ. law; while the material element is purely subjective and grounded in self love.

Hence, the highest law of morality is, "act so that the maxim on which thou actest would admit of being adopted as a law by all rational beings."

Actions are moral, not by reason of the good sought for, not by reason of the pleasurable, or outward law, but only through the form of *obligation*, law fulfilled for the sake of the law. The subjective motive in the moral is not inclination, not even the love of God; it is pure regard for the law given in reason (not empirically, but a simple fact of pure reason, to man, as also a sensuous being, in the form of the "Categorical Imperative;" (self-interest is the hypothetical imp.).

The aim of the will, the sum. bon., is virtue as the conditioning, happiness as the conditioned. The concept has these two elements nec. and inseparable.

(2) *Postulates of pure practical reason* are

(*a*) *Moral freedom*, from the natural law of causality; this is contained in the concept of the will's "autonomy," without which no morality;

(*b*) *immortality of personal existence;* for the moral idea involves an endless progression;

(*c*) GOD as moral ruler of nature, and reconciler of it with reason, giving that harmony to happiness and morality which nature does not provide. This postulate also nec. to morality. These postulates are given by practical reason, not as cognitions, not in the relations of phenom. and noum., but as realities serving practical ends. Rational faith is a necessity of man's nature.

Legal duty and right, though, like the moral, taking their form from pr. R., have reference only to the outward act. Right is the "collection of the limitations, under which the free will of one can accord with the free will of every other under the univ. law of freedom."

Legal duties being outward, are compulsory; and this postulates the state with power to that end, a union of men under civil laws made by their united will. In this they are sovereign; the executive acts in the name of the people; the judicial power is in the hands of their chosen representatives.

Religion is the moral in its relation to GOD as the lawgiver; a need of pract. reason; it is not the source, but the result of the moral. The Son of GOD is the ideal of man.

(K) *Critique of the judgment.* By this the particular is conceived as contained under the universal;

(1) The univ. (rule, principle, law) given, the faculty of judgm. is determinative, "subsuming" the particular.

(2) The part. given, in order to find the univ., it is reflective; (this the subject of the "critique";) (1 & 2) belong to the understanding; but in (2) theor. and practical reason find a connection.

The univ. laws of nat. have their ground in our understanding; the particular are empirical, contingent; the latter assume the former as given by some intelligence, (not ours); for the reflective understanding needs an *à pr.* principle, the concept of final cause, giving unity to the emp. laws when the univ. law does not determine them, a regulative principle.

Thus, in thought, the uniformity of nat. becomes compatible with ends sought by free intelligence.

The two-fold moment in the concept of final cause, is

(1) subjective, formal, *æsthetic* judgment of the harmony of the form of the object, with the faculty of intuition, which excites a feeling of pleasure and satisfaction, disinterested, univ., nec., (the beautiful; cf. Schiller, and distinguish the agreeable, sensuously pleasurable).

The *sublime* awakens the idea of the infinite, and pleases through the contrast between the thought and the merely sensuous.

(2) *Teleological judgment,* (objective or material), considering nat. in the light of adaptations, the agreement of the form with a given concept of an end;

(*a*) external, the relation of one thing to another, the mechanism of nat.;

(*b*) internal, in organic products, the parts, ends, and means reciprocally for one another.

Art is free production ; fine art, the art of genius, the work of human freedom delighting in the beautiful.

In teleology we ascribe obj. causality to concepts, borrowing for nat. phil. a causality from the analogy of ourselves. But our reason has no power to unite the mechanical relations of nat. with its final causes ; both mechanical laws and ends, are regulative princ. of thought, the result of the constitution of our understanding.

(L) Among the numerous followers of Kant, most prominent are

(1) *Reinhold,* (1758–1823, A. D.) prof. at Jena, which became a centre for Kant's phil. ; he wrote " Letters on Kant's Phil.," and " New Theory of Human Thought :"

(2) *Beck,* (1761--1842, A. D.) ; in his "Princ. of the Crit. Phil." he endeavored to dispense with Kant's Ding-an-sich, leading to "subjective idealism," which found its chief defender in Fichte.

2. Fichte.

(A) *Johann Gottlieb Fichte*. (1762--1814, A. D.) b. in Lusatia, his life a remarkable contrast to the calm unvaried career of Kant. Of humble parentage, a most precocious child, meditative, imaginative, sensitive, he attracted the attention of influential friends, through whose means he was educated. He studied theol. at Jena (1780), was private tutor in Switz. At first Spinozist, he embraced Kant's phil. with great enthusiasm, and sought his acquaintance with his "Critique of all revelation," (1791). He succeeded Reinhold at Jena (1794), and made known his doctrine of science ; but, incurring the charge of atheism, retired to Prussia (1799), lecturing at Berlin before a numerous circle of educated men. In 1809, he was prof. at the univ. there; but in 1813, dismissing his students, he enlisted with the volunteers; he died of a fever the next year.

His numerous *works* are marked by energy, eloquence, and a vigorous logic; most prominent may be mentioned, those on the "Wissenschaftslehre," "On the Destination of the Scholar," "On the Dest. of Man," "The Sun-clear Statement" of the latest phil.; "The Way to the Blessed Life," etc.

(B) Science demands a rigid *method*, assuming nothing beyond its first principle. Scientific truth must have self-evident basis, and proceed by demonstration. Kant fails to harmonize phenom. and noum., subj. and obj.; he takes for granted the obj. reality of sense-intuition, but there is no logical nec. of assuming the Ding-an-Sich.

(C) The first *principle* is the *ego*, given with absolute certainty in consciousness (subjective idealism); its representations are unquestionable; their verification can be only other repres.; we cannot transcend our own thought. "Thou art thyself the Ding-an-Sich—all that thou seest without thee, thou art ever thyself; in all consc. thou beholdest thyself.—Consc. is an active *hinschauen* of that which thou gazest at (anschauest), an *herausschauen* of thee without thyself." (Best. d. Menschen.)

The ego is absolute, infinite. But it is active, and becomes conscious of itself as both agent and product of its activity.

(1) *Thesis.* The ego posits itself, and exists in and through this act; being = thought; existence = consc. This primitive act of the mind is the principle of identity,

A = A; ego = ego; obj. and subj. are identified. This gives the categ. of reality.

(2.) *Antithesis.* While the absolute ego seeks to posit itself, it finds in itself a barrier, an opposition, (Anstoss) and is obliged to posit a non-ego, without which it cannot be self-conscious: not-A is not = A; non-ego is not = ego; the categ. of negation, the second condition of thought = existence.

(3.) *Synthesis,* the ego opposes to the divisible ego, a divisible non-ego; the categ. of limitation.

(*a.*) Theoretical, the ego posits itself as conditioned by the non-ego.

(*b.*) Practical, the ego posits the non-ego as condit. by the ego.

The "inexplicable absolute limitations" we objectify and call matter. Substance is a mental synthesis of accidents.

(D.) The problem of *theoretical* science is to explain the phenom. of the mind's activity, *i. e.*, relations of subj. to self-affirmed object. (1) So far as the ego posits itself as conditioned and determined by the non-ego, so far is it *intelligence.* Sensation = ego, produces this limitation of its own activity; understanding = power of fixing a sensation.

(2) So far as the ego posits the non-ego as conditioned and determined by the ego, so far is it *will* acting freely.

Reason = ego, is raised above all limitations in its free producing power.

(E.) *Practical science* (cf. Kant) concerns itself both with *rights* and *morals,* on the basis of ext. and int. freedom.

(1) The abs. ego while determined by the non-ego, is

also obliged to posit a plurality of det. egos. As det. it posits itself one of many; its own freedom involves the freedom of others, and these limit one another. The right is the sum of these limitations; "thou must limit thine ext. freedom in such manner and measure that thou with others, and others with thee, can make a community."

(2) The ego strives endlessly after self-development, freedom from the limitations of the non-ego. This is the essence of morality.

The moral order of the world is the result of the activity of the will in thus freeing itself from the determination of the finite. This is the Divine; what we name GOD is this moral order of the world.

To seek for this we need *faith* in this moral order, in the reality of ego and the outer world; but this faith is a resolve of the will.

Fichte, in his later works, inclined to abs. idealism, (cf. Schelling) a theory of identity; the ego and non-ego are equally real, but identical = the absolute, the subj.-obj., = GOD, who ever reveals Himself in and through human consciousness. (Note Fichte's five eras of history, and see Coleridge, Biog. Lit. c. viii; Carlyle's Hero-Worship, Lect. v.)

3. SCHELLING.

Fichte's spec. phil. tended to nihilism (Hamilton's Reid, i., p. 129). He had argued from the subjective, *ego*, to the objective, the former producing the latter; why is it not equally valid to proceed otherwise, the objective producing the consc. ego; laws of consc. = laws of nature?

(A.) *Fr. Wm. Joseph von Schelling*, b. in Würtemberg (1775), ed. at Tübingen, Leipzic, pupil of Fichte at

Jena, succeeded him there (1798); member of Acad. Sc., Munich (1807–1842); Prof. at Berlin, opposed by the Hegelians, soon retired to Switz., d. 1854.

(B.) The reality of nature is to be re-established against subj. idealism, by a phil. of nature (obj. idealism). Proceeding subjectively we obtain a transcendental idealism; but both are limited and rest on a higher principle, the absolute as the identity of subj. and obj., given in immediate intuition of abs. existence (Sein), (phil. of identity). Schelling himself did not lay down and adhere to an exclusive system; his imaginative genius maintained a continuous progress, in which three distinct periods appear; (1) Phil. of identity; (2) of Neo-Platonic intuition (Plotinus); (3) of theosophic mysticism (Böhme, Gnosticism).

(C.) *Philosophy of Identity.* ("Phil. of Nature," 1797; "System of Transc. Idealism," 1800; "Zeitschrift für spec. Physik," 1801, etc.)

(1) A valid *method* must be pure *à priori,* grounded on immediate intell., intuition of the Abs.; this alone gives an absolute science in which all things, secondarily, are known in their eternal ideas.

(2) *Principle.* The subj. or ideal, and the obj. or real, are only two poles of the same abs., which reciprocally posit and manifest one another; they are the differentiated revelation of one and the same intelligence, their only substance. All knowledge rests on the harmony of these two; hence, two fundamental sciences;

(*a.*) Of *nature*, "spec. physik," how the ideal originates from the real. "How does the subj. arise from the obj., spirit from nature?"

(*b.*) *Transcendental;* one assumes the subj., and inquires, "how an obj. arises from it, nature from mind?"

(*a.*) Dead nature is a crude intelligence reaching towards self-consc., which in its highest and last reflection is man, or universal reason, whereby nat. has wholly turned back on itself and its identity with intell. and consc. is established.

(*b.*) (*α*) *Theoretical.* Matter is mind viewing itself making itself obj. ; *e. g.*, sens. is mind's activity producing a distinct image ; in reflection mind contemplates the process of its own productions : self-consc. produces thus the concept (Begriff).

(*β*) *Practical.* The ego, self-consc., freely produces a kingdom of freedom, the moral order, the order of rights in the State.

(*γ*) *Phil. of Art,* is founded on the unity of the real and the ideal; its task is the bringing before intuition the identity of the conscious and the unconscious. In the teleology of nature the ego beholds this identity externally ; in art, in the ego itself. The ego is thus at once consc. and unconsc. in this free production. These two activities are represented as united in the product : the Inf., finitely represented, = beauty. This is the norm of nat. beauty.

(3.) *Identity.* S. seeks a principle on which to found the duplicity of the ego and non-ego, of spirit and nature This princ. is the absolute, in which they are identified ; knowledge = being ; abs. ideal = abs real ; abs. = ego = inf. all = mind. It is manifest in the forms of ego and non-ego, which are relative concepts.

(*a.*) *God* is the absolute indifference of contraries ; the unity of being and thought, of subj. and obj., of ideal and real ; this is the potentiality of the actual from which the two opposites differentiate themselves without losing their unity in the absolute.

(*b.*) In *nature*, the Abs. diff. its own essence as form, making the subjective objective.

(*c.*) In the world of *spirit*, the Abs. "subsumes" the form into its own essence, the objective becoming subjective. These are only separated in concept. The difference is only quantitative; the whole abs. ident. being in the one in the form of reality, in the other, of ideality. In nature the Inf. veils itself in the finite; in the ideal is a regress to the Inf. The Abs., reflected in being, is the eternal body; in thought, the eternal soul of the world.

Distinguish, then, in knowledge and being, two poles and an indifference,

The Three Potencies ("Potenzen");

(*a.*) expansive, progress outward, reflective, the inf. becoming finite;

(*b.*) attractive, regress inward, "subsumption," the effort of the abs. in the finite to return to the Inf.;

(*c*) Indifference, potency of reason, blending of (*a*) and (*b*).

In *Nature* (obj., real): (*a*) matter, (*b*) dynamics, (*c*) organic union;

In (*a*) (α) expansion, (β) attraction, (γ) gravity;

In (*b*) (α) magnetism, (β) electricity, (γ) galvanism;

In (*c*) (α) reproduction, (β) irritability, (γ) sensibility.

In *Mind* (subj., ideal): (*a*) knowledge, (*b*) action, (*c*) reason;

In (*a*) (α) feeling, (β) reflection, (γ) freedom;

In (*b*) (α) individuality, (β) the state, (γ) history;

In (*c*) art. (See Morell).

Finite things then differ only relatively; in the abs. all are identical (Pantheistic idealism).

The *soul* is the ideal of the body, finite relatively to it, inf. as one with the Abs. *Morality* is grounded in that free life in which the soul exalts itself by immed. intuit. of the Abs., which lives in us and we in it.

The *state* is not a work of chance or free choice; it is a special manifestation of the Abs., a harmony of univ. necessity with the freedom of the individual, a moral organism.

(D) *Second* (*Neo-plat.*) *Period.* ("Phil. and Rev.," 1804, etc.). The Abs. is pure ideality, eternally intuiting itself; it renders this ideal real; this reality is its form, its image, to which it gives power to change its own ideality into objective forms, *ideas*. How then to pass to the finite? There is a gap, only conceivable as a falling off, through the freedom (selbstständigkeit) of the ideas. But ideas can beget only the images, unreal, the ruins of the higher ideal world.

This is the case with the human soul, not as it is in itself, but so far as it is related to the sensible world, and this is its individuality; and thus the soul may, in its freedom, turn to the abs., or set its limited ego against the univ. and inf. In the former case it raises itself, by immediate intellectual intuit., to the absolute; this is its true freedom, its true morality.

Immortality of the soul is not ever-enduring individuality; it is a turning back and reconciliation with its source. This at length accomplished in all souls, and the sense-world lost in the ideal, difference will terminate in identity, the union of the real and ideal.

The eternal Son of GOD is the finite itself as it exists in the et. intuit. of GOD, manifested as a GOD suffering and subjected to the fatalities of time. The Incarnation is an eternal fact.

(E) *Third, Theosophic Period.* ("Nat. of Human Freedom," 1809). The princ. of imm. intell. intuit. of the Abs. was by S. finally developed under the influence of Böhme and St. Martin. He seeks to construct a cosmogony which is also a theogony, based on the "self-realization" of GOD in the process of creation of the world.

Existence = will. In GOD are three momenta:

(1) Indifference, the primordial basis, incomprehensible, of His reality.

(2) Duplication of this indiff., as cause and existence, nature, blind, unconscious, and intelligence, the Word. His actuality is thus conditioned; the primordial basis is differentiated as two eternal contradictories.

(3) The reconciliation of these, as Love, Spirit.

To this theogony corresponds the development of the world: from the illumination of dark, unconscious matter by thought, of the real by the ideal, originates the world. Thus GOD reaches perfect actuality. Man is the consummation of nature; in him GOD is manifested as spirit, *i. e.*, as become actual. But in him the two principles are separable, and the particular will can oppose the universal will; hence the possibility of good and evil. Man at present is subject to necessity, having made himself what he is, in an "intelligible act before time."

GOD is at once transcendent and immanent with respect to the world. "Positive phil." begins with GOD to prove the divinity of the existent. In "the unpremeditating, blindly necessitated being" of GOD are three potencies:

(*a*) Unconscious will, *causa materialis*. (Nature in GOD.)

(*b*) Conscious will, *causa efficiens*, the Word, the Light, in GOD.

(*c*) The unity of both, *causa finalis*, "secundum quam omnia fiant."

To examine how S. pantheistically developes his theogony, applies it to the dogma of the Trinity, and derives the principle of evil from the concept of God, would detain us too long. We need only add that S., as Fichte, distinguishes a Petrine christianity, a Pauline, and a "church of the Future," Johannean.

S. is the head of a numerous school. (Here note the relations of idealism to art, politics, lit., morals, etc.)

4. Hegel.

[See Ueberweg; Morell; Sterling's "Secret of Hegel," 1865.]

(A) *Geo. Wm. Frederick Hegel*, b. (1770) at Stuttgart, ed. at Tübingen, tutor at Berne and Jena, then prof. at the latter place; ed. "Crit. Journal Phil.;" director of a gymnasium at Nuremberg until 1816; prof. at Heidelberg until 1818, then lectured at Berlin; d. 1831.

His works were edited, after his death, by his pupils; most important are "Phenomenology of Spirit," (1807: battle of Jena); "Science of Logic," (1812-1816); "Encyc. of Phil. Sciences," (1817).

(B) Hegel gives to idealism its full systematic development; adopting at first the principles of Schelling, he avoided his mystical "imm. intuitions," and soon separated himself, by his strict dialectical method. The work of phil. begins with the logical concept, and its method is *à priori* (ontological). The development of thought is the development of being. True logic is the very process of the abs. itself. (Absolute, logical idealism.)

(C) The real is the absolute, the universal, but not motionless, blank existence; it is a perpetual process, thought (denken = Sein) unfolding itself as two opposites, and their reconciliation by a second negation: understanding views the finite as distinguished from its opposite—(A is determined by not-A)—separates subj. and obj.; reason unites them in the concept, whose essence is negation and negation of that negation. This is thought, but it is also being, and actual finite things result from the mutual relations which the abs. contains; the universe is a universe of relations. The finite out of the inf., the limited out of the abs., is for understanding only; in the idea of the reason they are one.

In the absolute everywhere, in thought, in sens., perc., in reflection, we find a three-fold movement: (1) the thought in itself (an sich); (2) it passes over into its opposite (aussersich sein); (3) it turns back upon itself, the union of the contradictions (in sich sein): (1) God, (2) Nature, (3) Spirit.

(D) *Logic* is the science of the pure idea, the abs. = God (in ansich sein); it includes ontology, since thought and being are one.

The abstract concept sets limitation to itself, and so denies its universality, and then, through negation of that negation, becomes the perfect, concrete "idea."

We begin, then, with pure being, indeterminate, = nothing: their unity = becoming (Werden), whence results determinate being (Dasein).

(1) Science of *being* = thought; it embraces three steps: (*a*) *quality*, being limited by negation, through the three steps of sein, dasein, für-sich-sein, the reconciling of the first two, independent being, the ideal of the determinate; (*b*) *quantity*, the outward form, in its three momenta of pure quantity, particular quantity, and degree; the union of quantity and quality = "Mass," measure the relation of one to another.

(2) Science of the *essence*, or the concept reflected

on itself by negation, being "sublated" (für-sich-sein).

(*a*) Ground of existence: (α) pure notion of existence (identity, difference, ground); (β) essential existence; (γ) the thing.

(*b*) Phenomena: (α) phenomenal world; (β) matter and form; (γ) relation.

(*c*) Totality, reality, union of (*a*) and (*b*): (α) relation of substance; (β) rel. of cause; (γ) action and re-action.

(3) Science of the *concept*, (in-sich-sein), the union of being and essence, thought returned on itself.

(*a*) Subjective, in its three momenta; (α) universality; (β) limitation; (γ) unity.

This gives us (α) the concept as such, (β) the judgment, (γ) the inference.

(*b*) Objective; (α) mechanism; (β) chemism; (γ) teleology.

(*c*) Idea, union of subj. and obj. as concrete reality: (α) life; (β) cognition; (γ) abs. idea = GOD.

(E) *Philosophy of Nature* is the science of the idea as passing over to "other;" the abs. in its determined being by free movement externalizing itself. Logic is thus the princ. of the phil. of nat., and nature itself is a system of successive steps; it is the process by which union with the idea is recovered, which union is accomplished in spirit, the goal, the end. The first step, answering to Being, is:

(1) *Mechanics*, of empty, indeterminate forms;

(*a*) Abstract mathematical properties of (α) time, (β) space, (γ) matter, their union;

(*b*) Concrete, mechanical, (α) attraction, (β) repulsion, (γ) gravity, weight, the union of (α) and (β);

(*c*) Absolute, of free motion in space:

(2) *Physics*, of matter individualized in

(*a*) General forms of matter, sun, and planets, elements, meteorology;

(*b*) Relative forms, specific gravity, cohesion, heat;

(*c*) Total individuality, specific forms, properties, etc.:

(3) *Organism*, combining the other two movements, nat. elevated above the chemical process;

(*a.*) Universal organism of the earth (geological); here the idea of life appears as the result of a past process of life;

(*b.*) Vegetable organism, from present life;

(*c.*) The plant is not a totality, a unity; the organizing unity is the animal process, as soul, self-feeling (selbst-gefühl).

In man nature becomes self-conscious, the ego: thus the idea, from its "otherness" becomes conscious of itself.

(F.) *Philosophy of Spirit, Mind* (Geist), the science of the idea returned from "otherness," developed from natural determination into freedom, the independent idea (für-sich-sein), which is conscious of self.

Man's spirit is united with his body in the unity of the concept. Soul and body are one; body is the reality of soul, soul the ideality of body.

Spirit becomes manifest to itself in negation of universality and negation of that negation; this development is called its faculties: it *is* not spirit, but the abs. idea is spirit in the dialectic process of contradiction. The three momenta are,

(1) *Subjective spirit* (an sich); it is at first

(*a.*) Blended with natural determination, the soul in its

relation to the body, the object of *Anthropology* (Naturgeist), which is (α) purely natural, the immateriality of nature; (β) sensitive soul; (γ) actual, the union of (α) and (β); distinguishing the world from it and itself from the world, it becomes

(*b.*) *Consciousness*; it frees itself from the form of mere being, gives itself the form of essence, and becomes *ego*, (α) consciousness; (β) self-consc.; (γ) reason. This is the object of *phenomenology*. Finally, reconciling the contradiction of (*a*) and (*b*), the soul arrives at consc. of its unity with the world, and becomes,

(*c.*) Proper *spirit*, the unity of subj. and obj.; its three momenta are (α) theoretical, *Intelligence*, giving to separated and contingent objects a subjective, univ., necessary and rational princ.; (β) practical, will; (γ) free spirit, the actual, the union of int. and will. This is the object of *Pneumatology*.

(2.) *Objective spirit*, free will producing from itself a world of freedom; this freedom of the abs. consc. is the univ., rational will which produces in the individ. will the consc. of rights and morality. Its three momenta are (*a*) *Pure indeterminateness*, rights (jurisprudence);

(α) Property, (β) contract, (γ) penalty, (strafe,) vindication of rights;

(*b.*) *Morality* (subjective), will reflected on itself, determined against the univ.; (α) purpose in the action, and responsibility, (β) aim, intention, and well-being (general advantage), (γ) good, the unity of the univ. and the particular. Evil is the inmost reflection of subjectivity upon itself against the obj. and univ., the asserting of the finite against the infinite.

(*c.*) *Social morals* the unity and truth of (*a*) and (*b*), regard (α) the family relation raised to a spiritual determination; (β) society, spirit abstracting itself in many personalities; (γ) the state, the actuality of the moral idea (politics), "the self-consc., ethical substance developed into organized actuality;" divine will as present spirit. The highest duty of individuals is to be fellow-members of the State.

History is the development of the consc. of freedom following the momenta of (γ).

(3.) *Absolute spirit,* the unity of subj. and obj., has its three momenta: it knows itself in

(*a.*) *Art,* in intuition and image;

(*b.*) *Religion,* in the form of emotion and imagination;

(*c.*) *Philosophy,* in the form of thought and concept.

(*a.*) The beautiful is "the actuality of the idea in the form of limited manifestation." Its two inseparable factors are idea and material; hence three art forms, (α) symbolic art, in which material preponderates over idea; (β) classic, content and form being adequate to one another; (γ) romantic, in which spirit overmasters material; (divide thus the fine arts, object., subj. and reconc.)

(*b.*) Religion is the form which abs. truth assumes for feeling and imagination; it is man's knowledge of God and God's knowledge of Himself in man, one and the same act.

(*c*) Abs. Phil. is the idea thinking itself, truth knowing itself, reason comprehending itself, the self-consc. of the abs. in man, in the form of thought and concept. The Hist. of Phil. is the strife of the abs. idea to arrive at adequate conception of itself; all previous systems are moments of this process, now perfected in the *Phil. of the Absolute.*

(G) *School of Hegel.* His numerous followers soon divided into what may be termed a "right," a "left," and a "centre;" the first endeavoring to reconcile his logical system with "orthodoxy;" the second developing on the same basis a logical pantheism, *e.g.*, Strauss, Bauer, Feuerbach.

5. OPPONENTS OF PURE IDEALISM.

Here we may conveniently introduce those philos. of Germany who, though basing their princ. on Kant or Schelling, yet introduced mystical or empirical elements, or a psychol. method, which rendered their philos. systems inferior in systematic form to those mentioned above. We may select

(A.) *Fr. Heinr. Jacobi,* (1) (1743–1819, A. D.,) b. at Düsseldorf, held an office under government at Munich, afterwards Pres. of the Acad. there, devoting his leisure to philos. questions, producing occasional papers, the (philos.) romance "Waldemar," etc.; "the Plato of Germany."

(2.) J. detects a radical defect in Kant's system, the need of a connecting link between the thinking subject and the transc. obj. Sensations are not caused by phenom. for they are in the mind; nor, according to the "Critique," by things in themselves (transc.), for cause and effect are only in the phenom. world. Thus the Crit. is self-destructive. Fichte's subj. idealism is logically valid. Phil. ends in Spinozism, for demonstration may lead up to the world as a whole, not to its author; it passes from the conditioned to the conditioned, not to the unconditioned.

But the obj. of perc. is believed real, though this cannot be proved. *Faith* is an immanent conviction, a rational intuit. of the supra-sensible; this gives direct conviction of God's existence, etc. God is present to man through the heart ("myst. of sent."). "There is light in my heart, but when I try to bring it to the understanding it is extinguished."

(B.) *Jacob Fr. Fries*, (1.) (1773–1843, A. D.) Prof. of Phil. at Heidelberg and Jena; his chief work is "New Critique of the Reason" (1807); but he wrote also, "Wissen, Glaube und Ahnung" (1805), etc., etc.

(2.) Psychol. is the basis of phil., for only through internal experience are we conscious how we possess *à pr.* cognitions. With Kant he recognizes space, time, the categories, as subj. *à pr.* forms. As with Jacobi, the sphere of the understanding (Wissen) is merely subj. phenom. Things in themselves, the ideas, are the object of direct intuition of the higher faculty (Vernunft). This is faith.

Bouterwek, (1766–1828, A. D.,) adopts essentially the same principles; ("Nat. Realism;" see copious quotations from Jacobi, etc., in Hamilton's Reid, p. 793, seq.)

(C.) *Fr. Ern. Dan. Schleiermacher* (1) (1768–1834 A.D.), b. at Breslau, at first a Moravian preacher at Berlin, etc., Prof. at Halle, Prof. of Theol. at Berlin; his numerous works discuss religion, ethics, politics, phil., etc.; they exercised a great and lasting influence on the Lutheran rel., and on German ethics. (see a highly appreciative review in Ueberweg.)

(2.) Following Kant, S. tried to avoid the extreme idealism of Fichte, Schelling and Hegel. There are two factors in thought, the *à pr.* and the empirical. Distinguish the matter and the form of cognitions; the former is given in sense-perc., the latter by thought, but both are real obj.; space, time, the categories, are forms of things themselves.

The forms of development of knowledge are induction and deduction, but the latter must proceed from princ. given by the former.

The plurality of objects has obj. unity. The totality of them is the world; their unity is Deity (Spinozism). Reason and consc. in us are GOD. In the idea of GOD is the abstract unity of the ideal and the real; in the concept of the world, on the other hand, is their relative unity; it embraces (as opposed to one another) nature, in which the real preponderates, spirit, in which is more prominent the ideal.

In GOD is no difference between power and will. The div. causality is complete in the world. He is for us not thinkable, as the abs.; we can use only negation and anthropomorphic expressions.

(3.) "Science is the existence of things in human reason, and the exist. of human reason in things;" *religion* is the consc. of the unity of reason and nature. Every part of the world is related to the rest in action and passion. From the latter in us results our feeling of dependence in which religion is rooted; from the former a feeling of our freedom, which is the ground of *morality.*

(*a.*) We have a feeling of entire dependence on the Infinity of the universe: "to feel one's self in the imm. unity of intuition and feeling one with the eternal is the aim of religion" (subjective side). This feeling is manifested in religious ideas and dogmas: objectively, religion is the being of GOD manifested in our feeling. Rel. can and must take definite forms in reaching perfect actuality. These are the positive religions, each based on some one of the many relations of the finite to the Inf. To make obj. the subj. feeling is mysticism and mythology.

(*b*) S.'s specialty is *ethics:* the moral task of man is the reconciliation of nature and reason, the latter becoming the conscious lord of the former.

(*α*) Theory of *goods.* A good is a partic. unity of nature and reason; the sum. bon. is the univ. unity of these, of the real and the ideal.

(*β*) *Virtue* is the force from which issue moral actions.

(*γ*) *Duty* is progress towards the highest good: its most universal law, "Act constantly with thy whole moral force, striving to fulfil thy whole moral task."

(D.) *Arthur Schopenhauer,* (1) (1788–1860, A. D.) b. at Dantzic, ed. at Göttingen, under Schulze (Ænesidemus); taught at Berlin (1820–1831); his career cannot be called successful, though he had followers. His principal work is, "The World as Will and Representation," (Notion, Vorstellung.)

(2.) No subject without object, no obj. without subj.; "The world is my notion, my represent.," (Vorstellung.) But this is the subj. aspect of the world, in which all is relative; (princ. of suff. reason.) Kant's Ding-an-sich is a mere assumption; universal forms of existence are, *à pr.*, in our consc., and can be discovered there. Space, time, the categories, are subjective, valid only for phenom. The innermost essence of the world is something most known by us; it is *Will,* Univ. Will, which is known to us through int. perc. in our own will. It includes conscious desire, unconscious instinct, natural forces.

The objectivity of the will = represent. (Vorst.); but will everywhere is one. Between will and represent. is the eternal unchangeable idea, will in its primary objective form. In cognition of it the subject ceases to be merely individual.

In man, volition and its result are one and the same. The body itself is objectified will. This is the key to the essence of all other things. Abstracting their limited being (Dasein) as notions, represent., there will remain their essence as will.

Art is the work of genius, the highest step in the objectification of will, in which the eternal idea is known and repeated.

(3.) The world is not the best, but the worst possible, (pessimism). Will, existence, is perpetual suffering. It must cease to affirm, to will itself, in order to escape : as simple represent., in enjoyment of the beautiful, it is free from torment; this is the aim, imperfectly accomplished, of genius.

Conscious, then, of the identity of our will with the Univ. Will, the first point in ethics is sympathy with suffering; but next, the mortification in ourselves of the will to live, so that volition may cease. (Nirvana.)

Hartmann follows in S.'s steps.

(E) *John Fr. Herbart*, (1) (1776–1841, A. D.) b. at Oldenburg, studied at Jena under Fichte, tutor in Switz., (Pestalozzi), Prof. at Göttingen, (1805,) at Königsberg, (1809) ret. to Göttingen, (1833) ; besides writing on "Pedagogik," he produced numerous philos. works, *e. g.*, "Psychology, founded on Exp. Metaph. and Math."

(2.) He offered a system of *realism* grounded on Kant and Leibnitz. The basis of phil. is the sum of all emp. phenom., its aim is to "elaborate concepts ;" for, as derived from exp. and the ego, they involve contradictions (*e. g.*, extension, action in time, many attributes in one subj.) which need to be explained ; the emp. concept must be explained, methodically transformed. This is the province of Metaph. Phil., then, has three parts; Logic, Metaph. Æsthetics.

(3.) Exp. gives us the materials of knowledge, but not *what* things are ; but its forms are objective, for we have no control over them. Logic aims to render distinct its concepts, to render them co-ordinate. Met. then corrects and transforms as

(*a.*) *Ontology*. There are a multiplicity of real essences, each with a simple quality. The real is abs. position, (monad, math. point), neither in time nor space, (phenomenal, in the mind) ; "intelligible space" is that in which it is conceived as existing. Things are complexes of these, standing in diff. relations to one another; all supposed qualities or properties are these *relations*.

How comes it to pass, then, that exp. seems to give us unity in things? One of the many simple essences has a central position, and the others appear in relation to it. The real cannot change; but their relations in a thing may; we may view the thing in diff. rel., *e. g.*, a line in Math. This activity of the real is due to the effort of "self-preservation" against disturbing influences from without.

(*b.*) *Synechology*, explaining the contrad. involved in the idea of matter. The real essences by internal energy interpenetrating one another and re-acting, a sort of attraction and repulsion arises from which the atom, the mass, matter.

Time, space, motion are not actual, (obj. phenom. only) but relations of obj. : thus the relation of the monads gives the line ; then follow the surface, extension in three dimensions, space.

(*c.*) *Eidology*, elucidating the phenom. of the human

mind, its multiplicity and unity. The central real of the *ego*, as a thing, a limited being, is soul. Faculties are log ical names in classifying psychical phenom. Its one activity is " self-preservation." The soul is affected by the real essences which surround it; its act of self-preserv. is the notion (Vorst.).

The " *Sum of arrest*" is found in the uniting of several notions (Vorst.) in the soul; continuing to exist, then, if opposed, each loses part of its intensity, and the math. total is " the sum of arrest:" and thus, where there are several, the weakest may be forced out of consc. On this is based his application of Math. to psychology not to the abs. but the rel. intensity of the Vorst.). H.'s psychology of will, desire, etc., applies these princ. The orderly relations of the simple, real essences imply a Div. Intelligence. (Teleology.)

(4.) *Æsthetics*, set forth the ideas on which are based the satisfaction or dissatisfaction produced by relations: they include ethics, when relations of will are con cerned; the moral is based on the int. satisfaction from harmony between will and judgment; this is the morally beautiful, virtue as ideal.

Benevolence is harmony between one will and that of others.

Legal right arises from dissatisfaction at conflict of will.

Herbart had a widely extended school.

(F.) *Fr. Ed. Beneke*, (1) (1798–1854, A. D.) b. at Berlin, added to his studies in Germ. Phil., Eng. and Scotch, forbidden to lecture at Univ. of Berlin, (which interdict he attributed to Hegel,) he taught at Göttingen, (1824–1827), then returned to Berlin. His works give special atten tion to Psych., *e.g.*, "Elements of Psych." (1833); "Nat. System of Pract. Phil." (Ethics, etc.) (1837–1840); "Metaphysics," (1840).

(2.) Against Hegel and Herbart, he proposes to base Metaphys. Phil. on Psych. We have direct knowledge of our own psychical activities, of our own psychical being as it is, by sense-perc. of our own bodies; and sense-perc. of other bodies, by analogy, gives us the idea of other souls like our own.

Emp. consc. does *not* involve contradictions; but int. sens. and perc. must be elaborated by the inductive method, analyzing the complex contents of consc., and synthetically uniting them in a system.

(3.) *Psychology.* The soul is active powers, for a thing is the sum of all its forces. "Faculties" are elements of the soul's substratum, not *in* a substance; what bear the name are "hypostatized" class-concepts of complicated phenom.

The soul is the totality of these united powers; but analysis gives four primary groups of psychical processes:

(*a.*) Various elementary powers in each sense appropriate excitations from without (Reizaneignung), whereby are formed sensations and perceptions;

(*b.*) New elementary powers are developed and added to these;

(*c.*) Adjustment (ausgleichung) or transfer of "excitations;" some of the exc. remain as "traces," in unconsc.; in various psychical combinations they may unite with others and elevate them to consc., etc.;

(*d.*) Mutual attraction and blending of homogeneous psychical products.

Powers of the developed soul are from "traces" of previously excited psychical products of sense-perc.; *e. g.*, instead of a faculty of memory, each representation has its own memory, the effort at reproduction.

(4.) *Metaphysics* are based on psychology. From psychical powers having inferred an immaterial soul, by *analogy* we infer the being, *an sich*, of our own body: then, similarly, of other souls, and other bodies; so also the concepts of substance and accidents, space and time, etc.

(5.) *Ethics*, are based on the relative worth of the psychical functions as given in feeling; morality requires that we choose the higher, the more worthy, as subjectively felt and objectively desired.

(G.) German Idealism, as will be seen, has run its course; some of the Hegelian school, like Feuerbach, have adopted materialism; others (as J. H. Fichte; see Morell), have endeavored to apply its methods to realism. Or else, in despair of Phil., German thought, on an empirical or materialist basis, has devoted itself to the Nat. Sciences. (Büchner, "Form and Matter," Lond. 1864.)

Among opponents is, especially worthy of notice, Ulrici. (Consult Erdmann, and see trans. in Am. Ed. Ueberweg.) See also Lange, Gesch. d. Materialismus.

Others have tried to reconstruct phil.; as Trendelenberg on the basis of Aristotle; Lotze after Leibnitz. (See Erdmann, ubi. sup.)

CHAPTER XVI.

ENGLISH AND FRENCH EMPIRICISM IN THE NINETEENTH CENTURY.

[*Ref.* Morell; Cousin; Whewell; Mackintosh.]

1. UTILITARIAN ETHICS. 2. SPECULATIVE EMPIRICISM IN ENGLAND. 3. FRENCH IDEOLOGY AND POSITIVISM.

1. UTILITARIAN ETHICS.

We resume Eng. phil. at a period when the influence of Locke was almost supreme, and begin with a writer who, though unsystematic, yet through his temperate good sense and his practical views has exercised a remarkable control of English thought.

(A.) *William Paley*, (1) (1743–1805, A. D.) Fellow of Christ's Coll., Camb., in 1765 defended Epicureanism in a prize essay; in 1785, produced his "Principles of Morals and Politics." (See Dug. Stewart.)

(2.) He denies a "moral sense," because it would involve innate ideas; obligation is founded on the will of a superior; the supreme law-giver is GOD, whose will aims at the production of happiness among His creatures.

Virtue is "the doing good to mankind in obedience to the will of GOD, and for the sake of everlasting happiness." But what is duty is to be determined by the criterion of universal happiness; whatever is on the whole beneficial is right.

(B.) *Jeremy Bentham*, (See Mill's Disc. vol. 1, and Autob. (x.), and Whewell's Hist. Moral Phil., Lect. xiii–xviii.) (1) (1748–1832, A. D.) ed. at Queen's Coll., Oxf., wrote "Fragment on Government," "Principles of Morals and Legislation" (1789); Dr. Bowring published in 1832 his "Deontology." More consistent than Paley, of great analytic power, of witty and sarcastic style, he became the leader of a school of liberal thinkers in politics, the school of "Philos. radicalism." A man of fortune, he founded the *Westminster Rev.* (See J. S. Mill's Autob. c. iv.) His chief influence, however, has been on jurisprudence.

(2.) Man is governed in practical conduct by—

(*a*) Selfish passions, (*b*) sympathy and antipathy towards others. The good = pleasure measured by (*a*) magnitude of intensity and duration, (*b*) extent, *i. e.*, number of persons. On this is based B.'s ethical criterion, "the greatest happiness of the greatest number," as the sum of remaining pleasures, after subtracting pains, (*a*) of ourselves; hence the virtue of prudence which is (α) "self-regarding prudence," (β) "extra-regarding prudence," for others; (*b*) of others, whence is derived the virtue of beneficence.

(3) B.'s jurisprudence condemns the "compact" theory as a mischievous fiction; it is especially notable in its classification of offences with minute subdivisions;

(*a*) Private, against individuals; (α) person, (β) property, (γ) reputation. (δ) condition, (ε) against (α) and (γ); (ζ) against (α) and (β);

(*b*) Semi-public, offences against a class;

(*c*) Self-regarding off.;

(*a*) Public, against the community ;

(*c*) Multiform ; (α) by falsehood, (β) against trust

Punishment has for its object to prevent offences, to prevent the worst, to keep down the mischief, to act at the least expense, in fine, to prevent suffering and, to promote happiness.

2 Speculative Empiricism in England.

Here we find no new principle, but a development in certain directions, (*e. g.*, assoc. of ideas, (Jas. Mill), a far wider induction from phenom. ; an attempt to pass from physiology (and even *craniology*, under the influence of Gall, Spurzheim, Combe), to physiology ; the new impulse given to phys. investigation creates a tendency to " naturalism," sometimes restrained by the influence of Scotch and German systems, (J. S. Mill), while again material phenom, are used almost exclusively as the key to fundamental princ. of Phil. (H. Spencer) ; sociology and politics occupy a more prominent place in spec. phil. than in any previous age.

(A) *James Mill.* (See J. S. Mill's Autob. ; Moll.)

(1.) (1773-1836, A. D.) b. at Montrose, Scot., ed. at Univ. Edinb., min. of the Scotch Kirk, gave up his profession, entered the service of the E. Ind. Co. ; he wrote " Hist. Br. India," (1818), " El. Pol. Econ.," (1821), " Ess. on Gov." (1828), " Anal. Phenom. Human Mind," (1829).

(2) The only objects of knowledge are (*a*) sensations, (*b*) ideas, copies of (*a*) ; sensation and " ideation " are the two ultimate mental processes. Consc. is a generic name for these. " To be conscious of the prick of a pin = to have the sensation," (Anal. c. iii). ; conception is a generic

name for ideas only ; imag. for trains of ideas. Memory is complex, (*a*) the idea of past sens., (*b*) present self, past self, and the train of consc. (c. x.).

In *Classification*, naming at first an individual, we apply the name to another like it, and so on : *abstract* names are concrete names with the "connotation" dropped.

Judgment is recognition that two names stand for the same things, (analytical ?) (c. xi.) ; this explains ratiocination.

(3) *Association of ideas* will explain all terms ; some of the latter denote sens., others connote the associated ideas. Sens., ideas, are coincident or successive ; successions are fortuitous or constant. Hence

(*a*) cause and effect, constant antecedence and subsequence ;

(*b*) Substance, coalescence of a certain number of sens.: this "concomitance" is between color and figure, solidity and form, etc. ;

(*c*) Time, an abstract for three abstracts, past, present, future, given in successive sensations ;

(*d*) Muscular sens., and those of touch, in a certain order, are named line ; assoc. of ideas gives the idea of added length, and lines in every direction, *extension ad inf.*

(4) *Active powers* are analyzed as pleasurable and painful sens. The idea of pleasure is desire (c. xix.) ; will is desire of means to an end.

Moral sentiments begin with assoc. of pleasure to ourselves with certain ideas, then of pleasure from praise.

(B) *Alex. Bain*, Prof. Univ. Aberdeen, ("Senses and the Intellect," 1864 ; "Emotions and the will ;" "Mental and Moral Science," 1868 ; etc.,) adopts the same principles, with special applications of physiology. Solidity, extension, space, exist in our minds as sensible impressions with feelings of force. The idea of extension originates in the duration of muscular effort, as given in musc. sens. "Belief in ext. reality is the anticipation of a given effect to a given antecedent." Self is a complex of feelings, actions and intelligence. Will is the name for collective impulses to action.

The moral sentiment is due to education and experience ; remorse and self-approval, by assoc. of ideas, are transferred from experience of results to the inward antecedent disposition. (See J. S. Mill, Disc. v. iv.)

(C) *John Stuart Mill.* (See Autobiography, Mansel, "Phil. of the Cond. etc." ; McCosh, " Examination, etc." ; " Intuitions, etc." ; Porter, " Human Int." on causation, §§ 591-3.)

(1) (1806-1873, A. D.), son of Jas. Mill, clerk in the India House, ed. West. Rev. (1835-1840) ; distinguished as a writer on the " Liberal " side, (" Pol. Ec.," " Liberty," " Subj. of Women," etc.). His most important philos. works, are " System of Logic," (rejecting ontology, but arguing for his phil. theory,) " Ex. of Sir Wm. Hamilton's phil." " Utilitarianism" in " Discussions," " Comte," " Three Essays on Religion," (posthumous) ; Note especially the last, " Theism," (1870).

Mill's transparent clearness and precision of style, apparent fairness and sincerity, render him one of the most attractive and influential of his school.

(2) *His theory of knowledge* is strictly empirical ; all general propositions and concepts come from experience according to the laws of induction, which he develops with great skill in his Logic. In his " Exam. of Sir Wm.

Hamilton's Phil." having, with his usual precision and clearness, exposed the weak points in the "phil. of the conditioned," he proceeds, (c. xi.) to lay down the "psychol. theory" (associational) of belief in an ext. world.

(*a*) The idea of "*substance* or *matter*" is reduced to "permanent possibilities of sensation;" *i. e.*, the mind not only receives sens., and associates their ideas, but is capable of expectation, of forming the concept of possible sens. An existing sens. brings up, by the law of assoc. of ideas, the ideas of others as possible, and this collected group, with the idea of permanent possibility, is the concept of body.

These groups of possibilities are thought of as diff. from the actual sens., as the cause of it. This theory cannot be proved, but the law of parcimony gives it the preference over that of intuit. of a *non-ego*. (cf. Idealism of Berkeley).

Extension would be a complex of successive sens. if given by touch only, but through sight they are thought of as simultaneous. (cf. Bain.)

In primary qualities of body, the predominating idea is these possibilities; in secondary, the actual sens.

(*b*) Self, *ego*. We know feelings, *i. e.* sensations, emotions, thoughts, volitions, (the last three are not in groups, are of the individ.); the belief of the existence of mind is a belief of the permanent possibility of these states. (Ex. c. xii.) But M. confesses that memory and expectation are inexplicable on this theory; feelings have "a thread of consc."

(*c*) The idea of *cause* and effect, of power, activity, is due to a fixed order of sequence in these groups of possibilities of sens. The idea, like all others, is formed from exp. of these sequences; but yet, in his "Logic," causation is *unconditional* relation of succession. "Efficient causes—not phenomena—are radically inaccessible to the human faculties."

(*d*) Axioms, *general principles,* are due to ind. from exp. "All inference is from particulars to particulars; general prop. merely register such inferences." (Logic, cc. iv. v.)

(3) *Ethics.* (*a*) The law of causality applies also to human actions. *Will,* the "active phenom., is an off-shoot of desire, the passive sensibility" (Util. c. iv.); it is determined by desires, etc. (Ex. c. xxix.); we are *not* consc. of ability to act against our strongest preference.

(*b*) The *morality* of actions depends on their consequences, (cf. Jas. Mill and Bentham); the good or evil of these consequences is measured by pleasure or pain; for pleasure and freedom from pain are the only things desired as ends, and this therefore is the standard (relative) of morals. In pleasures, however, we must consider both quality and quantity, (Epicurus). Ethics an induct. science.

(*c*) Moral feelings are not innate, but acquired capacities; yet they are natural as based "on social instincts;" they are developed by ext. sanctions, *i. e.,* hope of favor, expectation of reward, popular opinions, institutions.

Justice (Util. c. v.) is based on the natural feelings of resentment and sympathy (sentiment = animal desire widened); its morality is from enlarged human sympathy and intelligent self-interest; hence the desire to punish a person who has done harm. "Legal constraints" from this sentiment generate the idea of justice. Like veracity, it is "of artificial origin." (Ess. on Nature.)

(*c*) In *politics,* M. rejects the theory of natural rights;

for "general good" is determined by induction from expediency; political rights are relative to the state of society.

(*d*) Reason finds in the appearance of design in nature probable evidence for the existence of a *Creator*, not of matter or force, but of the present order, a Being of limited power. (See remarkable Essay on Theism, 1870).

(D.) *Herbert Spencer*, (1) (b. 1820) published Social Statics (1850); in 1860, undertook a "System of Phil.;" (*a*) First principles, (1860, rev. 1867); (*b*) Biology, (1866); (*c*) Psychology, (1872, rev. of 1855); (*d*) "Principles of Sociology," to finish the scheme.

(2) S.'s primary doctrine is *evolution*, both in psychical and physical phenom., a change from "an indefinite incoherent homogeneity to a def. coherent heterogeneity." This princ. is an induction from exp. of which no further account can be given, for the absolute in any form is unthinkable, although there is an ultimate reality (x) in which subject and object coincide; yet our concept of the Abs. is positive though indefinite.

Truth is perfect agreement, throughout the range of our exp., of all represent. of things (Princ. § 40), and the test of truth is inconceivableness of the contradictory; but the "nec. truths" are the result of countless experiences of ancestors transmitting a *tendency* in the nervous system, the store-house of impressions.

(3) Neither matter nor mind can be known in themselves, but only phenom. in their relations of sequence and co-existence; time and space are abstracts of these; body adds concept of existence from exp. of force, the unknown cause. Psychical states are included in its transformations; heat, light, etc., are transformable into

emotions, thoughts (Psych. § 71); materialism = spiritualism, (sc. phenomenalism).

(4) *Psychology* is a branch of biology (life a continual adjustment of int. to ext. relations), and "considers the connection between the organism and its environments." The term mind represents a "circumscribed aggregate of activities;" these are evolved by outward conditions which produce states of ever-increasing energy, a tendency to renewal, eventually a permanent condition of the nervous system. Memory is an incomplete automatism, partial instinct. Reason arises out of instinct when the environments are very complex. Volition is "imperfect connection between the ext. impressions and the consequent action;" "cessation of automatic action = dawn of volition." (Psych. § 218.)

3. French Ideology and Positivism.

At the end of the Rev., French Phil. was almost purely sensualistic. Either physiology was the only ground of psych. (Cabanis; sens. an affection of the nerves, the brain secreting thought), or else, (subjectively) sensualism took the form of "ideology," while Volney's catechism presented "self-preservation" as the end and criterion of morals.

(A.) *Destutt de Tracy*, (1754–1836, A.D.), produced, in 1804, his "Elements d' Idéologie," distinguishing four sorts of feelings (ideas), (1) actual sensations, (2) feelings of past sens., (3) feelings of relations, (judgment, etc.,) (4) feelings of want, danger, etc.

(B.) *Laromiguière*, (1756–1837, A.D.) Prof. of Phil., Acad. de P., published in 1815 "Leçons de Phil." or "Essais sur les Facultés de L'Ame." (See Cousin's rev. in Fragm. Phil. v.)

Following Condillac, and aiming at the same unity of system, L. finds that analysis gives attention as the fundamental faculty of the mind, (reaction from sensualism.) The development of faculties is, (1) attention, (2) comparison, attention to two impressions, (3) judgment, etc., from (2); memory, etc., products of sens.; (1), (2), (3 united, constitute the understanding; add the sens. of need and there arise (1) desire; from this (2) preference, (3) liberty; (1), (2), (3) united constitute will. Materials of knowledge are supplied by *sensibility* (includes reflection, judgment of relations, and moral sense.)

A spiritualist and religious reaction followed the Restoration in France, (vid. inf.) until *Positivism*, as the negation of all Phil., claimed the prominent place which it now holds there.

(C.) *Augustus Comte.* (See Mill's Comte (West. Rev. 1865), H. Martineau's (abridged,) trans. of "Phil. Positive," 1853), Lewes.) Metaphysics, the search for first or final causes, must be abandoned for "positive" science.

Nothing but phenom. can be known, and the phenom. of consc. must be relegated to biology, as a part of physiology; phrenology, scientifically evolved, is the organon for the study of mental functions.

Consequently all knowledge is relative; as the mind is *evolved*, so also knowledge. The only province of true phil. is the study and classification of phenomenal laws, *i. e.*, the sequences and resemblances of phenom.

The *Classific. and co-ord. of sciences* correspond to the principles of C., and are ingenious and thorough.

Begin with the simplest and lowest order of phenom., and so advance to the more complex; (1) Math., (2) Astronomy, (adding new facts), (3) Physics, (4) Chemistry, 5) Biology, (6) Sociology.

In *history*, trace the evolution of mind through three stages, (1) theological, (*a*) fetichism, (as in brutes). (*b*), polytheism, (*c*) monotheism; (2) metaphysical (abstractions viewed as real entities); (3) positive.

(Note Comte's later career of "Positive Religion" with its cultus of the "Grand Être.")

Positivism has its later representatives in Taine, Littré, etc. (See Harrison, Cont. Rev., 1876.)

CHAPTER XVII.

ENGLISH AND FRENCH PSYCHOLOGICAL AND SPIRITUALISTIC SCHOOL OF THE NINETEENTH CENTURY.

1. Psychological Spiritualism in England and the United States. 2. French Eclecticism.

1. Psychological Spiritualism in England and the United States.

The marked re-action towards spiritualism in phil., lit., arts, etc. (See Wordsworth's Exc., B. ii.), which may be dated from the year 1815, contains, both in Eng. and Fr., three special elements:

(1) German phil. in (*a*) idealism, (*b*) criticism (" phil. of the cond.," "relativity of knowledge,") the former of which in Eng. exerted a remarkable influence through the (fragmentary) writings and the conversations of Coleridge; (cf. also Cousin ; see also Carlyle, Misc. Ess. v. 1.);

(2) Psychological method, and the prominence of

psych., almost to the exclusion of ontology; (so also Scotch phil.);

(3) A mystical and theosophic element, more or less based on Jacobi and Schelling, sometimes taking the form of pantheism (see Shelley's Adonais, 41 seq.)

(A) *Samuel Taylor Coleridge*, (1) (1772-1834, A. D.) ed. at Christ's Hospital and Cambridge; Unitarian preacher, radical, spent a year in Germany (1798), pub. in 1817 his "Biog. Lit." under influence of Kant and Schelling, "The Friend," (1809-1818), "Aids to Reflection," (1825), etc. Though his published work is unsystematic and fragmentary, yet its depth and thoughtfulness, and still more, the power of his conversation, gave him an extraordinary influence in aid of the spiritualist reaction, throughout Eng. and the U. S. His special office, like that of Socrates, to awaken thought. (J. S. Mill, Disc. v. 2.)

(2) Adopting some essential princ. from Kant, for a time largely influenced by Schelling, (the Friend, Biog. Lit. xii.), at a later period, he more nearly approached to Jacobi's standpoint. Of special note among his princ.,

(*a*) *Reason*, distinguished from understanding, is intuition of univ. and nec. truths, self-evident, supersensual princ. (Friend, Introd. Ess. xv. ad fin.; Aids, etc., Sp. Rel. Aph. viii. App.); understanding = discursive reason, is the regulative power, which generalizes sense-perc. and proceeds by inference from them. (cf. Par. Lost. v. 483.)

(*b*) *Conscience*, practical reason, adds free will, directly attests the reality of an immortal freely acting soul, of an absolute good, of God.

C. earnestly and effectively opposed Paley's morality of expediency. (Friend, § 1. Ess. xv.) Only the moral being, the spirit and the religion of man, can fill up the gap between the absolute and the phenomenal.

Faith is the synthesis of reason and will; an inward light of reason, a direct beholding of eternal truth.

(C) Coleridge has had a remarkable influence upon the phil. of the *beautiful.* Disting. fancy, the representative faculty, from imag. which analyzes and re-creates, idealizes, unifies. (Biog. Lit. iii., ad fin.)

(B) *William Whewell,* (1795-1866, A. D.) ed. Trin. Coll., Camb., fellow, Prof. Moral Phil. (1838), Master Trin. Coll. (1841), pub. " Hist. Ind. Sc." (1837); " Phil. Ind. Sc." (1840-1858); " El. Morality," (1845); Hist. Moral Phil., (1852) etc.

W. adopts the phil. of Kant, and applies it with great logical skill to the phil. of physics. " Ideas" are forms under which sens. are viewed by the mind: ground forms are "fundamental ideas," *à priori* truths of intuition implied in Gram., Arithm., (space, time,) in Mech. Sc., (cause, the fund. idea of force, matter,) etc., superimposed on sense-perc. by the mind; the idea of substance is an irresistible conviction of a substrate to phenom.

Secondary ideas are " ideal conceptions;" *e. g.*, number is a necessary concept, based on sense of succession. (cf. Mill's Logic.)

In *ethics* W., though indebted to Kant, fails to give a consistent and systematic form. (cf. Mill's rev., Disc. v. iii.) Will is the mind's internal act, stimulated by "springs of action," viz. appetites, affections, desires, "moral sentiments," (approb. and disapprob.), reflex sentiments; he adds also rules or laws; practical reason guides in applying them. Conscience is desires, aff., etc., cultured through rules of duty. Duties are based on rights, obligations, moral "ideas," *sc.* benevolence, justice, truth, purity, order; these latter are forms of action given to man by GOD, and express the supreme law, the will of GOD. They are the five cardinal virtues. Virtue is a disposition to acts conformed to law, (cf. Scotus); this is the right, and reason's rule is to do what is right because it is right.

Happiness and duty are identical; the former is the rational object of man's aim; the latter, the obligatory law of action; reconciliation of these is the aim of ethics.

Rights are based on man's nature as a social animal, and defined by positive laws. The idea of order implies a State, a government, as necessary to the existence of rights and freedom. The patriarchal theory and the "social compact" each view one side only of the complex reality.

Among the latest Eng. exponents of spiritualism, and opponents of empiricism, or of materialism, need be named only—

James McCosh, Prof. Logic and Met., Belfast, Irel., Pres. Coll. N. J. (1869), as an able opponent of both pure idealism and of sensualism; "Methods of Div. Gov.;" "Typical Forms, etc.;" "Intuit. of the Mind, etc.;" "Ex. of J. S. Mill's Phil.," etc., and *Jas. Martineau*, whose phil. essays have been collected and pub. (See Cont. Rev., 1876.)

(C.) *American Philosophy* has taken a practical direction from Eng. thought, and been chiefly devoted to psych. Five impulses from abroad or from within may be noticed:

(*a.*) The *Calvinistic* thought of N. E., raising especially questions connected with human will and Div. Gov.;

e. g. Jonathan Edwards (1703–1758, A. D.), "Treatise on the Will." (1754.)

(*b.*) French *liberal* spec., in its applications to the sc. of Gov. at the Rev. (cf. Federalist and Thos. Jeff.)

(*c.*) *Coleridge,* (Prof. Marsh's Ed. and Preface, 1829, Dr. McVickar's Ed. and Pref., 1839), and *Cousin.* (Prof. Henry's (1834) and Wright's trans.)

(*d.*) German *Idealism.* (Boston Unit. school, Journal Spec. Phil., St. Louis).

(*e.*) *Empirical* School, evolution. (Draper, Fiske, "Cosmic Phil.," aiming at scient. arrangement of H. Spencer's princ. of cosmology.)

This last has, as yet (1876), but little hold on Am. thought, and numerous writers, of whom Dr. Porter (b. 1811, Prof. Moral Phil., Yale Coll., 1846, Pres. 1871), may be taken as a distinguished representative—("The Human Intellect" (1868), etc., admirable for precision, clearness and scientific breadth. See, especially, Pt. IV., cc. v., viii., Causation, the Absolute) — have developed psychology on a spiritualistic basis, recognizing intuitive princ. of reason having objective validity, and the essential freedom of man's higher life from the nec. which rules nature.

2. French Eclecticism.

In France the reaction against materialism took a form which may be called psychological, largely based on Scotch Phil.; at a later period Cousin, under influences derived from Germany, founded a school to which he gave the name of "Eclectic."

(A.) *Royer-Collard* (1) (1763–1845, A. D.), whose life

was chiefly political, was Dean of the Fac. of Let., Normal School, Paris (1810). Fragments of his lectures were ed. by Jouffroy, app. to his trans. of Reid; the founder of the new psychol. school. (See Sir Wm. Hamilton's Reid, app. note D).

(2.) In sense-perc. we learn by nat. induction (necessary) external objects, their reality and their properties; *sc.* externality, extension, substance, duration, causality: by the same nat. induction we pass also to the knowledge of unlimited space.

Substance, space, etc., then, are *à pr.* ideas; so also are right and wrong.

Mind may act unconsciously. (See Hamilton's Met. Lect. xvii.)

In R–C. and his associates we find the Scotch phil. with little variation, (the same "fund. laws of belief,") but with improved analysis and system.

(B.) *Maine De Biran,* (1) (1766–1824, A. D.) Deputy and cons. d'État after the Restoration, at first a disciple of Cabanis and DeTracy, in 1805 was already abandoning them, and soon followed, with great phil. skill and precision of thought, the rising Scotch School. Cousin ed. four vols. of his works, (1840); three more appeared in 1859.

(2.) (*a.*) As early as 1803 M. dist. with great clearness between sens. as a passive affection, and perc. as a result of voluntary activity, of the mind; habit "weakens sens. and strengthens perc."

(*b.*) He finds, then, an active element in the will, the personality of the *ego*, given in "imm. int. apperception;" the *ego* knows itself in causal action with an effect, for muscular effort of will is known as producing musc. sens. Thus to will is known as to cause; personality, will, cause, are here identical. In continuity of effort is direct apperc. of the unity and identity of the *ego*.

(*c*.) This is our first knowledge of cause. By "nat. induction" we transfer the idea to outward obj.; thus the idea of substance is reduced to that of cause, (Leibnitz); (see Porter's Hum. Int. § 596.)

(C.) *Jouffroy*, (1796–1842, A. D.) Prof. Moral Phil., Normal School at Paris, trans. and ed. Dugald Stewart and Reid; pub. "Mélanges Philos." (1833); his "Cours d'Esthétique" appeared in 1843; "Cours de Droit Nat.," in 1845. J. is the principal moralist of the Ecl. school. Distinguish in man the personal life, free will, from the impersonal, in which he belongs to nature.

Good and evil exist; their ground, in each creature, is what aids or prevents the fulfilment of its destiny.

(D.) *Victor Cousin*, (1), (1792–1867, A. D.) a pupil of Laromiguière (1811), then a disciple of Royer-Collard and Maine De Biran, Prof. Phil., Normal School (1815); in 1820 was compelled to retire, reinstated (1828), in 1840 was made Min. Pub. Instr.; his brilliant eloquence gave him vast influence in France, and, indirectly, in Eng. and the U. S.

He pub. his course of Lectures, (1815–20 and 1828–1830); "Fragm. Philos.," etc.; of special value his rev. of Locke (trans. Prof. Henry), and Lect. on "The True, the Beautiful and the Good," (trans. O. W. Wight).

(2.) His method is analysis and induction applied to the facts of *consc.* (psychol. method); this is the fund. princ. of all knowledge, of intell. life; in it we apprehend ourselves, through it the external world, the Absolute = GOD. Analyze the facts of cons. but stop at them.

(3.) C. calls his phil. *eclectic;* no phil. is absolutely

false, but many are incomplete, one sided ; (see the three Pref. to Fragm. Phil.) Let us consider and analyze *all* the facts of consc.

They are of three orders, sens., will, reason.

(4.) *Reason* develops itself in two ways, (*a*) spontaneous, (*b*) reflective; error is in reflective thought, giving contingent truths, general principles: (*a*) discerns in particular, determined facts, even when first presented, the univ. and nec. principles in which the Abs. appears to it. In thinking the finite, the imperfect, reason spontaneously proceeds to the Inf., the perfect, the Abs.; herein reason is impersonal.

(5) Thus we may pass from psych. to ont. The primitive facts of consc. are—

(*a*) affection, volition, determinate modifications of the *ego ;* relation of these to the *ego ; ego ;*

(*b*) successive affections, etc. ; relation ; identity of *ego ;*

(*c*) determinate effects willed ; relation ; power of *ego ;*

(*d*) intention, det. means to det. end; relation ; end. Eliminating the conditioned, the finite element, reason's spontaneity possesses as its prim. princ.—

{ (*a*) attribute and subject ;
{ (*b*) plurality and unity;
{ (*c*) cause and effect;
{ (*d*) relations of means to end.

The finite, the conditioned, plurality, is only conceivable in and with the Inf. Unity, the Abs., *sc. God,* essential activity, first Cause, Creator, the True, the Beautiful, the Good. Because the Abs. falls under the consc. of a finite being, GOD does not become relative, determined.

Cognitions of reason are not relative, but absolute.

(6) In *Ethics*, the method and results are the same. Dist. the contingent, sentiments, emotions, instincts, from the nec. princ. of spontaneous reason, imposing univ. obligation. This implies free will, for duty supposes power. Dist. will from desire ; the one, aiming at morality, the other at happiness : true ethics will harmonize these, the antecedent and the consequent : thus GOD is found to be holy, as the creator of a moral being. From princ. of merit and demerit derive (necessarily) the immortality of the soul.

(7) Of *Æsthetics*, Cousin treats with the same brilliant eloquence as of ethics. Following the psychol. method we shall disengage ideal beauty from the real which are blended in the spont. prim. synthesis. Unity and variety are general marks of beauty ; physical, intellectual, moral, its three chief forms. The true and absolute ideal is GOD Himself. *Art* is the free reproduction of the beautiful, aiming to reach the soul through the senses, to express the ideal, the inf., in material forms.

In Cousin's second period (1828) was a marked influence of Germ. thought ; in his "Lect. on the True, etc." (re-ed. in 1853), he returns to the Scotch phil. of "Common Sense" and psych.

(*E.*) A thoughtful school of religious sceptics, in despair of human reason, sought, in the first half of the nineteenth cent., to substitute a traditional revelation as the princ. of all true knowledge ; chief is *De Bonald* (1754–1840, A.D.), "Récherches philos." (1818). *Count Joseph de Maistre* (1753–1821, A.D.), produced in his "Soirées de St. Petersburg," a thoughtful and sometimes eloquent theodicea, with mystical tendency. More remarkable for eloquence and personal influence is the *Abbé de Lamennais* (1782–1854, A.D.), who, in his "Essai sur L' Indifférence en matière de Religion" (1817–1827), gave a wide impulse to the religious reaction in France, while exposing the fallacies in every source of individ. knowledge: But univ. consent does not err. His "Paroles d'un Croyant," basing pure democracy on the N. T., being condemned by the Papal chair, he entered on a new career, producing (1841–1846), his "Esquisse d'une Philosophie," an all-embracing ontology, which had no lasting effect.

INDEX.

www.ingramcontent.com/pod-product-compliance
Lightning Source LLC
LaVergne TN
LVHW020239110826
845151LV00003B/969

* 9 7 8 1 4 2 5 5 3 0 0 0 6 *